Transitions

Development Through Symbolic Resources

a volume in
Advances in Cultural Psychology:
Constructing Human Development

Series Editor:
Jaan Valsiner

Transitions

Development Through Symbolic Resources

by

Tania Zittoun
University of Cambridge

INFORMATION AGE PUBLISHING

Greenwich, Connecticut • www.infoagepub.com

Library of Congress Cataloging-in-Publication Data

Zittoun, Tania.
  Transitions : symbolic resources in development / by Tania Zittoun.
    p. cm. — (Advances in cultural psychology)
  Includes bibliographical references.
  ISBN 1-59311-227-0 (hardcover) — ISBN 1-59311-226-2 (pbk.)
  1. Adolescent psychology. 2. Developmental psychology. 3. Popular culture. 4. Culture—Psychological aspects. 5. Change (Psychology) 6. Symbolism (Psychology) 7. Identity (Psychology) in adolescence. I. Title.
  II. Series.
  BF724.Z58 2005
  305.235'501--dc22
                                                            2005026072

Copyright © 2006 IAP–Information Age Publishing, Inc.

All rights reserved. No part of this publication may be reproduced, stored in a retrieval system, or transmitted, in any form or by any means, electronic, mechanical, photocopying, microfilming, recording or otherwise, without written permission from the publisher.

Printed in the United States of America

Pour Milan

CONTENTS

Editorial Introduction
   Jaan Valsiner   ix

Introduction   xiii

1. Young Adults in Blurred Fields of Changing Media   *1*
   Change and Development   *2*
   Looking for Youth Transitions   *8*
   Qualifying Youth: Symbolic Responsibility   *14*
   Moving Away From the Study of Youth and Media   *24*

2. Modeling Cultural Experiences and Symbolic Resources in Development   *33*
   Semiotic Processes in Cultural Experiences   *34*
   Semiotic Elaborations of Emotions and the Unconscious   *44*
   Cultural Experiences and Changes Beyond the Sphere of Imaginary Experience   *54*
   The Five Aspects of Cultural Experiences   *58*
   Semiotic Processes in Youth Development   *64*

3. Accessing Personal Cultures   *69*
   Epistemological Issues   *69*
   Methodological Issues   *75*
   The Reconstructive Interpretative Method   *79*
   Generalization   *89*
   An Overview of 29 Possible Case Studies   *90*

4. Young People's Uses of Symbolic Resources   *101*
   What Transitions, What Resources?   *102*
   The Aboutness of Cultural Elements   *104*

Time Orientation	*113*
Levels of Semiotic Mediation	*119*
5. Symbolic Resources in Developmental Transitions	*127*
Pop Lyrics for Grieving and Changing School: Julia	*130*
Hesse to Come Back: Eli	*141*
Scout for Defining a Job: Pat	*149*
Bible and Biographies to Sketch a Life: Thomas	*157*
The Ambiguities of Propaganda: Max	*164*
A Discussion of Five Case Studies	*171*
6. Conclusions: Youth Transitions, Symbolic Processes and the Life-Span	*185*
Development Through Symbolic Resources	*186*
Developing Uses of Symbolic Resources	*189*
Expertise in Using Symbolic Resources	*202*
Openings	*206*
Concluding Words	*210*
Appendix A	*215*
Appendix B	*221*
References	*223*

EDITORIAL INTRODUCTION

The Bearable Aboutness of Development: How Persons Make Culture

The publication of Tania Zittoun's *TRANSITIONS: Development Through Symbolic Resources* as the first book in our series *Advances in Cultural Psychology* is an appropriate tribute to new theoretical trends in the discipline. Zittoun's theory is a novel synthesis based on different perspectives that have been clustered together in the area of cultural psychology over the past 2 decades. With meticulous care she dissects these theories, and reassembles her own that overcomes the weaknesses of their predecessors.

Cultural psychology today is in great need for new theoretical perspectives. The overwhelming empiricism of psychological research has limited the capacities of psychologists of our time to create their new general tools for thought—theories. Instead, psychology is involved in a mortal dance around the issues of methods—setting up evaluative preferences for quantitative over qualitative, or preferring sample based research to that based on individual cases. The readers of this book will find out that such oppositions do not stand in contemporary cultural psychology where the creation of highly abstract theories and focus on complex human life phenomena are being returned to their prominent place. Methods are derivates from theory and must fit the relevant aspects of phenomena—rather than stand alone as consensually set arbiters of science.

The central breakthrough in ideas on culture in human psychology is the focus on processes of development as involving qualitative breaks—ruptures—which need to be refilled by new construction by the person who constantly lives through these turmoils—big or small—in a state of readiness facing the uncertainty of future. This readiness guarantees that all human psychological functions are operating in a state of aboutness—something is *more-or-less*—but not precisely—*like* something else; something possible may happen at the next moment—but it also might not happen. The person may set up long-term future goals that look fixed—until these are altered, by will or circumstances. Our ways of recording our psychological experiences—language—sets us up to attempt to describe precisely what we live through. Yet it is in principle impossible since the process of living through any moment in one's life involves the aboutness of having come from the past, and facing the becoming into a future moment.

It is in this field of inevitable aboutness of life experiences that culture enters into the psychological worlds as an organizing device. Aboutness makes affective processes of living with uncertainty to be the core of creating temporary certainty in human lives—through the making and use of symbolic resources. The process of moving through a rupture, and creating one's future orientation through the *bricolage* of use of symbolic resources is the core of all human psychology. The human mind is constantly affectively constructive—by creating imaginary possible—desired or treaded—scenarios for the future.

Aside from being made up by persons in their lives, symbolic resources once made become carriers of socially encoded cultural possibilities through human history. Books written over 100 years back are potent symbolic resources for young people in a society very different from the origin. The architecture of temples, or the imagery in classical paintings carry culturally encoded affective suggestions forward through centuries. Some books—even ones that do not read easily—have been the source of inspiration for human generations to organize their sociomoral lives over long times. The continuity of histories of societies and those of persons becomes united in the act of making of the personal-cultural bricolage. This bricolage is built through semiotic mediation—contemporary cultural psychology incorporates into it perspectives that emphasize sign-mediation of human life experiences.

Zittoun's empirical evidence seems very ordinary at the first glance—young people telling their ways of living through ruptures by way of use of symbolic resources. Yet there is deep complexity in these descriptions that is being theoretically central—the affective trajectories of the persons' life spaces are expressed through the description of their relating with books, movies, social contexts, and possibilities for their futures.

Zittoun's theory provides new light to the processes and practices of education. When seen through the angle of her symbolic resource theory, all educational activities—informal and formal alike—are management efforts by educators to bring the young into contact with socially prioritized sets of symbolic resources (and keep them away from the disallowed resources). Educational goals are attained through setting up environments where the symbolic resources are set up in the background, as well as introduced into the activities of children (in the foreground). Yet the crucial integrator of the promoted ways of using these resources is the developing person oneself—educational efforts may succeed only if the imagination and activities of the young are dedicated to the kinds of uses of the resources that converge with the educationally desired ones. The whole context of development needs to orient the active learner in the generally desired direction—leaving it then to the developing person to assemble one's actual life experience trajectory.

The present book deserves careful reading as a new theoretical treatise in the advancing science of cultural psychology. It is a new symbolic resource for our developing science.

Jaan Valsiner
Chapel Hill-Worcester
January, 2005

INTRODUCTION

> *But, objects the gemara, if the verse of Exodus indicates that even a solitary student deserves the divine presence, why was it needed to call upon the verse of Malachi to show that God listens to the words exchanged between two persons? The verse in Malachi, answers the gemara, teaches us that when two persons devote themselves together to the study of the Tora, their words are written in "the book of memory."*
>
> —A. Steinsaltz (Ed.). *Talmud, Berakhot, 1* (2001)[1]

This book examines transitions in the life course—periods that follow ruptures, and during which people define new identities, new skills, and confer meanings to their trajectory and their world. Specifically the book examines the symbolic resources that people use to support these changes: the movies they see, the novels they read, the pictures they look at and the music they listen to. My main argument is that young people use movies, books, songs, and so forth, to help them work through transitions, and thus organize psychological development. Such movies, books, or songs are thus used as *symbolic resources*.

The theoretical framework for this argument is cultural developmental psychology. It is interested in processes of change, and examines the role of *semiotic devices*—signs—within thinking, feeling, and acting. The empirical domain is youth development, and this book aims to redefine our current understanding of that period. It examines situations of *everyday education* as crucial for the life course. It also addresses cultural experiences and invites reader and researchers to consider seriously their role in development and everyday life.

This book has theoretical aims. It proposes and defends the notion of the use of symbolic resource. Because novels, films, or songs are made out of signs, or semiotic units, they are understood as affecting other semiotic constructions or processes—those that occur in, and around, people. Consequently, the changing human person is understood as acting through signs. The book proposes a model of the semiotic architecture of self, of the semiotic dynamics that link the person, others, and the world, and of the evolution of such dynamics through the life course.

This book also opens avenues for applied research or work: it documents the diversity of youth trajectories, and the requirements likely to turn ruptures into positive changes; it offers a simple model to analyze what promotes or hinders the use of symbolic resources; it thus elucidates ways to support the processes through which symbolic resources are used for development.

The developmental perspective of the book is defined in chapter 1; a *rupture-transition* unit of analysis is proposed. Transitions imply identity changes, skill acquisition, and meaning construction. The notion of *symbolic responsibility* is proposed to characterize youth transitions, so as to account for development occurring in everyday life, for the fact that young people have to make choices within the cultural objects society presents them with, and for humans' craving for meaning.

A semiotic model of mind is proposed in chapter 2. A basic *semiotic prism* is presented to understand both the microgenesis of meanings, and the interactions people have with artifacts within their sphere of experience: it always implies a person, others, a symbolic object, and the meanings it acquires for the person. This model integrates the embodied, emotional, and unconscious qualities of human experience. In turn, *cultural experiences* are defined so as to account for their power to engage people's embodied, emotional, and unconscious experiences, together with their conscious understanding.

Chapter 3 is epistemological and methodological. It discusses the status of the theoretical metaphors used in the book. It also argues in favor of case studies in psychological research, and discusses the conditions through which these can become a fundamental part of constructing knowledge. The 30 cases through which the models are developed are then summarized.

Uses of symbolic resources are investigated in chapter 4. Three dimensions for describing their efficiency are proposed—their *aboutness*, their time-orientation, and their level within people's system of orientation—and analyzed in their different modalities and relationships. Pursuing this exploration, chapter 5 presents five cases studies. It illustrates the diversity of personal trajectories and uses of symbolic resources, and the similarities of such uses and their outcomes. The theoretical notions thus reveal dynamics of continuity and change within life-trajectories.

Finally, chapter 6 discusses these findings in a broader picture: how is development supported through using symbolic resources? How can the use of symbolic resources be promoted? What constrains such uses and their outcomes? And how does symbolic expertise enhance these processes and outcomes?

The ideas developed here have been cultivated and formulated through interactions with many colleagues and friends, starting with my old Geneva friends, who taught me to think through movies. Ideas presented here owe a lot to discussions with my Cambridge thinking partners —Flora Cornish, Alex Gillespie, Charis Psaltis, Daru Huppert, and Gerard Duveen. I thank them for their attentive, constructive, and friendly disagreements. Gerard Duveen, as well as Paul P. Baltes, and Jaan Valsiner, have offered me the hospitality of their institutes, in which these pages were written. I especially thank Jaan Valsiner for the trust placed in this enterprise, and the generosity with which he guided, and offered space to these explorations. I also particularly thank the 30 young people who agreed to discuss the role of cultural experiences in their lives. Finally, Simon Grimble patiently edited this book and I thank him for his work.

The research reported here and the redaction of this book have been supported by: a European Marie Curie Research Fellowship; a Corpus Christi College (Cambridge) Research Fellowship; and a fellowship from the Swiss National Foundation.

NOTE

1. My translation on the basis of the French edition, as follows: *Mais, objecte la guemara, puisque le verset de l'Exode nous indique que même un étudiant solitaire est digne de la présence divine, pourquoi fallait-il recourir au verset de Malachie pour montrer que l'Éternel écoute les paroles de Tora échangées par deux personnes? Le verset de Malachie, répond la guemara, nous apprend que dans le cas où deux personnes s'adonnent ensemble à l'étude de la Tora, leurs paroles sont inscrites «dans le livre du souvenir».*

CHAPTER 1

YOUNG ADULTS IN BLURRED FIELDS OF CHANGING MEDIA

"Unsere heutige Jugend ist es anders als wir es früher waren!"[1]
—Walter Friedrich & Adolf Hossakovski, *Zur Psychologie des Jugendalters*, Berlin: Volk und Wissen, Volkeigener Verlag (1962)

In the psyche, as in the real world, nothing happens without leaving a trace, nothing disappears.
—Lev S. Vygotsky (1926)

We all spend a significant amount of time reading novels, watching movies, listening to songs, contemplating images and so on. We experience these things with varying degrees of awareness, and often think about them afterwards. Sometimes we are sad, and put on that little sweet melody, and sometimes we are just happy to watch an action movie to change our mood. On the other hand, many people consider such practices as not so serious—are young people not spending too much time in consuming such pleasures? Are adults not too easily satisfied with low quality and superficial cultural artifacts?

In this book, I try to take seriously all these cultural experiences. I am rather sympathetic to them, I must say, and I try to give people—especially young people—credit for their choices. After all, do we not all have good reasons to like that stupid little melody that pops up in our mind, those three rhymes, or that children's book? I even go a step

Transitions: Development Through Symbolic Resources, 1–31
Copyright © 2006 by Information Age Publishing
All rights of reproduction in any form reserved.

further: I claim that, where modern society, education or politics do not provide us with the symbolic tools we need to address the issues that life presents us with, we do, in fact, find these by ourselves—we learn to use these movies or books as symbolic resources. Because I am a psychologist, I also argue that, in some conditions, such uses of symbolic resources are excellent tools to support development. How this might happen is what I will examine throughout these pages, focusing on young people's uses of symbolic resources.

This first chapter introduces my perspective on developmental psychology. I define *rupture-transition* as a unit of analysis for studying psychological change. I then present *youth* as the particular transition that will be examined in this book. The study of development through symbolic resources aims thus to address meaning-making processes, one of the less explored aspects of transitions, and an equally overlooked feature of young people's life—their new *symbolic responsibility*.

CHANGE AND DEVELOPMENT

The study of human development can take many forms, and operates within various constraints: it depends on the sociocultural context in which a study takes place, the funding sources supporting it, and on the scientific community to which the researcher feels belonging. It also depends on a researcher's assumptions about human beings, the world, or the nature of change. The study of human beings is thus exposed to classic difficulties: a researcher's enquiry is always partly guided by his or her experiences as a human being, and therefore possesses the blind spots that go along with that (Perret-Clermont, 1997). Also, in dealing with everyday matters, the scientist might be tempted to use common language, with the risk of becoming merely commonsensical. There are two basic remedies to avoid such sources of confusion: self-reflection, as well as defining the notions with which one works. The former may stay in the researcher's private domain; but the latter has to be exposed to one's readers, and this is what I will do in this first chapter.

Change in Human Development

First of all, I need to expose my working assumptions. I am going to talk about *change*—but change, to start with, might have opposing implications. Etymologically, change comes from low Latin. It had first a commercial meaning: change is *exchanging* something for something else, substituting one thing for another. Later, change took on the meaning of the *process* of alteration of a state or a quality. These two definitions immediately open two opposing avenues for a developmental psychology. In *change*$_1$, a stage B of understanding can succeed to a state A, or a novice can turn into an expert.

In *change*$_2$, the process of transformation comes to the fore: the irreversibility of time becomes central. Such a time-infused notion of change grounds the developmental approach I propose. In doing so, I accept the tutelage of authors like Lev Vygotsky and Jean Piaget, readers of Pierre Janet (1928, 1929, 1934/1935), Henri Bergson (1911), William James (1892), John Dewey (1910, 1917, 1934), Charles Peirce (1868a, 1868b) and later Kurt Lewin (1951) and Alfred Schütz (1951). These authors have nourished the work of many contemporary researchers with whom I will dialogue here (Benson, 2001; Gillespie, 2004; Perret-Clermont, 1997, 2004; Valsiner, 1987, 1997, 1998, 2003).

In short, these authors admit, first, the sociocultural, historical, and material situatedness of human thought and action and, therefore, the mutual constitution of the individual and the social (Duveen & Lloyd, 1990; Perret-Clermont, 2004; Valsiner, 1987). Second, they acknowledge the ever-dynamic nature of the world, the constantly moving nature of the human psyche, and, therefore, the necessarily evolving nature of the transactions between the person and the world. These two assumptions bring us to see development as an open-ended process, located in a systemic whole (Valsiner & Connolly, 2003). Third, to account for these transactions, they admit the radical specificity of human worlds as being largely made up of semiotic texture (based on the use of signs, both in the world and, in some form, in the mind) (Moscovici, 1973; Nelson, 1981; Piaget, 1964/1967; Peirce, 1868a, 1868b; Tomasello, 1999; Toomela, 1996; Vygotsky & Luria, 1994; Wertsch, 1998).

Endorsing these statements, and allowing me not to systematically refer to their authors, my psychological enquiry examines change as it occurs in time—it is developmental; and it examines changes as they are mediated by semiotic form—it is therefore a cultural psychology. Such a psychological enquiry has to admit the interdependency of human actions, thoughts, and emotional dynamics, all of which have been artificially separated by main traditions of research. The notion of *conduct* offers a holistic unit of analysis for human located experiences, in time and space (Diriwächter, 2003, 2004; Janet, 1928, 1929, 1934/1935; Salomon, 1993; Schütz, 1945; Valsiner, 2004a). A person's conduct always engages a person positioned in a material, social, and symbolic location. Conduct is an embodied activity or experience that involves emotional, representational, and bodily dynamics. Conduct thus always involves *composites* of emotions, memories, thoughts and actions.

Acknowledging the ever-changing nature of beings does not prevent the researcher from having preferences for some kinds of changes rather than others. Talking about *development* always implies such a preference, a normative stance. I wish to make explicit my own norms and preferences. Development is, etymologically, a particular form of change that implies a process of unfolding, or a progression. In these terms, psychological development can be understood as a *qualitative* transformation of the person's thinking and linking abilities.[2] Often, a clear and superior restructuring of a person's state of understanding qualifies as development (Durkin, 1995; Piaget, 1964/1967).

To be able to account for changes in adults' lives, I will employ a weaker characterization of development. I would say that a qualitative change is optimal, if, first, it opens new ranges of possible conduct, that is, it is *generative* for further transitions (see chapter 2). Second, to be developmental, such changes should not prevent a person from maintaining a sense of *continuity and consistency*. Third, these changes must enable the person to maintain satisfying relationships with her social, material, and symbolic *environment*. If these two last conditions are not fulfilled, changes can bring the person to feel alienated (from herself or from others), which reduces his or her degree of freedom to generate new possibilities. In that sense, such changes could not be called developmental.

Ruptures, Transitions, and Uncertainty

If life is ever changing, we do not want to study outcomes of particular events, but processes of change. How, then, to isolate relevant processes in an ongoing flow? What can be the segment of time that should be the unit of a psychological enquiry?

There is a long tradition in psychology that considers ruptures as privileged *loci* for the observation of processes of psychological change. Peirce, Dewey, Piaget, Schütz, and Moscovici have proposed models based on ruptures such as conflicts, strange tasks or transitions. Their very different works employ, based on the analysis of phenomena of various degrees of generality, a simple sequence: it includes a continuous state, a rupture, and a possible process of restructuring allowing a new balance. In each case, it is not the outcome, but the process that is interesting. The base units have been explored in various sciences, from mathematics—in René Thom's catastrophe theory (1975), ruptures brutally modify a system and endanger it; the system survives if it can be structurally modified, while maintaining its identity—to embryology and semiotics (Sebeok, 1994; Van Geert, 2003). In my study, the proposed unit of analysis for psychological development is the unit *rupture-irruption of uncertainty-transition, implying processes leading to a new form of stability*. Such a unit of analysis opens a window on a wide range of psychological processes linked to change (Zittoun, Duveen, Gillespie, Ivinson, & Psaltis 2003).

In people's lives, *ruptures* might be due to various reasons. Psychologists have examined a few types of ruptures, according to various levels of the social reality in which the origin of the change is identified (Doise, 1982; Perret-Clermont, Carugati, & Oates, 2004). First, a rupture can result from an important change in the cultural context (a war starts, a new ideology is spread, a new technology changes lives). It can also come from a direct change of a person's sphere of experience (a person moves away from a country), or a change within a person's sphere of experience (a new boss enters the department). Alternatively, ruptures can be due to changes in the relationships and interactions the person has with others and objects (a child leaves home, a computer refuses to function). Finally, a rupture can come from within the person herself: she grows or gets older, her body changes, her ideas and her feelings bring her somewhere else.

The various locations of the origin of the rupture matter less than the fact that they do affect a person's ongoing *spheres of experience*. In effect, in complex societies, our lives are usually divided into various microworlds of experience. A person participates in many fields of activity (De Rivera, 1976; Lewin, 1939), or social or symbolic frames (Goffman, 1975)—for example, his professional, and his religious life, in each of which he meets specific actors, talks a given language, follows certain rules, develops certain intentions, and has as references some imaginary others. I will call such fields *spheres of experience*. This metaphorical notion is based on Von Uexküll's concept of *Umwelt* (1934/1956, 1940/1982). It suggests that we are generating our own worlds within the limits of some constraints, according to the scope of our perceptual and meaning-making abilities. Thus, in the same living room, Jules[3] and a fly are in two different *Umwelte*: because of their perceptual systems and cognitive abilities, for the fly the world is defined by the heat of candles and the sweetness of the drinks on the table; for Jules, there is a whole romantic scene which is going to take place. On this basis, it is possible to say that a person lives in various spheres of experience (successively, or at the same time, some being more in the foreground, others in the background). Jules's living room becomes indeed a different space when he is in a reading mood (then the bookshelves and its collection of rare prints, the sofa, and the low lamp become relevant), as opposed to when he has to fix the table and is looking for the hammer forgotten under who-knows-what pile of documents (then he just sees obstacles to his goal). It follows that a person's conduct in two spheres of experiences can be organized by different values, which can be incompatible—a rational accountant during the day can be a member of a trance group at night. This supposes that humans maintain a kind of impermeability between these spheres of experience. Thus, ruptures can occur within only one of these spheres, or in many of them at the same time. They can emerge when a person loses one particular sphere of experience (one encompassing activities linked to a deceased grandfather), or when one has to create a new sphere (moving home). Ruptures can result from the unexpected fusion of various spheres of experience—when a person known as "trance group member" becomes a professional colleague, or when a child, having learned a specific operation at school, is asked to do it at home.[4] Finally, the societal field in which these spheres are embedded can also exert new, or threatening forces on the spheres. Ruptures created by the change from one sphere of experience to another, and the societal forces exerted on a sphere of experience, are addressed in chapter 6.

In all these cases, a rupture is something that is *experienced by a person*: usually, everyday changes are limited and remain unnoticed. In a situation of rupture, changes are disquieting experiences (Simão, 2003), which suddenly endanger customary ways of doing things, put at stake relatively taken-for-granted routines and definitions.[5] The obvious suddenly comes into question. In other words, there is an irruption of *uncertainty* within everyday experience, which, retrospectively, reveals the degree of certainty that one had in one's spheres of experiences prior to that point of rupture.

Uncertainty is thus an experience of blurred personal reality, *relative* to a person's previous state of apprehension of things. *Uncertainty can be defined as a representational ill-adjustment between a person's current state of understanding and the given of a situation*:[6] a person can mobilize or generate representations about a state of affairs, but because of lack of criteria, information or experience, these representations cannot be stabilized. They may be oscillating rapidly, or remaining partial and therefore unhelpful for making meaning or directing conduct, or, finally, are coexisting and thus creating a field of ambiguity (Abbey & Valsiner, 2003b).

From a phenomenological perspective, uncertainty is generally perceived as a form of tension or anxiety, but can also be felt as an excitement. Some people do not tolerate uncertainty, while others actively challenge their lives in order to generate more ruptures and uncertainty. Experiencing uncertainty might be paralyzing, but in most cases, because it brings to some form of oscillation, it marks the beginning of the deconstruction of previous understanding, of the exploration of possibilities, or of the genesis of newness. Thus, if not paralyzing, uncertainty might be seen as an experience that calls for some new psychological activity.

Ruptures and irruptions of uncertainty can affect one's experience with *various degrees of generality*. Uncertainty can thus affect both single actions (which sandwich to choose for lunch) and very abstract beliefs, which offer guidance for a whole range of such local actions (holding a belief in an alliance with the divine, which forbids the consuming of certain sorts of meat) (see Valsiner, 2001a, 2001b, 2003, in press; these points will be discussed in chapters 2 & 4). A rupture occurring at a higher level of generality is likely to change more aspects of one's life— for example, losing one's faith in God after a car accident can modify many actions (going to church, giving to charity) and various categories of meaning (thinking of oneself as a Christian, committing oneself to help others). Reciprocally, however, ruptures at the level of actions might, in some conditions, modify conduct in a more general way. For example, the sudden death of a close friend in a car accident (a unique occurrence) can bring a person to renounce to his previous belief in the justice of the world (higher, generalized level).

Uncertainties and ruptures can finally vary in their *time-extension*: a rupture can be sudden, or emerge out of a repetitive situation or a slow process; uncertainty can appear brutally or as an extended cloudy period; and the work of transition can be a short-ranged one, in microadjustment, or might need months or years.

Transitions that follow ruptures *revealed by a consecutive experienced uncertainty* thus differ from transitions defined on a normative or psychosocial basis (e.g., getting married *should* be a turning point in one's life. Only the latter type of transitions are clearly felt to matter by the person, and they need to be clearly felt to matter in order to trigger the psychological work required in such changing circumstances.

The *work of transition* is thus the psychological work that may be triggered by a person's experienced uncertainty. It implies processes aiming at new forms of equilibrium, or satisfying adjustments to the situation (Valsiner, 1997). One might thus think that part of the psychological work that takes place during transitions is directed at reducing uncertainty, primarily through the creation of meanings and representations. For example, the work of transition to parenthood implies elaborating representations of the unknown child to come (Zittoun, 2004b), the work of transition before visiting a very different country implies mobilizing images from cinema and guidebooks to create representations of that country (Gillespie, 2004).

LOOKING FOR YOUTH TRANSITIONS

In our modern, so-called democratic societies, youth is a period where persons change social spaces, occupation, and sometimes, civic status – all this separately or simultaneously. Youth can be defined as implying multiple ruptures and transitions, changes within and of spheres of experience, which constitutes part of its interest for social scientists.

Through her developmental story, a person interacts with things, objects, persons, and signs. On the basis of these interactions with the collective culture (Valsiner, 1998), meanings attached to semiotic elements in the world find progressively a form of translation "in the person"; this is the process of *internalization*, through which shared meanings can become more or less central to the person (Lawrence & Valsiner, 2003; Valsiner, 1997). The unique result of a person's internalizations constitutes her *personal culture* (Valsiner, 1998). Youth can be seen as a catalyzing period of revision, or active creation of such a personal culture. Symmetrically, youth transition can be seen as a period in which a person starts to have a role of full societal participant, that is, a responsible expressive role. From now on, a person is expected (more than as a child or as an adolescent) to participate in the consumption and the production of circulating opinions, ideas, information, symbolic goods—as a worker, voter, holder of opinion, consumer, or parent—and the person is suppose to stand for her *externalization*. To designate the fact that a young person thus becomes responsible for her internalization and externalization, I will consider youth transition as a period characterized by the accession to a symbolic responsibility.

Before building on this idea, I have to signal that the existing literature on youth usually emphasizes the many difficulties of youth transitions, and rarely examines processes. I might, as Tudge (2000) proposes, be economical and ignore a literature based on very different assumptions than mine—much of the research on youth focuses on the normative outcomes of changes (employment, relational commitment), rather than processes. Also, most of the literature examines culture as influencing passive young people, rather than examining them as constructors of their personal culture. Yet, I consider that the existing literature offers a thematic landscape; reviewing current trends highlights consensus and blind spots. In turn, it facilitates the positioning of my perspective, and may illuminate my own blind spots. In this section, I present current studies on youth. The lack of definition of the end of youth transition (the beginning of adulthood) will bring me to particularize it: this is how I will come back to the notion of *symbolic responsibility* in the following section.

Youth as a Psychosocial Transition

As the period during which children are turned into adults, adolescence and youth have been of special interest for psychologists and researchers in human sciences for many years. Adolescence does indeed appear to reflect wider changes in societies (Mørch, 2003). Over the past 20 years, as the outcome of social, economical, and technological changes, a new age group has been identified by social scientists: *young adulthood* or *postadolescence*, an uncertain period between adolescence and adulthood. Adolescence had previously been consensually defined as starting with puberty, and young adulthood as starting *after* the physiological changes of adolescence,[7] and their related emotional (Sayer, 1998), cognitive (Keating, 1990; Keating & Sasse, 1996; Steinberg, 1993)[8] and symbolic developments (Anastasopoulos, 1988; Labouvie-Vief, 1992). Young adulthood has progressively acquired its own scientific status. Generally, young adulthood is defined as a psychosocial transition period. Such a notion of transition is understood in a different manner than the more generic *transition process*. It can be said that the *psychosocial youth transition* (as a stage) includes multiple *processes of transition* as defined above. Youth becomes interesting for developmental research because of its concentration of processes of transition.[9]

The psychosocial transition to adulthood has been examined from three main perspectives: (a) As a sociocultural phenomenon, in a given societal state and historical context (at the turn of the twenty-first century, in democratic societies where new technologies play an increasing role); (b) As a self-perceived phenomenon by *young adults*; (c) As a period implying specific psychological tasks, as defined by psychologists. These three perspectives are interdependent: the relations between (a) and (c) reflect the distance between social representations and scientific discourse (Moscovici, 1973; Valsiner, 1989); and the relation between these discourses and the *youth perspective* questions the self-fulfilling prophetic power of public and scientific discourses (Griffin, 1993; Hacking, 1999). Psychological development is constrained by these three dimensions.

Youth Transition as a Social and Cultural Phenomenon

Over the past 20 years, in the United States and in European countries, sociohistorical events, economic, and technological changes, migration movements, and the modification of the structures of families have reshaped the average life-path. Obtaining a stable job, creating a separate home, having a family and children, have thus lost their value as thresholds to adulthood. Young people can indeed leave their parents without creating a new family, stay partially financially dependent on their parents while having a job and children, engage in numerous short-time professional contracts, or opt for unstable relationships, at an age that their parents would have considered as adult. It thus seemed that at some point corresponding to the end of the classical adolescence, young people's lives became engaged in a long and unclear period, more or less extended, characterized by multiple changes of role and status. Given the multiple fields of experience of a person, it started to become difficult to speak of one single transition through a clear threshold into adulthood. Social scientists have instead started to speak of various *role-transitions* (Carugati & Selleri, 1996; Jaffe, 1998). Some authors distinguish the school-to-work transition from the domestic transition and the housing transition (Cole, 1995; in Coleman & Hendry, 1980/1999; Galland, 1997; Palmonari, 1993), or more simply, separate social transitions (i.e., professional) from more private ones (i.e., sexual and relational) (Durkin, 1995). These various transitions appear not to be addressed at the same speed, or in the same order for everybody (Carugati, 2004).[10] Although such facts suggest individualized trajectories, youth transitions remain bounded by social, economical, and historical landscapes. Given national variations in the structure of education and professional training (Fouquet, 2004; Iacovou & Berthoud, 2001), in the modalities of social support (unemployment support, minimal allowance, etc.), or in its tolerance of young people's exploration of alternative or artistic life-styles, each nation creates specific constraints and enabling conditions for young people, and thus produces various forms of pathways to adulthood (Resnick, 2004). Finally, social expectations about young people's role, place, expected abilities and achievements have changed as well (Anatrella, 1988; Bideaud, Houdé, & Pedinelli, 1993; Freund, 2003; Grob, 2001).

Pragmatically, such psychosocial transitions appear to satisfy psychological needs: a *floating* period allows for periods of trial-and-error, for the exploration of possible pathways and for variations in personal change. Prieur (2002) even suggests that going through adulthood thresholds more conventionally may have negative consequences: in France, young people in jail were more likely to have fulfilled normative tasks (such as having a family) than average young people,[11] which suggests that an absence of an exploratory period impedes a person's satisfying adjustment to the exigencies of modern life. It thus finally seems that a long period of uncertain delayed youth transition, or institutionalized "moratorium" (Erikson, 1975), has emerged out of functional purposes, as enabling a longer maturational process to the individual for a life in a more complex and changing society (Anatrella, 1999; Clémence, et al., 2001; Perret-Clermont, Pontecorvo, Resnick, Zittoun, & Burge, 2004).

Thus, speaking of psychosocial youth transitions accounts for a particular period during which some of the psychological needs of human beings living in modern societies can be satisfied.

Youth as a Self-Perceived Phenomenon

Some social scientists have been interested in documenting how young people would consider themselves in transitions. Given the sociocultural and economical constraints they are presented with,[12] it seems thus that young people develop a sense of what is possible, or suitable to happen for them, which is likely to differ from the representations held by their parents at the same age (Heath & Yi Cheung, 1998; Coleman & Hendry, 1980/1999; Grob, Krings, & Bangerter, 2001; Bangerter, Grob, & Kribgs, 2001).[13] Interactions between society and youth go beyond the socioeconomical constraints perceived by young people. Every society secretes its representations of youth; in modern, democratic societies, these are diffused widely through various means—through official policies, the media and the arts (Esprit, 1997). Young people are both directly exposed to these social discourses about them or addressed to them, and indirectly, through the way their parents and other adult address them. More general societal discourses also indirectly participate in young people's representations, particularly those that relate to the economy, ageing, health, violence, leisure, an so forth. These social and symbolic constraints are thus part of the construction of a person's representation as a young person, and in turn, participate in the shaping of her conduct and commitments (Griffin, 1993; Clémence, et al., 2001; Mørch, 2003; Hacking, 1999).

Youth as a Psychological Phenomenon

Various approaches have considered youth as a psychological issue, of which I will describe three general groups of studies. In lifespan and longitudinal approaches, youth is examined as part of the general course of life. Life-span writings on youth can thus be based on data gathered when a studied cohort becomes adolescent (Steinberg & Morris, 2001). Longitudinal studies are wide, methodologically complex, and costly projects, that have both fundamental ambitions and implications for policy makers. Their categories of analysis are chosen in a way that allows the possibility of identifying continuities and change over time, and that allow cross-cohort or international comparisons; information deemed irrelevant within such a wide enquiry is usually lost. Results and outcomes, rather than processes, can be observed on this kind of scale; phenomenon are understood as depending on general variables affecting wide samples, rather than in terms of personal logics of change. Longitudinal approaches have considered three main sorts of $change_1$: cognitive change, identity change, and change linked to a person's adjustment to challenges. In terms of development in thinking, most theoretical frames are still given by the work of Piaget (Inhelder & Piaget, 1955/1958), Kohlberg, (1981), Gilligan (1982/1983, 1988) or Elkind (1970, 1999). Rare alternative models are based on cognitive models (Keating, 1990), or are related to learning and assessment. Studies considering identity-development are mainly based on models such as Erikson's, Marcia's or John Hills' psychosocial development.[14] The processes of psychological change themselves are mostly understood in terms of stress and copying strategies, or adjustment and resiliency in challenging situations (for instance, Bangerter, Grob, & Krings, 2001; Coleman & Hendry, 1980/1999; Grob, Krings, & Bangerter, 2001; Seiffge-Krenke, 1997).[15] Longitudinal approaches mostly imply that some outcomes of changes are better than others, even if the notion of adulthood lacks clarity. Looking for causes of different outcomes of youth development in families, neighborhoods, peers, cliques, and siblings, school, leisure clubs, and workplaces, the more complex of these studies have acknowledged that simplistic causal explanations have had to be excluded.[16] Such studies have not contributed to our understanding of youth as much as we could have expected. On the one hand, the weight of longitudinal and life-span researches seems to have prevented exploration of detailed mechanisms of development. Examining cohorts at fixed time-spots enable comparisons through time, or across cohorts; yet, even when these time-spots become close to each other, the very nature of the processes of change are necessarily ignored. And if this is so, the process of development can only be, even in the best case scenario, an empirical reconstruction (like a film made by assembling pictures taken every couple of seconds) or a mathematical reconstruction (when all the observations are treated statistically so as to identify general patterns, such as a film generated by a computer). On the other hand, it seems that one of the reasons for supporting large scale longitudinal studies was that, through solid descriptions and by providing explanations of differences and changes, it would be possible to anticipate and predict people's evolution, with the hope of providing support to fragile sections of the population. However, as researchers have often stated, such predictions are very difficult to produce (and verify) (Lerner & Galambos, 1998; Steinberg & Morris, 2001). In short, given the costs of this kind of research and its methodological complexity, their outcome in terms of contributions to fundamental theory and to applied research may appear insufficient.

A second group of studies focuses on *youth problems*. Here, the notion of development is minimal: the cause of specific positive or negative behavior is looked for in other dimensions. Here, quantitative analysis tries to identify patterns of behavior and to predict the outcomes of *good* or *bad* developmental pathways, in regard to what seems to be an implicit norm of "'mature' adulthood—heterosexuality, marriage, parenthood, and (hopefully) a full-time job" (Griffin, 1993, p. 171).[17] Such studies may actually participate in the creation of so-called youth problems (Clémence et al., 2001; Griffin, 1993); they might also victimize groups of less standard people.[18] Such research can thus be suspected of producing self-fulfilling prophecies. Because of their absence of real consideration for developmental issues, they will not need to be further discussed in the frame of the present enquiry; it is enough to know that young people do have problems (as do many other people), that social scientists have good reasons to worry about these, but that most of this kind of research does not help us to understand the complex processes through which young people develop despite predictions to the contrary.

A third group consists of studies concerned with specific methodological[19] and theoretical questions about developmental, social, or thinking processes. Youth is, in many regards, used as a *laboratory* for the study of wider social phenomena (media-consumption, gender questions, new technologies, religious behavior, etc.) and psychological dynamics (identity construction, changes in personality, abstraction processes or creativity, or wisdom-thinking—(Csikszentmihaly & Larson, 1984; Heaven, 1994; Keating & Sasse, 1996; Pasupathi, Staudinger, & Baltes, 2001; Seiffge-Krenke, 1997; Steinberg, 1993; Turner & Helms, 1979/1989). Some of these studies bring useful insights into youth reality, sometimes precisely because they carry less normative expectations.

In short, the study of youth has been an abundant, but fragmented field. Its overall normativity has constrained it, and mostly prevented researchers from addressing new questions that may account for unexpected observed facts. Emphasis has been given to extreme maladjustments or deviancy, rather than to ordinary transitions. Change has been too often understood in its first meaning, that of substitution, and thus the research has mostly overlooked processes. Consequently, psychological processes that are specific to that period of life have not been identified, let alone explored.[20] One might have hoped that longitudinal studies would help in evaluating long-term consequences of specific changes, beyond a priori moral judgments; yet life-span studies mostly highlight the plasticity of life-paths (Baltes, 2000; Brandstädter & Lerner, 1999; Valsiner & Lawrence, 1997). In general, the specifically developmental part of youth psychology has been overlooked. Adopting a theoretical orientation of a kind with the third type of psychological studies just described above, I will try to reintegrate such a developmental orientation into the study of youth transitions.

QUALIFYING YOUTH: SYMBOLIC RESPONSIBILITY

From now on, I will concentrate on perspectives that understand change as processes. This implies that youth becomes a period rich in transitions, *as these might occur all through life*. First, I will break down the rupture-transition unit into three streams of interdependent change. Second, in order to distinguish youth from other periods of life, I will identify its *unique symbolic requirements*.

The Work of Transition in Youth

As with any other transitions during lifetime, youth requires processes of sociocultural relocation and identity changes, specific learning, and meaning construction processes (Perret-Clermont & Zittoun, 2002).

First, youth transitions involve changes in the social, material, or symbolic spheres of experience of the person. Transitions imply processes of *repositioning, or relocation* of the person in her social and symbolic fields (Benson, 2001; Duveen, 2001). Each of these movements creates new goals, orientations, possibilities, and constraints on action (Valsiner, 1998; Valsiner & Lawrence, 1997). Equally, any choice or orientation involves losses (Baltes, 1997). Relocations also confront a person with others, who are in more or less equal positions, who react and mirror that person's location. Thus repositioning implies *transformations of identities*—through one's own apprehension and through the mediation of others. These identity changes might be related to gender definition, to generational questions, to one's profession or to one's outside activities, to questions of social and cultural belonging. Each repositioning brings into question one's sense of continuity and coherency, and one's values and general orientation. Youth transitions include such repositioning. No longer adolescents, young people usually engage in movements in the social space: they move to new educational or professional settings, leave their parents' house or come back to their hometown, change accommodation, enter into new groups of friends, start new leisure activities, or move from an adolescent-wild life to a more settled-down life.

Second, such relocations imply new relationships with a given location, and new forms of conduct. People's conduct must take place in given material and social surroundings. It thus creates a set of constraints and enabling means for what one internalizes or learns, and what one can act or express. *Relocation goes along with the mobilization or the construction of skills and knowledge.* For learning to occur—which includes the construction of new skills and knowledge, or their actualization in new settings—past knowledge and skills must be mobilized and transformed through new internalizations, and thus, relocations can be linked to processes of restructuring knowledge. In the case of young people, social, cognitive, and expert forms of knowledge and skills might be required, for example, to be able to cook for oneself, to participate in the civic world, or to improve one's new academic or professional life.

Third, through these relocations, the encounters with various others, and learning, the person might experience uncertainty. This may, first, bring her to engage in *meaning-making*, that is, to elaborate, symbolically, what happens to her (Bruner, 1990, 1996). Second, she will need to maintain a sense of *continuity and consistency across spheres of experience* (Carugati & Selleri, 1996; Flammer & Alsaker, 2001; Malewska-Peyre & Tap, 1991; Palmonari, 1984, 1993). Third, the emotions and the nonconscious prolongations of these changes have to be acknowledged and symbolically elaborated, for the experience to be worked through, that is, linked and integrated to one's fabric of previous experiences (Zittoun, 2004b).

This third aspect is central for change to happen, and is often overlooked in youth studies.[21] Yet research on learning difficulties, or identity difficulties, suggests that meaning is an essential condition for learning to occur, or for essential psychical well-being (Bruner, 1990; Fabbri, Mari, & Valentini, 1992; Paìn, 1985). Also, emotional elaboration is fundamental for thinking through newness; conversely, nonelaborated emotions, absurd situations, can hinder thinking and acting. It is on this third aspect that we will focus: Meaning making requires thinking with signs and symbols: that is, it requires semiotic mediation. To understand youth transition, thus, we will need to understand semiotic mediation processes (see chapter 2).

An example given by the literature highlights the interdependency of these three aspects of the work of transition. In Tracy Chevalier's *Girl with a Pearl Earring* (1999),[22] Griet is a 16-year-old woman sent by her family to work as a maid in the family of the painter Vermeer in Delft, in the seventeenth century. The move of Griet out of childhood is concretized by many ruptures: her father having been left blind in a work accident, she has to leave her family to earn money; she moves to an new area of the town; in this new house, people are Catholics, while she comes from a Protestant family; and instead of being the older daughter of local artisans, she becomes the lower-rank maid in an established household, who sleeps in the basement. The novel describes the process of transition that brings her to this fallen position and then from there to the very special role of Vermeer's assistant and, eventually, model. We can observe processes of transition along the three dimensions identified above. First, during the first period of her new work at the Vermeer's, Griet has to work out her relation to the various inhabitants of the house (family, maids), and the network within which it is situated—that of art buyers, but also butchers and fish merchants. With them, and towards them, Griet defines and affirms her new *position*: she is a maid, but she does not let children direct her; she has to obey, but can suggest ideas. Second, she obviously has to learn new *competences*: how to wash, clean, cook, and buy food for such a large household, within the limits of her role and the requirements of the family. Third, she has to confer a *personal meaning* on her presence there, and find emotional support when she feels lonely and humiliated. This is where Griet discovers that she can mobilize three of her abilities as important resources for supporting the processes of transition. First, as she previously had to take care of her blind father, she learned to clean objects without changing their location so as to enable him to find them. She uses the same precision in Vermeer's atelier, where she has to clean the room without modifying the composition to be painted; and Vermeer notices this talent. Second, as a child she had developed the habit while preparing vegetables of separating them according to their color. Vermeer, who notices her gift, asks her to prepare his colors. She discovers that she is capable of being very sensitive to Vermeer's work, and progressively learns to understand the logic of colors and composition. She even comes to suggest some changes to Vermeer's work. Griet's discovery of the power of colors and painting, and her special relationship to Vermeer, soon enable her to overcome sadness and despair; she has a unique role and her action has a meaning within the work of the master. This will modify her social position—she will leave the basement and sleep in the attic, her role is kept secret from the family, which gives her some sense of exception. And through these new skills and identity, she also finds a way to reestablish links to her family of origin: she now narrates the paintings to her blind father, using her powerful imagination to translate physical impression into words. Eventually, the story will have a simple resolution—Griet, now 17 years old and secretly in love with Vermeer, finally decides to accept the courtship of a young butcher, to whom she is satisfactorily married—and thus seemingly terminates her transition to adulthood.

When Does Youth Finish? A Qualitative Definition of Youth Development

Recent research on youth generally admits that adulthood is attained when a certain number of psychosocial transitions have been achieved; these are linked to physiological maturation, the definition of personal goals, and social values in a given historical and societal context (Cavalli, 1989; Grob, 2001; Morrow & Richards, 1996). However, every clear-cut definition of thresholds to adulthood is necessarily ideological, for it depends on the scientist's orientations and values. Trying to avoid such a normative stance, Wyn and White (1997) note that many of the markers of adulthood (such as getting a job, leaving the parent's house, getting involved in an intimate relationship) are, in occidental industrialized countries, "transitory, reversible and impermanent" (Wyn & White 1997, p. 96). They thus see transitions as including both moves on a "horizontal" plan—(school-to-work, from family to a new household) and moves on a vertical plan, organized around age and generation cohorts. Adulthood would thus designate a person's belonging to a specific cultural-historical cohort that shares specific worries. Steinberg (1993) pushes one step further his scepticism about the possibility of defining a threshold to adulthood: it may be that a person goes through different stages of identity elaboration, many times, and regarding different domains, all life long (Harter, 1990; Meeus, et al., 1999). The question therefore becomes: is there a clear interest in defining adulthood at all (see also Resnick, 2004)? The idea of attaining adulthood is still powerful in everyday life, yet it might be redundant in scientific inquiries.

Constructing a System of Orientation and a Time Perspective

This slippery path can be avoided if one does not look for sociocultural criteria of adulthood, but for related *qualitative psychological* modifications. In effect, there are some psychological gestures that are required, both socially and psychically, for a person to move out of what is acknowledged to be youth, towards a zone of life generally identified as adulthood. These psychological gestures have been highlighted by clinical psychologists. Their clinical work made them aware of the minimal requirement for being able to live a good enough life in a given society. For Freud, to live a healthy adult life, a person must simply (!) be able to work and to love. For other psychologists, she must have a readiness to be confronted by intense, painful, and happy life events, thus developing an undeveloped part of herself, and she must have the resources to work through emotions (Waddell, 1998).[23]

Such approaches highlight three maturational processes. First, youth is a period for stabilizing values, choices, and orientations. This includes acquiring some psychical autonomy and constructing a hierarchy of values and orientations, based on the acceptance of one's conflictual side and linked to a sense of *personal dignity* (Anatrella, 1988; Blos, 1962/1966). Second, given societal requirements, this system of orientation must be turned into real options and commitments in *niches* provided by the environment, while renouncing (at least temporarily) other possible life choices (Waddell, 1998). Third, the person has to integrate a time perspective (childhood is seen as relatively timeless; adolescence is commonly depicted as the experience of the *here-and-now*) (Anatrella, 1999; Gutton & Jeammet, 1998).

Time inscription appears to have an especially great importance in youth in our societies. A personal sense of historicity, related to one's past and childhood and possible selves in the future, has to be found in order to define professional or personal goals, in the long term. Commitment to learning or working needs to be supported by such time orientations to be psychologically possible as they require the delay of gratification (Charlot, Bautier, & Rochex, 1992; Charlot & Glasman, 1998; Bajoit & Franssen, 1995). And a life in our societies is much more difficult without a clear professional or occupational choice. A transgenerational sense of history might have to be built as well, as a condition of generativity—both in the sense of being able to think about parenting, and in the sense of personal, professional artistic, or scientific creativity, all needing to be related to a type of tradition (Winnicott, 1989, 1971/2001; Erikson, 1975).[24] The ability to integrate conflicting tendencies, the organization and hierarchization of values and the construction of a time perceptive are central marks of the end of the transition to adulthood for clinical perspectives. Recently, other theoretical approaches have highlighted the importance of these dimensions on other grounds (see Brandstädter & Lerner, 1999).

The two dimensions that are time-perspective and a system of orientation, I suggest, constitute the system of coordinates necessary for meaning-making—they are required for people to define why they are in such an absurd time-spot, or whether it is worth enduring difficulties. Conversely, clinical studies document the difficulties of change in situations of rupture, and explain a dynamic that leads to psychic sufferance or social exclusion. Some of these difficulties can be read as linked to damaged time perspective and system of orientation. For example, in his psychotherapeutic work with immigrants, Tobie Nathan (1993) shows how African migrants in France, who have lost access to their traditional and symbolic system of orientation, and whose past ritual timescale has been totally modified by life in a big city, might suddenly be petrified when their adolescent children move away from home and choose a secular lifestyle: Nathan reports serious work accidents, such as falling from a high building, that can occur in such moments. Such falls can be read as the actualization of a "falling out of meaning": the choice of the child appears as a radical rupture to the parent; it cannot be interpreted within the traditional orientation system, and radically cuts intergenerational transmission and traditional time scales. Psychic sufferance and social exclusion (people lose their job) can follow such falls. The therapeutic setting, in that case, aims at restoring and renewing the system of orientation of the person (by discussing concerns with various other people coming from the same culture), and by creating a time-continuity (by narrating the new situation in terms of traditional stories, by engaging in ritual actions oriented toward future outcomes)—hence, to recreate a "net" of meaning around the person.

Hence, youth is defined as a period in which, through multiple transitions, a person defines a time perspective, a system of orientation, and the spheres of experiences in which these can be actualized. These are the basis for meaning-making, which are required for identity transformation and learning to be possible.

Resources in Transitions

People do not confront ruptures without enabling means or facilitators. They have some cognitive and physical abilities and dispositions. They have some experience of life, a history of past ruptures, and possibly a memory of past transitions. On this basis of this, they might thus have developed some skills or knowledge that can become resources.

People are part of social networks in which they can mobilize others to give them some expert or relational support; they can also draw on a more or less conscious social knowledge to determine how to act with various persons, in certain situations; the mobilization of such support can be said to constitute *social resources*. People can then mobilize forms of technical, reasoning or heuristic expertise and practical or formal knowledge, which we might call *cognitive resources*. These two broad families of resources have been widely studied in developmental and learning psychology (see Perret-Clermont, et al., 2004). Using such resources requires the associated ability to identify that a given situation requires mobilizing this or that form of knowledge so as to deal with the current issue.

Transition processes have been said to be made up of three types. Logically, we might think that *social resources* are mostly useful to address repositioning and identity changes in transitions. *Cognitive resources* are likely to support new acquisition of knowledge. But what can be mobilized to support the need to construct meaning, the growth of a time perspective, and the construction of a system of orientation? These psychic activities share one feature: they are possible only if one can take some distance toward the immediacy of the here and now. *Such distancing is precisely enabled by semiotic mediations*, be these elementary signs, language, or more complex symbolic entities (Vygotsky & Luria, 1994). Therefore, symbolic objects and culture are what we will need to consider for addressing such processes in youth (for similar moves see for example Fuhrer, 2004; Hundeide, 2004; Lightfoot, 1997a, 1997b).

Social and Interpersonal Constraints and Enabling Conditions for Meaning Making

What does culture offer to support processes of transition? Let us admit that there are two ways to approach meaning construction. On the one hand, macrosocial approaches can inform such processes; from that perspective, we need to consider symbolic systems developed by a given society in order to understand the making of people's system of orientation. On the other hand, we need to consider psychological processes through which people construct meaning. Of course, these sociogenetic, ontogenetic, and microgenetic dynamics are intimately related (Duveen, 1998)—even if they have been approached by different traditions of research.

In so-called *traditional* forms of societies, arriving at adulthood is, like birth or marriage, one of the turning points in a life-course. Becoming an adult is usually marked by ritual ceremonies that celebrate a person's cultural birth, his entrance into full participation to adult's rights and responsibilities. It implies a participation in the production of material goods (hunting, working, etc.), the maintenance of the group (begetting), and a symbolic participation (having a special role in the community, its changes and history, participating in collective celebration and rites) (Geertz, 1972; Moro, 1998; Nathan, 2001; Obeyesekere, 1963, 1977). Nowadays, religious and other forms of traditional strongly structured symbolic systems (with systems of rules, specific ritual objects, authorities and a form of organization of time) still confer shared meanings to changes and transitions and actions; they thus provide people with a consistent system of values and a time perspective, as well as social regulations for emotions linked to loss and uncertainty.

Out of such groups, in modern, open, and democratic society, the transition to adulthood is not systematically symbolically marked.[25] In his research on youth self-perception Grob, et al. (2001) shows that young people feel themselves to be the creators of their own possible lives; values, traditions, and experience from elders are perceived as exerting distant, nonconstraining power on their conduct and futures. It might be that people have not been explicitly transmitted such values; or that they affirm their independence because of social expectations of being autonomous. I suggest that they might be blind to the fact that intergenerational transmissions do leave deep traces in their orientation systems (e.g., moral and ethical values). Analyzing people's choices of first names for their children during the transition to parenthood suggests that transgenerational rules still guide processes of naming, even if they prefer not to see or to show these explicitly (Zittoun, 2001, 2004b).[26] If people pretend not to be guided by such values or guiding principles, they will have to find, at least on the surface, other ones, for life and its anxieties have to be regulated and made meaningful (Valsiner, 2003, in press). The next question is therefore: what cultural or symbolic means are available for nourishing and guiding everyday life changes?

Symbolic constructs are part of what societies provide individuals with to support their work of dealing with the world's changeability. At a collective level, when a society begets a certain collection of people—madmen, housewives, AIDS patients—it also generates, sometimes with some delay, social representations, myths and collective forms of discourse that confer shared meaning to these (Duveen, 2000; Jodelet, 2002; Moscovici, 1973). Extended youth or postadolescence has progressively been captured by shared representations. From the 1990s on to now, fluid forms of symbolic production—first low budget movies and experimental literature, and then, mainstream films and novels—have tried to create such symbolic forms. The market has also learned to have young persons, no longer adolescent but not yet established in the economical world, as target customers.[27] These representations, however, irrespective of whether they are produced by young people themselves or by older generations, offer a quite blurred view on youth, or picture a blurred youth.[28] Social scientists have thus seen much of young people's cultural behavior—formation of cliques and tribes, conversion to orthodox groups, consumerism habits and watching of undemanding television programs, risky behavior and addictions—as symptoms of young people's need for orientations and symbolic marking (Anatrella, 1988; Campiche, 1997; Dudzik, 1998; Esprit, 1997; Fornäs & Bolin, 1995; Giddens, 1994; Hundeide, 2004; Moro, 1998; Taracena, 1994; Warnier, 1999). But how these TV shows, movies, and films, might precisely be offering the symbolic tools to build the required systems of orientation, has not been discussed as such.

At the level of the individual, the emergence of structures for meaning-making depends on the same conditions as thinking in general. Without rewriting a psychology of development, I will just emphasize one point. Clinical psychologist, infant development authors as well as learning psychologist seem to agree on the fact that thinking is a fragile mechanism that requires complex and good-enough conditions to occur. The most favorable situations for development are of a social and interactive nature. As part of the environment of the child, elders are triggering, guiding, shaping, and/or scaffolding the child's conduct. Through coordination with the child, elders introduce the child to the range of possible behavior for humans, to the semiotic quality of the shared world, and to zones where the child can produce actions of which he had been unable until then (Goodnow, 1999; Lerner & Galambos, 1998; Perret & Perret-Clermont, 2001; Perret-Clermont, 2001; Pontecorvo & Pirchio, 2000; Stern, 1996; Tomasello, 1999; Tudge, 2000; Vygotsky & Luria, 1994). The emotional, embodied meanings the child attributes to a given situation, marked by these relationships, are deeply connected with the development of new understandings, the construction of new skills and new identity definitions (Aumont & Mesnier, 1992; Duveen, 2000; Hundeide, 2001; Perret & Perret-Clermont, 2001). Authors describe good-enough environments for learning; these require emotional and interpersonal attunement, fostering interactions with an object, in frames constructed on the basis of at least partially shared rules, and that interact with their surroundings. These early forms of triangulation are discussed more precisely in chapters 2 and chapter 6.

For now, Perret-Clermont's notion of "thinking space" (2001, 2004) summarizes the interpersonal and social conditions for thinking to occur. It designates a bounded symbolic space (simultaneously real and internal space), that enables new conduct (Valsiner, 1987, 1998, 2003). In the case of infants, such a space is strongly supported by the adults' activity. Pairs, or groups of older children can create among themselves interactive spaces for exploring and constructing new conduct (Grossen & Perret-Clermont, 1994; Hartup, 1999; Psaltis & Duveen, 2004). Finally, children can create such bounded spaces on their own: in play, children mobilize internalized experiences of prior shared bounded spaces and mingle them with productions of their imagination, within the limits of some material environment. Children thus create their own *zone of proximal development*, where they can attain new coordination, behavior, and skills (Haskell, Valsiner, & McHale, 2003; Vygotsky, 1933; Valsiner, 1989; Winnicott, 1971/2001—see chapter 2).

What structurally holds for infants and children is likely to be the case, in some respects, for young adults. Young adult development also requires bounded spaces for it to be oriented, canalized and enabled (Hasse, 2001; Zittoun, 2004a; Perret-Clermont, 2004). The question that interests us is thus: what equivalent specific bounded spaces can young adults find, so as to elaborate meanings and to develop both a system of orientation and a time perspective? Most of the research on young adult learning has been based on the model of child development. Amongst the researchers that acknowledge that young people grow in social worlds, most of the focus has been put on learning in the context of schools, community, formal, and informal groups, cliques and gangs (e.g., Perret-

Clermont, et al., 2004). One of the central features of youth has, to this point, only been considered in a marginal way: the fact that direct guidance of educators and parents might be no longer relevant as the person is engaged in worlds not only populated by forks, marbles, and electric trains, but in worlds of moral discussions, elections, movies, and hip-hop songs. Youth involves far more solitary interactions within symbolic worlds than childhood—the world of images, sounds, advertisement, computers, newspapers, beliefs, books, movies and so on (Fabbri, Mari, & Vasentini, 1992).[29] And this is exactly where we might find young people giving themselves bounded symbolic spaces where they might, as children in play, work on creating new understandings.

Given then, (a) that young adulthood requires complex restructurations in terms of orientation system, time perspective, consistency, and meaning—which are all highly culturally regulated; (b) that there is no overarching shared worldview that gives an already organized hierarchy of semiotic means; (c) that still, against predictions to the contrary, most young people go on growing, loving, and working; (d) that young people have a newly acquired access to what culture offers, where they can exercise their symbolic responsibility, we thus come to realize that, from an anthropological understanding as well as from a developmental perspective, one very good locus for observing young people's developmental work is the space in which they interact with symbolic objects such as books, movies, pictures, videos, that temporarily encapsulate shared ideas, meanings and beliefs.

Symbolic Responsibility

In the absence of comprehensive shared symbolic system, people have to improvise their system of values. It is quite likely that young people collect symbolic objects or discourses within the abundance of circulating messages. However heteroclite the self-made collections of symbolic elements by which people are constituted (a *bricolage*, see chapter 5), their orientation-systems are supposed to be efficient for living in society. For, even in the absence of consensus about the nature of adulthood, young people are still socially required to *behave as adults*. In particular, I propose, in the actual multiplication of discourses, people are asked to account for their symbolic conduct; I would say, they are implicitly charged with a *symbolic responsibility*. Symbolic responsibility is a two-sided notion. On one side, in our societies, the young person is given the theoretical freedom to choose what cultural experiences she wants to have, what objects she wants to interacts with, what she consumes; she also has an increased space for externalizing her thoughts, tastes, and opinions.

24 Transitions: Development through Symbolic Resources

On the other side, the young person is now asked to stand for and account for these internalization and externalizations. There is an age (which tends to change) where a child is not responsible for being accidentally confronted by shocking images; the young person can now be judged, or punished for downloading offending images from the Internet (she is personally responsible for making a *bad* choice). Similarly, a child's insult or testimony is generally not taken at face value; but there is moment where people are required to stand for what they say, vote, sign, sing, or even for their haircut.[30] Hence the following tension: young people are free to generate their systems of orientation and develop their own sense of the meaning of the world, yet they are responsible for the discrepancies between these and the consensual norms.

Finally, youth is the period during which a person lives through ruptures and transitions; she is required to exert her symbolic responsibility so as to confer a time perspective and a system of orientation to her conduct.

MOVING AWAY FROM THE STUDY OF YOUTH AND MEDIA

The proposition is to examine how complex symbolic objects that populate people's lives—images, paintings, novels, movies, songs, religious texts—can be used in a way that supports youth developmental process (Bruno, 2000). How can such cultural elements enter into people's processes of time-oriented meaning making? To address such issues, it is necessary to define a theoretical approach that renders visible processes of choice, understanding, internalization, transformation, or expression on the basis of cultural elements. This will force me to give some limited consideration to the abundant work on youth and the media.

In effect, as noted regarding studies on childhood (Hodge & Tripp, 1986), most of the literature on youth and the media has opted for approaches that cannot contribute to such an enquiry. It has been largely concerned with the immediate and long-term *effects* of cultural elements and the media on behavior, learning, and identity (see reviews in Anderson, Huston, Schmitt, Lineburger, & Wright, 2001; Johnson, Cohen, Smailes, Kasen, & Brook 2002; Tisseron, 2000).

Some studies have thus considered that time spent in front of the television was subtracted from time and energy that should be otherwise invested in homework, in socialization activities such as youth groups or in work experience (Blumer & Hauser, 1933; Flammer & Alsaker, 2000; Silbereisen, 2001a). Other studies were concerned about the role of certain aspects of the media in young people's behavior. For example, suggestive lyrics in songs have been said to have short-term effects on conduct (Fine, Mortimer, & Roberts, 1990). Content-based studies have examined the effects of specific groups of media-production on beliefs, attitude, and behavior, often in negative terms (contents are presumably negative and amoral). Studies on youth and violence in the media, or youth and the representation of gender in the media and belong to this type (e.g., Anderson, et al., De Bruin, 2001; 2001; Johnson, et al., 2002). Other studies have shown the lasting effects of media, at a higher-level of generality—on projects, values, and personality (in Bruno, 2000; Lutte, 1988). For example, media has been shown to participate in young people's socialization (to the adult world, to oppositional youth culture, or to oppositional adult worlds) and in one's gender definition (Fine, Mortimer, & Roberts 1990; Heath, 1994; Hundeide, 2004; Roulleau-Berger, 1991). Through identification with role models, an adolescent may thus redefine herself or define ways to behave and to live (how to kiss, how to behave as a loving woman) (Blumer & Hauser, 1933; Pasquier, 1999). However, most of these findings are based on correlational analysis, which have been shown to be highly controversial (Hodge & Tripp, 1986; Lembo, 2000; Livingstone, 1998), and inadequate to understand processes of change (Valsiner, 2004d; Valsiner & Sato, 2004). Among these studies, processes that have been identified to account for the influence of violence or sexual topic are: imitation, emotional involvement, role suggestion, or reality confusion. As Bruno concludes (2000), if it is the case that movies, role-playing, or musical bands can, in the absence of any other influences, shape our behavior, there is still no proof that a movie or a song can lead one to commit a crime, or to fall in love.[31]

In terms of processes, a number of studies linked to learning and cognitive development have examined how interactions with various artefacts modify and shape specific forms of thinking (Salomon, 1979, 1993; Tisseron, 2003). Such approaches assume that thinking occurs due to complex configurations of objects, peoples, relations, and actions, constantly modified by each other (Hutchins, 1995). A person's understanding is in that respect not only the product of his own mind, but is also enabled by his relationships to many other social and symbolic entities, or internalization of these relations. Salomon and others have shown that interactive new technology games or modern movies that enable experiencing spatial transformations such as zooming or travelling modify a person's available spatial metaphors. Visual transformations can be thus internalized and shape three-dimensional mental operations. In his research on people's resources for positive adjusting to various situations, Csikszentmihaly and his colleagues have pointed out that cultural elements such as books or movies can facilitate a person's avoidance of depression, because they play a role of "dissipative structures" helping "to relate isolated bits of information to each other, and ultimately to one's goals, for example the ability to see a passage from Shakespeare as pertinent for one's life" (Csikszentmihaly & Larson, 1984, p. 262). Even if they do not consider the specific meaning-contents of the cultural element at stake and the particular force of its relevance for a given person, such studies at least indicate a direction for an enquiry on transformative processes.

Hence most studies questioning the role of media in young people's lives have considered correlations between, on one side, the duration of a person's exposure to a cultural element or its contents, and on the other side, a given behavior of that person. The specificity of cultural experiences, that is, their semiotic nature, has been only scarcely considered by such studies (see for rare exceptions Hodge & Tripp, 1986; Salomon, 1979). My enquiry will, in contrast, examine how a person exerts her symbolic responsibility to choose cultural elements within her spheres of experience in a given society, how these cultural elements become part of her personal culture, and how she *uses* these as resources that become part of her apprehension of the world and herself.

In this first chapter, I have defined ruptures and transitions for analyzing development in youth. Transitions imply identity and positioning changes, knowledge acquisition and meaning making. Among the resources people might mobilize to support such processes, I have suggested to consider symbolic resource. Hence, instead of emphasizing failure in youth development, and instead of suspecting the mass media of negative influence, I will examine young people's everyday uses of cultural elements as symbolic resources, and the role of such uses in good enough processes of change. I thus will propose a psychology of *using* symbolic resources in everyday lives.

NOTES

1. "Our youth is different than it used to be!"
2. The notion of "act of synthesis" (Janet, 1926), or "équilibration majorante" (Piaget, 1964/1967; see Valsiner, 1989), express such ideas. Any such restructuration implies losses, and modifies the field of possible actions (Baltes, 1997; Lawrence & Valsiner, 1993; Valsiner & Conolly, 2003).
3. Jules and Jean are hypothetical characters; their names are used every time I invent an example for rhetorical or exploratory purposes. All the other first names mentioned in the text refer to actual empirical data.
4. The notion of sphere of experience is to be distinguished from A. Schütz's notion of "life world" (1951): life worlds are phenomenologically perceived, and evolve with changes in perception. A person in a given cultural community has one life-world. There, multiple realities can coexist—these require other cognitive modes: religious experience, watching a movie … —and passing from one to the other reality might require what Schütz calls a transition (1951, p. 254). It has also to be distinguished from Goffman's

"frames" (1975), which are purely socially defined. Sphere of experience as defined here try to include both the social-material basis of a given setting or frame of activity (à la Goffman), which imposes tensions, meanings, and positions unto the person, and the subjectively perceived world (à la Schütz). This enables us to say that a person moves from one sphere of experience to another—if the notion was purely phenomenological, we could only say that the sphere of experience was being transformed. This definition thus enables us to account for the sudden, radical, and shocking disturbance of a person's experienced world, due to external forces. In that sense, sphere of experience is much closer to Kurt Lewin's "fields of experience" (1951): there, one person can be at the same time in two overlapping situations, each of them being defined by a goal, various internal, and external forces, and a time-perspective including past memories, current experiences, and future orientations; a person can change situation, progressively or brutally. Here, the reason for not following Lewin's taxonomy is that I will not identify motivations and forces structuring a situational-field, and so forth.

5. The emphasis on rupture *being perceived as such by a person* brings the notion close to that of "turning-point" as defined by Rönkä, Oravala, and Pulkkinen (2002).

6. The idea of an ill-adjustment between the given and the state of a person's representational abilities is based on a semiotic metaphoric model of meaning-making inspired by Peirce (1868a, 1868b, 1878), as described in chapter 2. A semiotic understanding of psychological uncertainty is quite distant from that implied in the psychology of risk assessment where uncertainty is a form of risk that cannot be quantified (Gigerenzer, 2002).

7. Aspects of maturation held to be genetic appear to be mediated by sociocultural dimensions, such as the age of first menstruation (i.e., Crockett & Silbereisen, 2000; Silbereisen, 2001b).

8. Cognitive achievements in adolescence have been seen as: "(a) an increase in automaticity in automatic processes, which frees cognitive resources for other concerns; (b) a far greater breadth of content knowledge across domains; (c) an increased ability to maintain different representations of knowledge simultaneously, permitting new combinations of that knowledge; (d) an increase in the spontaneous use of cognitive strategies and procedures; and (e) a new appreciation of the relativity and uncertainty of knowledge" (Keating & Sasse, 1996, pp. 245-246).

9. Some authors describe youth as a period creating discontinuity in life-paths (Coleman, 1993), and other see it as being in the continuity of a person's life-story (Alléon, Morvan, & Lebovici, 1990; Canestrari, 1989; Laufer & Laufer, 1984). The cultural psychological approach adopted here highlights the tension between continuity and uncertainty of the outcomes of a period exposing the person to a multitude of events that can be experienced as ruptures.

10. These two facts have brought continental sociologists to speak about the "décloisonnement des seuils" (disconnection of thresholds): the processes of leaving one's parents house and creating a new family, leaving school, and getting a job, being economically dependent and then independent, occur at various times, may involve gaps, and may be reversible—which was not the case in Europe in for much of the last century, or in traditional,

initiation-type of societies (Anatrella, 1988; Cavalli & Galland, 1993; Charlot & Glasman, 1998; Evans & Furlong, 1997; Galland, 1995, 1997).

11. Study of the INSEE (Institut national de la statistique) on family life, in *Le Monde*, February 15, 2002.

12. The perception of the ages for adolescence (Flammer & Alsaker, 2001), adulthood (Arnett, 1998; Tilton-Weaver, Vitunski, & Galambos; 2001) and for specific developmental tasks are related to cultural, social, historical, and gender dimensions.

13. For example, in a narrative-based, cross-generational comparative study, Grob, Krings, and Bangerter questioned people from three Swiss groups, aged 25, 50, and 75, about their life-goals, retrospectively and prospectively, and their feeling of being in control of their life. It appears that broad changes in the sociohistorical context do not change the basic structure of people's narratives—their life is still seen as divided into childhood, a period of transition to adulthood, and adulthood. Yet the youngest interviewees take access to education for granted, confer a large importance to professional achievement and to leisure time, do not consider marriage as a priority, while the oldest participants had to struggle to get an education, and considered the constitution of a family as a priority. In contrast to their elders, who seem to consider that obstacles in their lives were due to external circumstances, the young people's language reveals a much stronger sense of being responsible for their choices, and for creating and using opportunities, as well as an affirmed sensitivity to their own mood and needs.

14. One difficulty is that these models have been developed on the basis of qualitative, clinical data; and recent studies have generally operationalized identity-related concepts in quantitative scales, thus losing access to the person's internal elaboration of identity matters (Adams, Montemayor, & Gullotta, 1996; Cavalli, 1989; Markus & Kitayama, 1991; Meeus, 1993; Meeus, et al., 1999).

15. Coleman & Hendry (1980/1999) identify two dominant theoretical frameworks characterizing longitudinal perspective. Contextualism is influenced by Bronfenbrenner's ecological theory (see Muuss, 1996) and includes recent development of the life-span theory (Baltes, Lindenberger, & Staudinger, 1996; Baltes & Staudinger, 1996; Rutter & Rutter, 1993), such as the selection-optimization-compensation (SOC) model (Baltes, 1996; Lerner, Freund, De Stefanis, & Habermas, 2001). These approaches share an awareness of the person in his and her context, of his or her active role, and of the ongoing processes and interaction between the person and his or her environments. However, most of the data supporting these approached are collected through broad surveys, which fail to capture the processes through which person-environment transactions take place. Second, focal models emphasize the various and successive tasks a young person must address on her way to adulthood; they suggest that these people have limited resources, and therefore have to face one at a time (i.e., changing school, puberty)—those forced to address more are in positions of risk. The focal model does not suppose a specific order of resolution of questions, nor an age-limitation, and admits context-malleability (Coleman, 1993), sociohistorical variability (Flammer & Alsaker, 2001), and personal agency (Cranach, 1992; see also Bynner, Chisholm, & Furlong, 1997; Meeus, et al., 1999).

16. Thus, biology and sociocultural dimension are mutually dependent; contextual elements appear interrelated in a complex manner; and interindividual differences cannot be explained by structural variables (such as household, social classes, or ages), but by subtler ones (e.g., parent-adolescent-conflict in intact versus divorced families; appropriateness of school) (Steinberg & Morris, 2001).

17. Studies have been considering young people's relationship to school and media, to new families, to siblings, to friends, and peer-groups, to violence and delinquency, to tobacco, drugs, and alcohol, to sexuality and sexual-transmitted diseases, to unexpected pregnancy and to romantic relationships, to social and political disengagement, to access to jobs and disaffection with schools, to food and clothing, and so forth (see for instance Amato & Booth, 1997; Bynner, Chisholm, & Furlong, 1997; Bynner, Ferri, & Shepherd, 1997; Csikszentmihaly & Schneider, 2000; Hendry, Shucksmith, Love, & Glendinning, 1993; Ryan, 2004; the latest additions to Coleman & Hendry, 1980/1999; or Muuss, 1962/1996). Often financed by institutions related to policy makers, these kinds of research have a shorter time-agenda than the earlier forms, and it seems, have generally reduced theoretical ambitions. Hence, many studies are oriented toward prevention or action without being necessarily grounded in developmental models. However, they mostly hold implicit assumptions about what is *healthy, normal, adjusted,* youth behavior.

18. Social or cultural demographic indicators predict such or such type of behavior; relational, intimate, violent, or cognitive style leads to such maturation and integration or marginalization (i.e., Barrett & Holmes, 2001; Williams & McGillicuddy, 1999). Low economical background, *poor* cultural baggage (often meaning, *lack of dominant culture*), lack of transgenerational transmission, youth culture consumption, external coping strategies appear to be a priori handicaps (if not threats). Conversely, problem-focused approaches oriented toward prevention indicate that young people can find some resources. Some peer or familial relationships, given elements of the sociocultural context (Amato & Booth, 1997; Heaven, 1994; Lerner & Galambos, 1998; Steinberg, 1993) can be positive factors in one's development, at times because of their interactions: the family can facilitate the school-to-work transition, by transmitting certain values, through enhancing one's self-esteem, and through the mobilization of social networks for a young job-seeker (Morrow & Richards, 1996).

19. For example, studies in narrative identities (Grotevant, 2001; Lightfoot, 1997a, 1997b; Neimeyer & Hevitt, 2001) or cultural studies (Marshall & Woollett, 2000).

20. See the pessimistic evaluation of Steinberg & Morris: "The study of psychosocial development—the study of identity, autonomy, intimacy, and so forth—once a central focus of research on adolescence, waned considerably, as researchers turned their attention to contextual influences on behaviour and functioning and to the study of individual differences. The study of cognitive development in adolescence has been moribund for some time now, replaced by study on adolescent decision-making and judgement…. No comprehensive theories of normative adolescent development has emerged to fill the voids created by the declining influence of Freud, Erikson, and Piaget, instead, the study of adolescence has come to be organised around a collection of 'mini-theories'—frameworks designed

to explain only small pieces collection of the larger puzzle. As a consequences, although the field of adolescence research is certainly bigger now than before, it is less coherent and, in a sense, less developmental than it has been in the past" (Steinberg & Morris, 2001, pp. 101-102).

21. The question of meaning elaboration has largely been ignored in recent Anglo-Saxon research on youth. The key-word *adolescence* counts 10241 quotations in Psycinfo, the APA review, between 1993 and 2004; *young adult* 1917, and *late adolescence* 619. The combination of *meaning* (15623) and *adolescence* deserves 219 records, *meaning* and *late adolescence* 10 references, and the junction of *meaning* and *young adult* 24.... However, there are studies considering such meanings-construction in terms of *narrative*, as linked to specific forms of thinking (Dominicé, 1985, Charlot, Bautier, & Rochex, 1992; Guichard, 1993; Kraus, 1996a, 1996b, 2000; Stern, 1996). Such studies mostly refer to Ricoeur (1985/1988), who admits that the process of narrativization creates a person's sense of temporality; however, clinical evidences suggest that one needs to have integrated a time perspective before being able to narrate one's life. Narrativization and meaning construction are both dependent on more essential semiotic processes, linked to emotions and memory.

22. I thank Muriel Gilbert for calling my attention to this novel.

23. Such criteria are obviously bounded by sociohistorical constraints. In a war or a famine situation a young person has other priorities than learning to deal with complex emotions! However, these criteria do not fix a particular form of *realized* person or *integrated* person.

24. Further in the book, the notion of *generative* will not be used in Erikson's (1975) sense of awareness of the need to transmit to next generation.

25. Although many people seem to be looking for forms of ritual passage to adulthood: see on the Web, the number of sites proposing people to create their own rite of passage; in Europe, in the mid90s, risk-taking behavior, extreme sports, body transformations, religious, and political commitments, have been largely interpreted as expressing the need for rites of passage to adulthood (Campiche, 1997; Nathan, 1992).

26. Hence traditional *naming rules* are still mobilized during the procedures of choosing first names, even if the final chosen first name will hide this connection (it is more likely to be visible in the second name) (Zittoun, 2005a).

27. In the early 2000s, media have turned late youth into a new social reality. In Britain, popular press, TV commercials, and movies have exploited the relational immaturities of *thirty-something*: see the success of *Bridget Jones' Diary*, or of "Sex and the City," or newspapers articles such as "Why Don't We Just Grow Up," (Bedell, 2002); "Maria and Matthew Live Miles Apart— Which Is Why They Are Staying Together," (Hill, 2002), and so forth. Yet similar worries appear to have been explored in nineteenth century literature (Jane Austen, George Eliot, etc.) (Waddell, 1998).

28. Young adults are often presented as having grown up in families and schools where adults, trying to implement egalitarian modes of relationships with their children, have avoided imposing strong models and orientations. During the 90s, adults would also have aimed more and more at *keeping young*, in their appearance, life-style, and relationships (Anatrella, 1988; 1999, Clémence, et al., 2001). These kinds of conduct can be seen as preventing the emergence of a representation of time as an irreversible

force that modifies and ends life-stories. In parallel, the discourse surrounding sexuality has been particularly confusing, around issues linked to conception (Zittoun, 2001), gender and homosexuality, pornography, incest, and child abuse (Anatrella, 1988, 1999). A general picture of *anything goes*, glorifying irresponsible actions, mostly emerges out of these representations. Current extreme political reactions (punishing abortion or homosexuality) might be seen as reactions to these anxiogene uncertainties.

29. Similarly, as Vygotsky and Luria (1994) explain, it is important to understand the acquisition of language in the development of thinking; but "the logical consequence of the recognition of the primary importance of the use of signs in the history of development of the higher psychological functions, is the inclusion of external forms of symbolic activity (speech, reading, writing, counting, and drawing) into the system of psychological categories.... From the new point of view we defend they are included into the system of higher psychological functions on an equal footing with all other psychological processes" (pp. 136-137). Examining the role of complex cultural objects as proposed here belongs to the same program.

30. Two facts reveal the importance and the fragility of people's symbolic, expressive responsibility (and freedom): in their growing need to predict and control unpredictable citizens, governments collect traces of semiotic expression—e-mails and uses of credit cards—more than traces of people's physical moves or concrete actions; also, people's shared anxieties—of losing control, or being invaded or contaminated—have e-mail as a locus (fears of viruses and spam). Highlighting these issues, the blockbuster *Matrix* pushes individual freedom one step further: it is not to choose one's action, but to choose one's epistemic stance towards symbolic production (I choose that this is a spoon and that I believe this spoon can fly, therefore the spoon flies); the radical enemy (which is, as most devils are, the other half of the hero) is specifically a bug (a computer virus, that is, something that escapes people's control of their symbolic expression).

31. Which needs to be repeated even in everyday newspapers, see for example Schone (2003) on *Matrix*.

CHAPTER 2

MODELING CULTURAL EXPERIENCES AND SYMBOLIC RESOURCES IN DEVELOPMENT

> *Imagination and creativity are linked to the free reworking of various elements of experience, freely combined, and which, as a precondition, without fail, require the level of inner freedom of thought, action and cognising which only he who has mastered thinking in concepts can achieve.... as Pushkin has aptly remarked, 'imagination is as necessary in geometry as it is in poetry.' Everything that necessitates artistic transformation of reality, everything that leads to inventiveness and the creation of anything new, requires the indispensable participation of fantasy.*
> —Lev S. Vygotsky, *Imagination and creativity of the adolescent* (1931/1994, pp. 269-270)

> *What holds for play also holds for the St. Matthew passion.*
> —Donald W. Winnicott, *Playing and Culture* (1968b, p. 206)

How can we comprehend what young people *do* with books, movies, and songs? There is no royal road to address this issue. Yet two pathways are visible. On one side, *using a book or a movie* implies a person's interaction with objects made out of organizations of semiotic units (signs) carrying meanings. Of course, such an object can be used in a material way—a book can be used to support a piece of paper on which one is writing. The same book can also be used for the fact that it carries meaning: using a book can thus be understood as *using semiotic mediators that come from a book*. It is this second definition of the idea of using a book which we will examine here. Accordingly, we are addressing a particular case of *semiotic mediation* of conduct. This leads to an examination of the role of semiotic mediation in the elaboration of emotions and unconscious thoughts. On the other side, using a book or a movie refers to a particular set of experiences—the experiences of reading a novel or watching a movie or listening to a song—which I will call *cultural experiences*. Based on a comparison with children's play, I will present characteristics of cultural experiences that might be relevant to understand how these cultural experiences change people's relationships to real-life issues. Cultural experiences change people, and can be memorized; they become internalized as part of peoples' personal culture; and these can be mobilized later on. *Symbolic resources* designate these books or movies as devices that are used by a person, with a degree of *intent*, in relationship to something that does not belong to the fictional reality itself, but that belongs to the person's other spheres of experience.

SEMIOTIC PROCESSES IN CULTURAL EXPERIENCES

Humans have the ability to use semiotic means—made out of signs that carry shareable meanings. Semiotic means exist in a material, perceptible form in the world; they can also be translated, so as to acquire an existence in a person's mind (Valsiner, 1997). Some material objects are primarily made to carry semiotic means (disks, pictures, books, etc.). To create them, humans attach meanings to specific semiotic units, in codes that are shared by others: musical, pictorial, verbal, embodied codes, and so forth. They follow (existing or new) rules of composition of the chosen code, to create new organizations of semiotic units. Often, trying to give a symbolic form to an intention modifies it—for example, it was the expression of my previous sentence that brought me to think of this present one.

Humans thus intentionally create *cultural elements* (or *artefacts*, Cole, 1995), loaded with meanings, that issue from their own experience of the world. Cultural elements such as movies, novels, art pieces, religious texts, or music are thus: (1) made out of the organizations of semiotic units and therefore carry encapsulated meanings (2) within the limits of a finite material support. These cultural elements enable humans to extend their intelligence and memory through time and space, and to elaborate and transform cultures and societies (Bruner, 1990; Hutchins, 1995; Salomon, 1979; Wertsch, 1998). Among the cultural elements that satisfy these conditions, I examine a very specific range of cultural elements that satisfy one more condition: (3) those that enable cultural experiences that have a strong imaginary component. Interacting with such cultural elements bring a person to leave the time and space of the here-and-now, to enter into another sphere of experience, where the social, material, and logical rules that apply in real life might not apply anymore; where thoughts and conduct in that sphere of experience have no consequences in the shared social reality; yet where a person's emotions are real (Crapanzano, 2004).

Such a definition leads to the examination of two classes of cultural elements: (a) cultural elements that are bounded by a discrete material support, such as a book, a song on a CD, a film on the screen, and so forth; (b) cultural elements that are part of a clearly defined symbolic system, that is, diffracted in time and space, across significant objects, rules and actors; these also exert a regulation of boundaries between what belongs to the symbolic system, and what does not. Hence, religious texts, practices specific to a minority group, some artistic happenings, might be considered as cultural elements as long as they satisfy the three criteria defined above: made out of organized semiotic units; bounded; and triggering imaginary experiences.

But what happens when thoughts meet semiotic mediators through a person's interaction with a cultural element? I will first present the elementary dynamic of semiotic mediations, that is, the microgenetic process through which all meaning can come to mind. I will then present mediations by cultural elements taken as a whole. One single model can describe the two scales of mediation: *the semiotic prism*.

The Semiotic Prism

Meaning-making can be described thanks to two interrelated dynamics: processes through which semiotic devices mediate objects and thoughts; processes through which objects and semiotic devices mediate relationships between people.

First, let us go back to the basics: human experience can be seen as a constant stream of perceptions and thoughts, originating from within and from outside the organism (Bergson, 1911; James, 1892/1984). For these constant stimuli to become something that is acknowledgeable, on which one's attention can be fixed, or which can be thought about, a portion must be delimited within this flow, fixed and somehow recognized. It is the property of semiotic units—signs, carrier of meanings—to render such processes possible. These have a social origin, and have been somehow translated, or transplanted (Vygotsky & Luria, 1994) within the person, where they can exist as part of her memories. Thus we can say that a person's thought is a continuous flow made out of internalized semiotic mediators that are there to help us apprehend new events.

How can new events be apprehended? Reading Peirce, one might think that it takes three things: first, it requires a person to already have some semiotic mediator in the mind; second, it requires the new event to be somehow grasped; third, it requires a link to be established between these two elements. This new link, in turn, usually modifies the new event and turns it into a new mediator; it modifies the existing one; and it modifies the whole state of understanding of the person (Peirce, 1868a, 1868b). Thinking is thus an on-going three-step dance. This elementary dynamic of linking (and unlinking and relinking) can be seen as the building block of every act of thought. Through this dynamic, the existing state of knowledge of a person can be transformed by new experiences, and the state of knowledge of a person shapes new experiences (as the assimilation and accommodation processes described by Piaget, 1967).

Second, these mediations also always have a social origin. Psychologically, the ontogenesis of semiotic thinking occurs within the child-others interaction (Piaget, 1964/1967; Vygotsky & Luria, 1994; Winnicott, 1971/2001). To greatly simplify, the child must have had the experience of being acknowledged, as a living being and in the quality of his emotional experience, by a caregiver. Within this acknowledgment she can explore her surroundings and discover objects or other things (e.g., she can discover a round soft red thing and put it in her mouth). Eventually, the caregiver can name, or offer a semiotic mediation, to *fix* experiences that the child has with these things in the world (e.g., "Mmmm.... You like it? This is good. This is a strawberry."). Thus the object mediates the caregiver child relationship; the semiotic mediation mediates the child-object relationship (Fonagy, Gergely, Jurist, & Target, 2002; Green, 2000; Moro & Rodriguez, 1998; Nelson, 2002; Vygotsky & Luria, 1994). Later on, people do not need to interact with caregivers to recognize or name new objects from their experiences. Yet, the internalized positions of specific *others* still play an important role in conduct, as nicely formulated by Vygotsky and Luria when presenting the case of children in their laboratory: "The child views the situation posed by the experimentalist, and he senses that, present or not, a human being stands behind that problem" (1994, p. 116).

Such reading of semiotic dynamics suggests that meaning always implies interplays between two forms of mediation. First, a symbolic/semiotic triangle links an existing semiotic unit, a new experience given to a person at time 1, and the meaning it acquires for her at time 2. Second, a psychosocial triangle links the person's experience, the meaning it acquires, and a real or an internalized other. Classical models of meaning-making have focused on one of these aspects only. On one side, the rela-

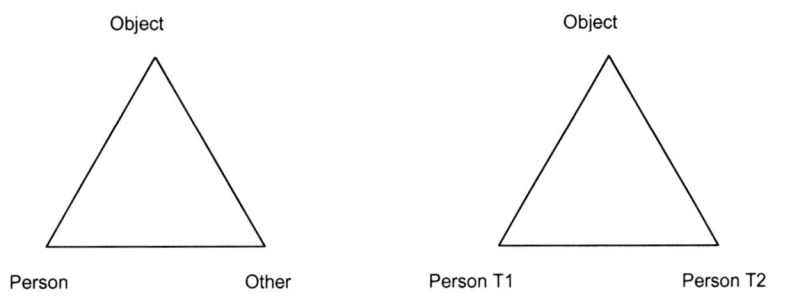

Modeling Cultural Experiences and Symbolic Resources in Development   37

Figure 2.1. Psychosocial and semiotic triangles.

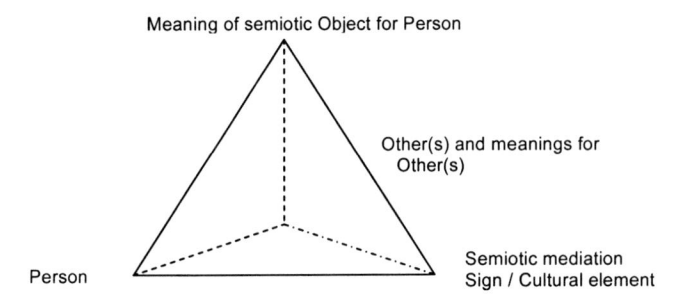

Figure 2.2. Semiotic prism.

tion between the experience to be signified and the existing signifier has been described in semiotics and, in various forms, in linguistics. On the other side, when the social dimension of the mediation is emphasized, a psychosocial triangle is offered to model the person, an other and an object (see for example, Moscovici, 1984/2003).

In contrast to these models, I propose that a full psychological description of meaning making must combine these two triangles. A *semiotic prism* will thus be the model used here for semiotic dynamics. Its poles are the *person* (and her thoughts and feelings), the *semiotic mediator*, the meaning it has for the person, and the *real or imagined other* for whom such a semiotic alliance exists.[1]

The prism is always focused on a given person, in a given situation. At the pole of the *person* is the diversity of her experience—images, emotions, perceptions, or previous meanings or understandings as given to her senses or her mind. A particular portion of this experience can have a *meaning for her*, if it is mediated by some *semiotic element* (a sign, or a symbolic object) (Peirce, 1968a, 1868b; Gillespie, 2004). Reciprocally, a *semiotic mediator, or a symbolic object* can *mean* something to a person's understanding only if it is associated with other thoughts, emotions, or perceptions.

By considering the *person* and *meaning for the person* as two distinct poles, the model suggests that the meaning that the element has for her can, at best, come to the foreground of her experience. It also suggests an ongoing intrapsychological dialogue (Abbey & Davis, 2003; Hermans, 1996; Josephs, 1998).

From the perspective of the *person*, the *other's* view on her or about a given object is constitutive of the meaning it has. The pole *other* creates the social and cultural dimension of the prism. A semiotic mediator functions *per definition* on the ground that its meaning (its association to certain experiences) has been acknowledged or shared by others. The paradox is that, in some conditions, the social dimension of the semiotic prism guarantees the *objectivity* of the meaning—people come to agree on the fact that there is some stability between a given sign and a referent. In other conditions, it is because of the social trace of experiences that some signs acquire a very personal emotional valence—what can also be called the presence of others in the unconscious (Green, 2002) (this is the double notion of *meaning* in Vygotsky 1936), (see Bruner, 1996; Wertsch, 2000). The difference might be given by the degree of generality of the social dimension—whether it is a defined social other, or a generalized social other (Gillespie, 2004).

Of course there are also private signs, such as when Jean[2] keeps in her room a stone that signifies for her the last encounter with Jules. Yet, genetically, the condition of a semiotic dynamics is social: it requires the coordination of two distinct human perspectives: also, logically, because it is located in the flow of time, a semiotic dynamic necessarily supposes the coordination of two perspectives as well: it can thus be said that the meaning of the stone is shared by Jean at time 1 (Jules and Jean on the stony beach), and Jean at time 2 (Jean in her room with the stone). However, for clarity's sake, I will concentrate on signs that are socially acknowledged as such, not on private signs.

Finally, the pole *meaning for the person* thus designates the subjective quality of a specific human experience, its double anchorage within embodied memories, affects and understandings, and in the shared world.

Memorials can thus be read through the semiotic prism (Zittoun, 2004d): Jules (*person*) stands in front of monument to the anonymous soldier of World War II (*symbolic object*), which is publicly shared: it is a national monument, placed on a crowded square, where everyone *knows* what it stands for (others). This makes him think about his grandfather, who died in the war, whom he never met (*meaning for person*).

Modeling Cultural Experiences and Symbolic Resources in Development 39

The prism model should not be seen as a list or a description of important dimensions. Rather, it pretends to be *functional* (Moscovici, 1984/2003). In order for this role to be fulfilled, it needs to be seen as an open-system of evolving relationships located in time. It implies that every modification of the prism modifies others aspects, and that these aspects necessarily change over time. In effect, semiotic dynamics occur in time; any sign can become the object of another sign (it can be *reversed*, Peirce, 1878; Vygotsky & Luria, 1994). Their uses enrich their meanings, and their uses can exceed or transform their original uses. Semiotic means acquire traces of their uses (what they designate, and for whom) and such traces are part of the richness and harmonics of shared and personal semiotic systems (Bakhtin, 1979/1986; Peirce, 1868a, 1868b, 1878).

Suppose, for example, that Jean (time 1) has to do a complex division at the baker's to know how many croissants she can buy (symbolic operation about the objects); imagine also that Jean (time 2) has a frightening and authoritative math teacher (other); Jean can suddenly feel paralyzed by the division, for she imagines the teacher's angry gaze on her back, and she renounces her croissants. This model can help us to observe the traces of social and affective dimensions of meaning making and thinking (Zittoun, Duveen, Gillespie, Ivinson, & Psaltis, 2003).

Also, at times, some poles or vectors linking them, rather than others, come to the foreground of one's experience. Sides of the prism can also be threatened; a prism that loses one side collapses, and becomes an impoverished triangle. *Cues*, defined by Peirce as semiotic elements that have a relation to a thing independently of human conventions, could be described by a triangle (rather than a prism). Young children ignore the fact that a map is more than just a nice object to play with, and that it is has a meaning of being the model of something in the world (Wiser, 2004; Wiser & Amin, 2001). In chapter 6 we will examine alterations of the semiotic prism.

This basic semiotic prism enables us to alternate between two analytical lenses: we can observe microgenetic semiotic processes; we can also examine semiotic processes mediated by cultural elements—books, films, pictures, each made out of the complex organization of such units. Let me pursue this exploration of microgenetic processes.

Semiotic Mediation and Architecture of the Self

A metaphor needs to be introduced in order to account for the fact that the person develops through endless conduct and interactions with others, the world and objects—and that these conduct and interactions are mediated through evolving semiotic prisms. The semiotic prism and other semiotic configurations are partly within the world, and partly internalized. At the level of their psychic translation, they necessarily have some form of organization. Psychology admits that the structure of mind, resulting from actions, interactions of the person in and with the world, reflects the organization of these interactions and actions.

Gillespie (2004) describes interpersonal relations as architectures of possible positions co-constructed by participants of interactions—a person's utterance from one particular perspective always creates a possible new position for another person, which she might momentarily attain, and from which she might reflect on herself; doing so, she might add a surplus of meaning to her previous understanding, and thus modify her position. Hence a traveller can mockingly describe the behavior of what he calls a *tourist* to an interviewer, before seeing himself from the perspective of the other and realizing that he acts exactly just as such a tourist.

The attaining of these positions is always a semiotically mediated activity. Gillespie (2004) proposes an *architecture of intersubjectivity* (drawing on Rommetveit, 1979) which describes the sets of possible positions created by a person in an interaction with an other, or a generalized other. A person can also engage by herself in moving across positions of real or imagined others, whose perspectives are imagined (or have become internalized). By extension, one might call this internalized structure of positions that a person temporarily adopts, drawing on previous interactions with real or imagined others, the *architecture of the self* (Gillespie, personal communication, September, 2004).

The metaphor of architecture suggests a tri-dimensional interiority, structured and organized along lines of forces, or axes reflecting a person's most important socializations and interactions—it is made out of memories of past semiotic dynamics having engaged real, internalized, imagined, and generalized others. The idea of an architecture of the self enables us to see consciousness as a focused point within that architecture, and constantly relocated (Benson, 2001). Moves of consciousness are constrained by the architecture; yet themselves modify the architecture. Some zones are easier to access than others; finally, there are hierarchies in the architecture, as we will see. [That metaphor thus builds on Hermans' (1996) idea of identity as "a multitude of I positions in an imaginal landscape," but gives some volume and structure to that landscape, and dissolves rigid I positions into temporary locations attained by the ever changing forefront of one's attention.]

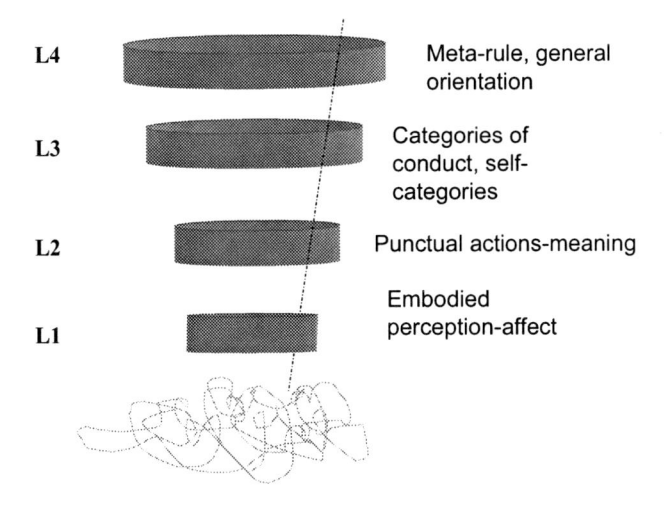

Modeling Cultural Experiences and Symbolic Resources in Development 41

L4		Meta-rule, general orientation
L3		Categories of conduct, self-categories
L2		Punctual actions-meaning
L1		Embodied perception-affect

Figure 2.3. Semiotic hierarchy.

Semiotic Mediation, its Levels, and Uncertainty

Semiotic means can designate punctual experiences, but can also be distant from the immediate experience and have a more general scope. They can thus be presented as part of a *hierarchy* of semiotic mediations within the architecture of the self, as Valsiner does in his theory of *enablement*, or theory of *bounded indeterminacy* (2001b, 2003, 2004c, in press), which is presented in Figure 2.3.

A person can be traversed by agitated and confused physiological states of discomfort—heartbeat varies, hands are cold, throat is constricted, confused ideas agitate one's mind, the world appears grey and hostile (Level 0).

A first level of semiotic mediation (Level 1), addresses the here-and-now of the given of an embodied experience. Semiotic mediation allows the person to distance herself enough from the experience to know that this state is unpleasant (*relative* to the memory of previous states).

At the second level, semiotic processes group and *label* such a field of impressions into known composites such as *sad* or *disgusted*; these can be named, but can also be fixed thanks to nonverbal semiotic means (Level 2). In doing so, semiotic mediations enable their evolution and termination (Valsiner, 2003, 2004c); the label leads to forms of conduct, such as crying in the presence of someone else (Tisseron, 1999; Obeyeskere, 1977).

At a third level, semiotic mediations can acquire a categorical function, conferring some permanency to properties of the self or of the world, beyond the here-and-now. When attached to the self, third level mediations can define properties of the self—such as "I am a sad person." When attached to the world, these offer representational categories that have a certain stability across situations (Level 3).

At a fourth level, semiotic mediations become generalized, more distant from the here-and-now of an embodied experience. These are standing beliefs, general orientations, and worldviews—for example, an idea about the senselessness of the world (such as "nothing is worth doing anyway"). Fourth level mediations can guide, or *promote*, lower level thoughts and actions; this is their *feed-forward* property (Valsiner, 2003).

Hence an over-generalized feeling can determine a person's physiological experiences (Level 0), and through it, will shape the whole hierarchy. Such a hierarchy finally has intransitive properties, that is, higher-level conducts can determine lower ones. In effect, both *lower* semiotic mediations (such as disgusted) as well as *higher* ones (such as "the world is unfair") will orient a person's future experiences, that is, promote certain experiences rather than others, or bound indeterminacy (Valsiner, 2003, Valsiner, 2004c). Hence, "I am disgusted" can enable a certain lower-level action (skipping one's dinner), or enable a particular fourth level position (adhering to the values of an underground movement). Semiotic mediations can thus be seen as organized into hierarchies of meaning within the architecture of the self.

As described in chapter 1, semiotic phenomena are interesting to study not so much within the ongoing-flow of mediated thought, but in ruptures, when uncertainty emerges. Uncertainty can occur at any of these four levels of mediation: at each level, one can miss the right mediation to think, or link, a current experience, or can oscillate between two ways of conferring meaning. Hence, at the first level, a person cannot be sure whether that particular state of the body is linked to emotions. At a second level, one can wonder whether this is angriness or depression; at a third level, one might wonder if one is happy or unhappy: and at a fourth level, one can examine his general life-orientation (i.e., "every experience is an occasion for growth"—or "life can only become worse"). I will call the process of attaching a given experience to a semiotic mediation at any one of these levels, and thereby reducing the corresponding uncertainty, *horizontal linking*. In contrast, *vertical linking* is the process of reducing uncertainty by changing the level of the hierarchy from which meaning is considered (see also Valsiner, 2004c). Hence, in the state described above, a person might have to consider a job offer, which has to be judged as "good for me" or "bad for me," both categories at Level 3. The person might use a Level 1 impression (feeling of constriction when thinking about the job) to decide that it is bad; or he might use a Level 4 principle, "every new experience is an occasion for growth," to decide that it is good. The semiotic mediation thus enables the reduction of uncertainty at a given level, by moving the mediation to an upper, or lower, level of the hierarchy.

More generally, semiotic mediations can bring distance towards the uncertainty of a rupture, and can project a little zone of known, symbolized experiences beyond it. They can thus *enable* or *promote* specific conduct (Valsiner, 2003). Hence, if a person confronted with the death of a relative or close friend can mobilize a traditional mediation such as the one associated with *ritual grief*, which is a high-level of mediation, her whole process of grief will be semiotically canalized for her. The uncertainty created by the rupture ("how will life be possible without him") is replaced by a clearly represented and organized suite of activities (for example, the Jewish prescription of mourning: 7 days of intense withdrawal from the world; 30 days of mourning; 12 months of daily prayers). Semiotic mediations distance the person from the immediate given of one's experience. Their enabling function is of great importance for a developmental enquiry: again, if development is studied within periods of transition—that follow a rupture that generates uncertainty—and semiotic mediations enable the creating of links that reduce uncertainties, then semiotic processes appear at the heart of our enquiry. Semiotic dynamics will thus be the processes to examine when understanding the work of transition: it is through these that, progressively, we may see the promotion of some forms of conduct rather than others, or the emergence of new forms of conduct.

Semiotic Mediations in Cultural Elements

We can finally change lenses of analysis and move from the microgenetic processes of semiotic mediation, to mediations enabled by cultural elements seen as a whole. In a cultural element (a book, a movie, or a painting), semiotic units are organized in a particular way (the structure of the story, the composition of the symphony, the arrangements of colors and shapes in the picture). Correspondingly, a person experiencing that book or painting is exposed to this particular configuration of semiotic units, which mediate her experience at various levels.

As semiotic organizations, cultural elements are submitted to certain rules and constraints; some are specific to their code (music vs. plastic arts); some have specific technical or conventional aspects (e.g., literary genres). These configurations constitute and transform meaning-contents. For example, the story of a person's transformation from a sad to a happy state, a meaning implying a succession in time, will be deployed differently in a folktale or in an epic novel, which determine specific *chronotopes* (spatial/temporal universes) (Bakhtin, 1937-1938/ 1981). It will also transform these contents when translated from a diachronic to a synchronic mode of symbolization, for example, when a tale is represented in a painting. Conversely, an instantaneous experience, such as "love at first sight" is, in poetry, developed as a time-enduring experience. Some symbolic elements play with complementarity and the contrasts between various semiotic codes—for example, some films show quiet scenes with music suggesting tensions, or bright colors emphasizing the dramatic and grotesque aspects of a character's discourse. Culturally-shared rules of genres and social representations allow people to call on additional meanings and expectancies during a cultural experience—a figure of innocence and purity generally suggests the opposing presence of a malevolent character (paradigmatic combinations), and two lonely male and female characters in a diachronic story might create the expectancy of a happy meeting (syntagmatic combinations) (for example Hodge & Tripp, 1986; Rowe, 1999; Phillips, 1999a, 1999b). The organization of the cultural element constrains the nature of the cultural experience: a book must be read in a certain order, while the viewing of a painting is freer (although generally guided by its formal composition). Finally, interacting with cultural elements enable the distance from, and the mediation of an experience at various levels of generality, at the same time or successively.

SEMIOTIC ELABORATIONS OF EMOTIONS AND THE UNCONSCIOUS

A person's experience, as it appears meaningful to her, can be described as a stream of conduct, or as a semiotic flow. Both ways, the *emotional quality* of experience is central (Diriwächter, 2003, 2004; Janet, 1926, 1928; Valsiner, in press). Emotions play a central role in most cultural experiences, which aim at triggering emotional responses.[3] Emotions strongly shape the memories that might be awakened by cultural experiences; and they finally may be important in situations of rupture and uncertainty. The role of semiotic mediations is to confer meaning to ruptures, but also to elaborate memories, emotions, and the unconscious prolongations of experience.

Here, I propose a model where emotions are seen as directly linked to physiological events, but also as resulting from physical or representational conduct: they most likely come out of, develop and terminate through the ongoing transactions between semiotic mediations and embodied experiences, conscious and unconscious thoughts.

Theorizing Emotions

In psychological models, the question of emotions is often treated after cognition and reflection have been theorized. Possibly as a consequence of this, emotions are often only conferred secondary roles in theories: as underpinning tensions, or as catalysts or inhibitors of thought. A long tradition of research that has drawn on the work of William James (1884) and Carl Lange (1885) (Janet, 1928; Laird, in press; Rapaport, 1942) has explored the relationships between the embodied component of emotions and their mental apprehensions.[4]

Along with most researchers on emotions, I acknowledge the embodiment of emotional experiences, and the fact that some experiences might affect the body in its more primary reactions. However, in common with a smaller number of researchers, I will consider that emotional experiences can be called *emotions as such* only once their very existence has been rendered meaningful, that is, attached to a mnemonic trace such as an image, a sound, or any other semiotic means, or in a few cases, a linguistic emotion label (Valsiner, in press). This does not mean, however, that these emotions need to be consciously acknowledged. The purpose of traditional religion, psychotherapy and art, crafts of binding signs, is mostly to capture and transform emotional experiences, with or without the full awareness of the person. Semiotic means have the power to capture, fix, regulate, or canalize emotional embodied experiences and memories.

The dynamic hierarchic model of semiotic mediation developed by Valsiner (2003, in press) presented above aims at accounting for the transformation of emotions. In that model, a hierarchy of semiotic mediations enables, first, to group and acknowledge a physiological event (Level 1 mediation); second, to name or label that emotional experience (Level 2); third, to give a categorical qualification of that emotion or a generalized feeling in link to a self-definition (Level 3); and fourth, to over-generalize the current experience at a level of vague beliefs or basic attitude (Level 4). Level 4 emotions have feed-forward properties; they define Level 0 possible events, and so can loop back and affect the entire hierarchy. Valsiner sometimes calls these various levels of mediation subconscious (embodied and beyond clear mediation), conscious (nameable and categorizable), and supraconscious (over-generalized and therefore, as little identifiable as Level 1).

The vocabulary used within that model triggers some connections with theories that acknowledge unconscious dynamics. Taking this proposition seriously, I draw on psychoanalytical theories that explore unconscious dynamics to complement Valsiner's propositions. Starting with Valsiner's model as a working basis, I adopt a strategy of *supplementarity* (Gillespie, 2003): models will be called on so as to complete each other. I justify my use of psychoanalytical models in the frame of a cultural psychology on epistemological and theoretical grounds. On the one side, the psychoanalytical models considered here aim at giving helpful metaphors to account for observed facts, just as semiotic models do. On the other side, these models are all compatible with my initial assumptions: they admit the ever-changing nature of the mind, examine conduct in their totality, and their semiotic mediations. This will bring me to make three arguments:

1. An hierarchical model represents *vertical* links; mostly, we see relations of subsumption (content A is subsumed under higher-level concept A—that might have merged out of A). Yet, empirical facts reveal that emotions are very labile and likely to create quickly *horizontal* relationships;
2. An hierarchical model tends to suggest that the lower levels are the less conscious ones, while the higher are more; as we have seen, Valsiner's over-generalized fourth level is no longer conscious, which suggests that there is a middle group of conscious mediations. Yet empirical facts show that even the level of middle conduct, which can be seen as self-related, and verbalizable, is only very partially conscious;
3. If semiotic mediations are, in great part, not conscious and are governed by the logic of the emotions, there must be some means to help convert or translate these mediations into conscious ones. Complex organizations of semiotic mediation such as pieces of art, statues, novels, and films, may have a function linked to these emotional and unconscious emotions and meanings.

Adding Secondary Emotions and Horizontal Links With Janet

A hierarchical model of semiotic mediation shows vertical relationships as well as feed-forward dynamics (Valsiner, 2004c). Yet, examining a comparable hierarchy based on clinical evidence suggests that this must be completed by horizontal linking. To show this, I will follow Pierre Janet's propositions (1926, 1928, 1934/1935).

In parallel to the development of the German *Ganzheit* psychology (cf., Diriwächter, 2003, 2004), in France, Janet developed his psychology of *conduct*, complex embodied perception-thoughts-feeling-actions, where emotions have a central organizing strength (Zittoun, 2004c).

Janet proposes a hierarchy of *conduct*. A hierarchy of conduct is not a hierarchy of semiotic mediations, but a hierarchy of *relational* conduct. Janet is in effect interested in relational acts that he distinguishes on the basis of *what* they link. The lower forms of conduct are actions that link things from the world; middle forms of conduct includes relations between actions and thoughts; higher forms of conduct are relationships between thoughts. Higher forms of conduct have a broader generality: a moral commitment, as a form of higher-level conduct, orients various beliefs and actions (middle conduct), and thus regulates local experiences of the world (lower conduct). For Janet, these relational acts have a social origin (Valsiner & Van der Veer, 2000), and thus his hierarchy of conduct and semiotic hierarchies can be said to be overlap in most cases.

Emotions are, for Janet, part of complex composites that constitute conduct. Janet distinguishes emotions linked to *primary actions*, from emotions linked to *secondary actions*. Primary actions are forms of conduct that are produced as reactions to the world—automatic actions, obedience, routines, verbal answers, or memories. These include bodily actions as well as forms of language or thought, and can be reflective (directed at other actions),[5] as long as they are directly stimulated by an encounter with a person or an event located in the world. Secondary actions are of the same type as primary ones—all the thoughts, expressions, behavior, which follow or are *caused by primary actions* (1928, p. 122). These are thoughts about thoughts, inner attitudes towards primary actions, tensions concerning the past or the future, spontaneous conduct, the production of new sentences, actions, grasp of consciousness, and so forth. Hence emotional composites are made out of both primary conduct, provoked by conditions determining one's possibilities of acting, and secondary conduct with their own emotional tone. A person "does not contemplate his or her perception like one contemplates a spectacle," but adds to that numerous secondary actions: "Sentimental regulation seems to be essentially made out of the addition of secondary actions which, by their presence, modify primary actions, increase or diminish them, or orient them in various ways" (Janet, 1934/1935, pp. 103-104, my translation). Emotional experiences are thus complex *composites*.

This hierarchical model combined with a definition of emotions as a composite of primary and secondary conduct leads to an understanding of emotion that supplements the one we have already developed. In effect, the first complication of normal emotions is that they are located in a particular time-spot. At this point, the person's conduct includes a physiological state, and thoughts and emotions linked to the perception of the situation. To this can be associated secondary thoughts, among which memories of similar situations or feelings. These associations might in turn provoke additional physiological reactions. The impressions and thoughts will be interpreted in that person's situation, together with possible thoughts and emotions about the future. On a happy day, Jules might see the scarf of a dear person and feel his heart beat—which would remind him of the intense moment of the gift of the scarf, and his related feelings of love; that would be reread in the present moment, with the knowledge that this person will not come back. Present sadness and past happiness create a form of regret. The general tone of an emotional state emerges out of that composite.

A second complication of emotions is that they are deeply social and involve not only low-level direct conduct in the world, but also always thought about actions (middle conduct), and high-level conduct (thoughts about thoughts and values); Janet thus sees love and hate as highly social and cultural feelings (1934/1935, p. 98). Each of these levels is submitted to a symbolic canalization, a person's conduct having been developed in symbolic worlds. Some kinds of emotional-related conduct are thus socially expected, wished for, or forbidden, and such mediations necessarily awake other secondary thoughts that might modify, downward, one's actions, or, upward, one's values or commitments. Finally, the felt emotion appears to be a complex resultant (not necessarily a reflective synthesis) of a vast composite of modified basic feelings, perceptions, mental conduct, memories, affects and so forth, that can be condensed and displaced (Freud, 1900). As in other holistic approaches, it is an overarching tonality that emerges out of a totality of an experience (Kulpe, in Diriwächter, 2003).

We thus see the interest of considering that emotions are not only linked or structured vertically (within the hierarchy), but that these also can be horizontally linked through secondary emotions. Usually, such lateral or horizontal links stay in the background of conduct, from where they add the thickness of harmonics of other times and places to the present (Bakhtin, 1979/1986). Here, I see two important reasons to enrich our initial hierarchical model, so as to be able to consider both vertical and horizontal links.

First, such enrichment is fundamental for us to be able to account for emotions that are not only triggered by real experiences, but also by imagined experiences and artefacts. Everyday situations indeed combine memories and interactions with cultural elements: it feels cold, and Jules feels cold, and last time Jules was cold he saw that advertisement for hot chocolate, and all this makes him think of his childhood's winter holidays in Swiss chalets, a memory that is very cosy and warming (which reduces his present sense of coldness). What occurs in the body (Level 0 or 1) can be produced by cultural experiences due to the power of vertical and feed-forward links, and due to the evocation of secondary thoughts.

Second, in some cases, these lateral associations can drastically modify the course of an experience. As Janet, Freud, and other psychopathologists have shown, secondary conduct can indeed invade and distort thinking. If the boss enters Jules' office shouting, it can trigger mnemonic traces of the dog jumping on his cradle when he was a baby, before he had access to means of verbalizing; every time someone shouts at him, he might feel utterly terrorized, to a degree not explicable by the current situation.

What we thus need to include in our hierarchies of emotional semiotic mediation, are *horizontal* emotional and mnemonic links. We also need to define an understanding of the work of *unconscious processes*. At this point two psychoanalytical contributions usefully supplement our reflection.

Adding Unconscious and Disorder With Green and Matte Blanco

A post-Freudian psychoanalyst, André Green has developed Freud's theory of affects (emotions) (see also Freud, 1920). Green's formulation of the *psychic apparatus* can be represented as divided into four metaphorical zones, the soma, the unconscious, the conscious, and the real, delimited by some qualitative boundary. Drives can be defined as embodied (somatic) desires or needs, tending to seek satisfaction in the world; affects are their visible aspects. Provoked by external or internal events, affects occur in the soma, beyond consciousness; they then tend to diffuse through different layers of the psyche where they are transformed, before eventually finding a form that can bring conduct within the socially shared reality. From the soma, they accede to the unconscious under the form of *psychic representation of the drive*, where they can be connected to *representations of things* (conscious or unconscious mnemonic traces linked to interactions with objects of the world), and progressively, be linked to *representation of words* (allowing reflectivity). Such doubly linked emotional experiences can thus enter consciousness, under a symbolic form (Green, 1973/1999, 2000, 2002).

This simple and elegant model of the elaboration of representations, presented as a model of *gradients* (Green, 2002), has surprising overlaps with our hierarchical model of semiotic mediations. We might thus say that the Level 0 of mediation corresponds to a given somatic experience, as it might possibly be apprehended by the mind; psychic representation of drives would belong to a sort of Level 0 of semiotic mediation. Representations of things, which are prelinguistic mnemonic traces, correspond to elementary, Level 1 mediations. Links to representations of words would designate semiotic mediations at Level 2 and 3. Level 4 mediations would be crystallized forms of relations that are attributed to the functions of the superego or sublimation.

This parallel is fundamental for extending the model of semiotic mediations so as to account for phenomena that cannot be understood without the hypothesis of unconscious dynamics, such as distortions of thought. In the psychoanalytical model, when affects subsist without link to representations, they cannot be acknowledged as such, and consequently threaten further semiotic elaboration. They can be subject to *cleavage*, as in traumas, where they cause zones of avoidance of thinking, or acted out, that is, they find a direct short-cut at somatic level (Freud, 1914). If affects are linked to representations, but are not tolerable for other reasons (such as *superego*, or higher-level values), these composites can be *repressed* or transformed to become consciously tolerable, and this can in turn modify deeper memories. In a semiotic model, we might say that cleavage operates at the Level 1, before these are attached to representations, and that repression operates at any semiotically mediated higher-level.

Green's model thus shows that semiotic processes can occur without becoming objects of awareness during emotional elaboration. For psychoanalysts, these unconscious processes have their own dynamics and life: they might create wild lateral links, intrude other thought-emotion configurations, or participate an unnoticed transformation of one's architecture of self and experience of the world.

We can now extend such a hierarchical-gradient model of thinking to define the *horizontal* linking suggested above with the help of Matte Blanco's conception of logics of thinking (Matte Blanco, 1975). In his reading of Freud, he highlights the difference of relations established by conscious and unconscious processes. In conscious life, relations between components of ideas have to be asymmetrical: A causes B, A comes before B, A is part of B—and not the opposite. Unconscious linking operations tend to treat any relation as bidirectional: if A causes B, then B causes A, if B can come before A, then B can also be part of B. The unconscious can thus be seen as creating symmetrical relationship between representations, whatever the nature of the relationship is in the conscious life (and in the real world). This distinction is a simplification of Freud's distinction between primary processes (characterized by timelessness, displacement, condensation, double contradictions, and absence of causal links, as in the dream work (Freud, 1900, 1901), and secondary processes (submitted to rules of causality, noncontradiction, and time).[6] In Matte Blanco's view, the logic of the unconscious can thus modify categorization relationships: if A is part of B, B can also be part of A, and of C of which A is also part. This brings Matte Blanco to consider the unconscious as made up of "infinite sets": if an object that normally belongs to set C, enters bilogic (combining symmetric and asymmetric) modes of linking, it can progressively become attached to any member of that given set; more abstract categories of that set become equivalent to that element, and thus any member of set C that can be described by that abstract concept becomes equivalent with that first object. Thus, in the unconscious of a mother, a baby can become subsumed under its property of being soft, and thus be treated as any other soft object—for example, addressed and treated as *it*, the towel (Rayner, 1995). Consciousness tolerates not much bilogic linking; only a very little part of such infinite sets become conscious.

For Matte Blanco, as for Janet, Valsiner, or Green, emotions are made out of two classes of phenomena. First, emotions are physiological; as such, they are for one part experienced as sensation-feelings, and for another part, as inciting actions. Second, emotions are made out of thinking. Among such thinking, Matte Blanco includes not only the acknowledgment of sensation-feelings, but also and immediately, their associated thought: being angry includes the recognition of a certain physiological state, but also *angry thoughts*—thinking badly about the person who provoked that reaction, thinking about his stupidity, thinking about things that might be said to him. Matte Blanco thus proposes an analysis of emotional events in terms of symmetrical links, that is, in terms of his analysis of the logic of unconscious linking. Examined closely though the bilogic lenses, these secondary components of emotions appear to have other characteristics. If Jean is angry about Jules's action, the action's property of being anger-causing might be generalized to all other aspects of Jules, and might be maximized: all of these aspects are absolutely stupid; finally, that might be extended to other objects that represent Jules (the book he lent Jean is so anger-causing that she has to throw it out of the window).

In this perspective, unconscious emotional dynamics are seen as *wild* linking and categorizing processes. Let us come back to our hierarchy of semiotic mediations: the bilogic proposition suggests that lateral associations create *absurd* semiotic mediations. Hence, Jean feels strange and tense (L1[7])—she does not like that person wearing a bow-tie (L2)—can symmetrically evoke a lateral link—she hates bow-ties—which becomes a labelled thought and object of awareness (L2). This might then be generalized and guide her further choices of clothes and of friendships (L3) (bow-tie example in Bandura, 1971). Thus, wild links might be created between a given element of thought, its horizontal associations, and their vertical links. Semiotic mediations could enter in anarchic enablements or limitations of conduct. Absurd higher-level mediations could guide a person's conduct, without her being able to justify these rationally.

Such a model excludes the possibility of a clear-cut division between unconscious (lower and over-generalized) and conscious semiotic mediations.[8] Rather, it seems that consciousness is a very limited zone rather located within middle conduct, itself surrounded by clouds of unconscious linking, both vertical and horizontal, accelerated by unbounded emotional dynamics. *Hence, consciousness would be the most privileged zone of attention within the architecture of the self.* However, such a model also sug-

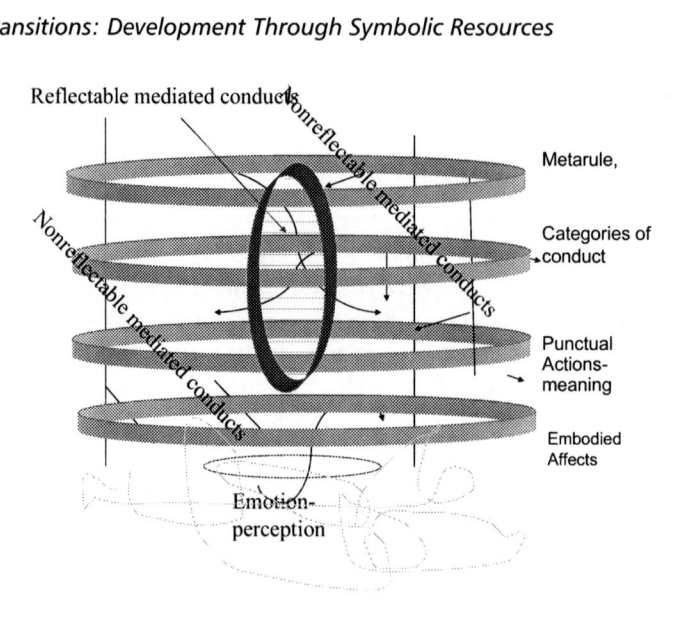

52   Transitions: Development Through Symbolic Resources

Figure 2.4.   Hierarchical models: The part of consciousness.

gests that other zones might become more conscious, if the right linking and translations processes occur.

Wo Es War, Soll Ich Werden

This leads to another important question for understanding thinking: how are linking processes that can extend consciousness possible? In other words, as Janet, Green, and Matte Blanco have asked, if unconscious primary processes and secondary processes are qualitatively so different, if symmetrical wild linking is so different from asymmetrical thinking, and if emotional dynamics are mostly unconscious, how can these unconscious emotional dynamics ever become object of awareness and observation? How can symmetrical processes be expressed, according to asymmetric principles (Matte Blanco, 1975)? Since Freud, most authors highlight the difficulty of linking language (which is asymmetric) and symmetric psychic processes.

This needs a form of *translation*. For Matte Blanco symmetrical thoughts cannot become conscious, but can nevertheless be translated in such a way that one becomes aware of their existence. These translation processes need to be supported one way or another—and this is where the importance of semiotic mediations, as well as that of therapeutic settings or cultural experiences come to the fore (Green, 1992; Nathan, 1992).

Green describes as *tertiary* the processes that enable the translation or linking of primary and secondary dynamics, and considers them as thinking *per excellence*. It is where thinking, enabled by semiotic mediations, encompasses both personal meaning and a time-structure (Green, 1973/1999, 2000). Psychoanalytical settings as well as cultural elements promote such tertiary processes.

Psychoanalytic therapeutic settings aim at facilitating the emergence of such tertiary processes. The particular relationship between patient and psychoanalyst, and the ways language is used between them, enables the creation of a *potential* communication, where things can be paradoxically simultaneously imagined and real (Winnicott, 1971/2001). Thanks to this transitional space, which is *between* socially shared reality and inner lives (with their fantasies and thoughts), links between primary and secondary processes can be assembled, unlinked and relinked by the patient, played with, and addressed to the analyst. The analyst becomes the presence of the other in the patient's thinking, thanks to which he can use semiotic mediations to address his interiority (*meaning for self*). The other can be also seen as imposing a particular form of socially ruled language (secondarity) by acknowledging the personal overtone and undertones it has for the patient (primary processes); from that particular position, he can reflect on the links between explicit and implicit discourse through interpretations, thus returning these in a relinked, tertiary way to the patient. The patient might eventually internalize that other's position to reflect on his own various embodied experiences and thoughts.

Cultural elements, such as myths or tales, offer comparable potential spaces and socially shared symbolic structures that enable tertiary processes (Green, 1969; Nathan, 1993; Tisseron, 2003; Winnicott, 1971/2001). Tales and myths submit unconscious primary linked themes such as birth, death, sexuality, to the structure of socially shared semiotic configurations: the language of tales, and the historically-matured, socially shared rules about how to deal with these issues. Tales and myths (*symbolic objects*) used by a person link her with the social others of her culture, to confer a symbolic and communicable form to intimate (but shared) fears and fantasies (De Rosny, 1981/1985, 1992; Grossen & Perret-Clermont, 1992; Kaës, 1996, 1998; Nathan, 1998).

Hence, therapeutic spaces or myths socially guide and support the creation of new semiotic positions within the architecture of self; they provide spaces to untie and deploy various forms of human experiences; and they offer a semiotic-configuration broad enough to encompass abstract as well as very concrete experiences, asymmetrical and symmetrical linking. Both support thinking and the elaboration of experience, for they offer three elements: a standpoint for reflecting, a space for exploring, and a semiotic structure to capture, articulate and communicate.

All sorts of cultural elements might provide the person with the same three elements: transitional spaces, semiotic guidance, and new positions within the architecture of self. Cultural experiences might thus enable tertiary processes: they might guide linking processes, both vertical and horizontal, between embodied experiences and more distanced mediations, between unconscious and conscious contents and processes. Cultural experiences might be seen as linking unconscious and invading emotions and images into new configurations. These can thus become preconscious, and likely to be reflected on. Nonconscious[9] or unconscious zones of our experiences might thus come to consciousness.

CULTURAL EXPERIENCES AND CHANGES BEYOND THE SPHERE OF IMAGINARY EXPERIENCE

When a person encounters a cultural element and interacts with it, she can have a *cultural experience*: reading a novel, watching a movie, contemplating an art piece, or participating in a religious set of actions. While being intensely personal, cultural experiences are also highly social, in the sense that they rely on socially shared semiotic systems and conventions. For Vygotsky, "Art is the social within us.... Art is the social technique of emotion, a tool of society which brings the most intimate and personal aspects of our being into the circle of social life" (1928, p. 249). A cultural experience is an active experience. Bakhtin (1979/1986) describes a reader or a listener that engages his responsiveness while having such an experience: he anticipates, questions, interprets, sees intentions, formulates possible answers to what he hears or sees. How do we break down these social aspects, this responsiveness and the possible changes that ensue?

In the two previous sections, I have shown change occurring through semiotic processes, and considered cultural elements as made out of semiotic configurations—*a fortiori*, cultural experiences should engage some processes of change. Yet cultural experiences offer a sphere of experience that is qualitatively distinct from other everyday life experiences: they give an *imaginary* access to a time and a space that stand out of the here-and-now of the person in the socially shared reality. Such a boundary between spheres of experience is even one of the conditions of the possibility of an imaginary experience. If it is so, why should cultural experiences have any efficiency beyond the duration of the imaginary experience? Why should anything imaginary have an influence on people's conduct in the socially shared reality and on their inner life?

In this section, I draw on literature on children's play, which has largely explored the developmental effects of playing as imaginary experiences.[10] Stating that children's play and cultural experiences share some *structural* features, I propose defining some similar *functional* qualities shared by the former and the latter. I thus argue that cultural experiences, occurring in imaginary spheres of experience, can indeed modify a person's subsequent experiences within her everyday spheres of experience (Benson, 2001; Freud, 1908; Koepping, 1997; Vygotsky, 1928/1971).

There is a fundamental structural similarity between children's play and adult's cultural experiences. First, they are both activities based on interacting with symbolic objects, carriers of shared social meanings. Second, children's play, as well as adult's cultural experiences, supposes a suspension from the here-and-now of the socially shared reality, and thus creates a "finite province of meaning" (Schütz, 1945). Third, that suspended reality is an *imaginary one*: in both cases, it enables free (not socially bounded) transformations of signs and memories of one's life in the shared world, and it engages real emotions. (In contrast, thinking about mathematics or physics requires a suspension from the social shared reality, but does not involve real feelings, and is bounded by socially shared systems of rules).

These aspects have been highlighted by authors from various orientations. For Winnicott, it is the status of reality *in between* the inner and the outer world that is shared by play and cultural experiences—the fact that the question of their reality status is bracketed, as is the question whether the event is *created* from the inside of the person or founded in her environment (see chapter 6). Vygotsky similarly (1928/1971, 1931/1994) sees the key-feature of play in the fact that it is imaginary, and that imagination supposes a suspension of the here and now, that allows exploration of past, future, and other possible worlds; he also highlights the importance of the social and cultural dimension of symbolic activities. For Janet (1934/1935), play is defined by its gratuity—it has no other direct function than that of enhancing a person's pleasure. Therefore, adult conduct such as well-eating, gossiping, and erotic games share with children's play the fact that they are ludic and pleasurable. For Harris (2000), both children's play and adults' cultural experiences suppose a type of bracketing of the reality; the ability to *hold in mind* and to modify these held information; a real emotional involvement; and the mobilization of past experiences.

Beyond a structural similarity between children's play and cultural experiences, authors saw a developmental continuity between these. Freud (1908) proposes that what is lived publicly by children has to become private when people become adolescents and adults. In effect, children's open manifestations of desires and fantasies in play would not be accepted by adults' social life. Imaginary experiences have therefore to become private. They become private through the mediation of cultural elements that are socially shared and acknowledged, such as novels or pieces of music. In contrast to children, Freud emphasizes the time orientation of adult's cultural experiences: they are always at the meeting point of one's past memories, present experience, and the direction of its resolution or its future. Harris (2000), who like Dewey (1910) notes the narrative structure of play, sees the main differences between children's play and adult's fiction experiences in the progressive complexification of the person's competences, knowledge about the world, and combinatory abilities (executive functions). Finally, adults progressively master their ability to modulate emotional involvement in imaginary zones. One main difference between children's play and adult's cultural is that children's play is carried through, or mediated by, objects of the real world organized by themselves and—generally—others with whom they directly interact, while adult's cultural experiences are made possible through external cultural elements, containing semiotic units, already configured by distant authors or other people.

Functionally, play can be shown to engage processes of transformation that participate in children's development. Commentators usually consider that Piaget (1951, 1945/1994) showed the role of play in cognitive development, whereas Winnicott and Freud insisted on play's emotional benefits (Sutton-Smith, 1997). Yet a closer look at these authors suggests that these two aspects are not dissociable. In Freud's account (1908, 1914, 1920), in play and in cultural experience, a person lives emotions that are forbidden in real life, thus liberating certain tensions (the *cathartic* part of the experience). She can experience mastery, rather than passivity (she performs the action, she has not been *acted on*, as is often the case in real life); by her (often repetitive) manipulations of objects and things that are part of the play, some emotions and ideas can be transformed. Janet was not satisfied with a cathartic explanation of play. Rather, he saw the specificity of play and cultural experiences in their being gratuitous (having no useful effect on reality); taking place in an unreal space, play and cultural experiences do not have the same consequences as in real life, where they would otherwise be too costly (killing someone in play is OK; killing someone in reality has annoying consequences). Play hence allows exploration of other possibilities, personally gratifying experiences; play is often a freeing, uplifting experience: a child coming back exhausted from a school day can, after half an hour of play, be full of energy again (Janet, 1934/1935). Similarly, for Winnicott, playing offers the creative pleasure of exploring new possibilities and new aspects of oneself. On his side, Piaget (1945/1994) saw play as an evolution of imitation; it offers a way to subvert the world to one's views or to engage in cathartic experiences; but more importantly, play offers occasions for schemes to be reinforced, developed, or restructured. These ideas are subsumed into the dynamic principle proposed by Vygotsky (1931/1994): the child creates, through his or her play, a zone of proximal development—a zone where skills or action not yet quite possible for a child at a given moment of his or her development in the social and material reality, are suddenly possible (Valsiner, 1989). Play hence enables explorations of skills or of their expressive possibilities, first, thanks to the location of play within an imaginary zone (the suspension of the reality status and its consequences); second, thanks to the guiding properties of the sociocultural setting, objects, and patterns of behavior enabling the play; and third, thanks to the fact that play draws on various emotionally-laden conscious and unconscious mnemonic traces, that can be thus transformed. For Harris (2000) these experiences enrich one's understanding of reality through the test of alternatives, the exploration of possibilities not given *de facto;* they may change ones outlook on the real, thanks to new perspectives that allow the focusing of attention on new aspects of situations. Additionally, for Harris, experimenting *deictic displacement* or counterfactual realities, changes a person—the same way that real experiences would change her, since it moves her, modifies her memories, and changes her knowledge of the world, of others, and of herself. Hence, the benefits of the play experience are not isolated and limited to the suspended reality of imaginary experiences; playing has consequences for one's apprehension of reality. For Piaget, play transforms schemes, which have transdomain properties; once acquired these can, in some conditions, be transferred to other domains. For Vygotsky, play enables distancing from the here and now and current understanding, and therefore, brings about new combinations and coordinations. For Freud, play unfolds, transforms, and thus neutralizes conflicts, unelaborated emotions or unlinked memories, that could otherwise have invaded one's relation to oneself or the reality; for Winnicott and Harris, play is a part of creative dynamics, one aspect of the possible field of development of the person.

Janet, Freud, and Piaget also indicate the importance of the modality of playing: play can, as any other human activity, be done either in an imitative, repetitive, automatic way (negative assimilation (Piaget, 1945), death-oriented repetition (Freud, 1914), automatism (Janet, 1926) or in an exploratory, creative way. Only the latter might bring disequilibria and complex restructuring of one's current state of understanding or thinking. Winnicott, however, is more optimistic about the ever-changing nature of thought: for him, in some conditions, imitation and repetition can have consolidating and transformative functions, and thus be part of the emergence of newness (Haskell & McHale, 2004; Haskell, Valsiner, & McHale, 2003). What makes for him the difference between a developmental outcome of play and a nondevelopmental one, is thus not the *imi-*

tative vs. *innovative* nature of playing: rather, it is the child's ability, or inability, to tolerate the uncertainty of the imaginary zone of playing.

If we assume that structural similarities between children's play and adults' cultural experiences are good enough reasons to think that there are some functional similarities between these, it is reasonable to think that adult cultural experiences can foster changes that last beyond the imaginary. Cultural experiences might enable the generation of alternative spheres of experiences. They might bring one to develop new perspectives within the architecture of the self, and be guided across positions; one might experience emotions that would be impossible to have in real life; one might become active rather than passive, and work through conscious, emotional, and unconscious contents that would otherwise invade or impede on ones' activities in real-life spheres of experiences. One might elaborate emotions or ideas that affect one's conduct in the shared reality. However, this also suggests that the developmental effects of cultural experiences might depend on a person's ability to tolerate the openness of imaginative spheres of experience, which depends, in turn, on the work of emotion and memory.

To support that deduction, I must now examine cultural experiences, and distinguish what they entail, to show what might indeed change people's understanding not only within the temporary imaginary province of meaning—as Schütz suggests (1945)—but so as to transform their very apprehension of their world.

THE FIVE ASPECTS OF CULTURAL EXPERIENCES

If we admit that cultural experiences are likely to affect people's relationship to the real world, we must identify the ways through which this is accomplished. Literary and art critics, philosophers, artists, educationalists, have written a great deal on the developmental potential of cultural experiences: for education, for assisting the development of morality, for self-discovery or discovery of the world, for self-survival in adversity, for healing or for many other transformations of the person (for e.g., Benson, 1993; Bruner, 1990; Freud, 1908; Levi, 1985/1991; Ouaknin, 1994, 1986/1995; Vygotsky, 1926 for a review). Here, in summarizing this literature, I break down the notion of cultural experience into five aspects. This division corresponds both to various aspects highlighted by authors from various allegiances, and to a theoretical analysis. Each of these aspects has indeed been identified as requiring particular psychological processes, limited by some constraints, and likely to participate in the creation of momentary or durable change in the person.

1. *Location: cultural experience as a sociocultural positioning.* A person's interaction with a given cultural element is constrained or bounded by social and cultural dimensions (László, 1999), her story, and her past cultural experiences. The choice of a given cultural experience can be seen as a function of social belongings, social markings, or identities (Benson, 2001; Duveen, 1998). When approaching and *choosing* a cultural element *as a socially located object*, a person constitutes himself as a consumer of that object. Conversely, choosing a certain type of cultural experience can modify social locations, and identities: reading a lot of *Beat Generation* novels constitutes a British student as a certain type of *cool* person. The *symbolic relocation* of a person is thus a function of the symbolic distances between the positions of the person and of the symbolic element, inscribed in shared networks of meanings, and linked to the positions of imaginary others related to its production, diffusion or consumption (Jules reads this book because his idol, David Beckham, has written it). At this level, the constraints on changes are psychosocial: psychosocial dynamics determine who is in what sociocultural (symbolic) position, what cultural elements are available for him, and what he or she can do with these. Hence, economically deprived young people watched motion pictures, through which they developed an aspiration for luxury, and learned technical-burglary skills (Blumer & Hauser, 1933); religious students approached their reading assignments with the idea that any book is a way to improve oneself and one's relationship to others (Zittoun, 2004e). Legitimating processes linked to locations are discussed in chapter 6.

2. *Framing and manipulation.* A cultural experience implies embodied conduct that precedes it, accompanies it, and concludes it. Such conducts are part of the *framing* of the cultural experience itself, as has been shown by anthropologists and cultural critics (see Koepping, 1997; Lembo, 2000; Nell, 1988). As *embodied manipulations*, these are also constituents of the cultural experience itself (Tisseron, 1999). A storyteller traditionally *frames* his tale, both in terms of setting (at night by the fire), and by a specific introductory *call*; such physical, symbolic, and social processes do more than frame the experience itself. They might also accompany and modify the cultural experience's general tonality, one's commitment to it, and the degree to which one accepts entering the proposed imaginary zone. The more the context is present, the less the imaginary experience appears as real (Blumer & Hauser, 1933; Grodal, 1997; Cupchik, 2002; Lembo, 2000). Hence doing something or talking while watching a movie de-realizes it (Lembo,

2000; Livingstone & Lunt, 1994). Manipulations linked to the cultural experience, such as playing with the remote control, or surfing on the Web, are part of the processes that bring the person to the state of mind required for an imaginary experience to be the case, and might modify the nature of that commitment. In the short term, framing and manipulating conduct are enabling conditions for accessing an imaginary experience that requires the mobilization of memories and emotions independently from the real, here-and-now situation. Framing and manipulating conduct might also engage changes that have longer-term consequences: surfing on the Web, following zoom movements on a screen can be internalized and become possible metaphors for guiding mental transformations; playing with material frames can reinforce one's ability to *hold in mind* (Salomon, 1979; Tisseron, 1998, 1999, 2003).

3. *The imaginary experience.* This is at the heart of interaction with the cultural element. It requires an encounter between the collective culture (Valsiner, 1998) and the most intimate part of a person, which occurs in one's interiority (Poulet, 1972/1980; Zittoun, 2004b). It supposes both a status of nonreality, and a real emotional participation (Freud, 1908; Harris, 2000; Koepping, 1997; Vygotsky, 1931/1994; Winnicott, 1971/2001). Cultural experiences do not *transfer* meaning from an author to a reader: they require the person to recreate an experience on the basis of meanings encapsulated in the semiotic configuration offered by the cultural element. The person must provide memories of images and emotions to nourish the proposed experience and in order for it to make sense (Vygotsky, 1931/1994; Zittoun, 2004b). In that sense, every cultural experience requires a reconfiguration of a person's embodied memories, emotions and thoughts.

The interaction between a person and a cultural element takes a certain time, and imposes a certain sequence of exposure to perceptual stimuli (sound, image, rhythm, etc.). The evolution of the image on the screen, of the sound, the montage-effects, the narrative effects, and the specificities of the characters, provoke and guide complex composites of embodied experiences (physiological and muscular reactions), mnemonic processes, emotional states, and constructions of future oriented hypothesis (Grodal, 1997). This complexity is, for example, expressed in the description of Madame Bovary's experience at the opera:

> [Waiting the beginning of the play, then watching the scene]. Emma, remembering her early readings, found herself caught up into the very heart of Sir Walter Scott. It was as though she could hear through the mist the sound of Scottish bagpipes echoing in the

Modeling Cultural Experiences and Symbolic Resources in Development 61

> undergrowth. Her recollection of the novel made it easy for her for follow the libretto; and she traced the movement of the story, phrase by phrase, while the vague thoughts thronging her mind vanished, almost as soon as formed, beneath the gusts of music. She let herself be lulled by the melodies, and felt her whole being vibrate as though the bows of the violins were being drawn across her own taut nerves.... Lucie [the main feminine character], with a look of extreme seriousness, began her aria in G major. She bewailed her love, she begged for wings. Emma, too, would have liked to escape from life and flyaway in an embrace.... From his very entrance [Edgar Lagardy, the male character] enraptured the audience. He clasped Lucy in his arms, left her, then returned, always, apparently, in a state of despair.... Emma leaned forward, the better to see him, scraping the velvet of the box with her fingernails. Her heart drank its fill of his melodious lamentations.... She recognized all the intoxicating delights, all the agonies, of which she had herself almost died. The voice of the singing heroine seemed but the echo of her own consciousness, the illusions which haunted her, part of her own experience. But no one in the world had ever loved like this! (Flaubert, 1857/1999, pp. 241-242)

Or in the changes of mood and state of mind of Quangel, sharing his prison cell with Dr. Reichardt, a former musician, in Hans Fallada's novel written under the Nazi regime in Berlin (1947/1965/2002):

> During this morning walk, which would last from ten to noon, Dr. Reichhardt would sing very low, and Quangel become used to lend an ear to what he was humming. At times, he felt he was becoming strong enough to overcome any ordeal, and Reichhardt would then say "Beethoven." At times, Quangel would feel an incomprehensible joy and lightness, as he never had felt before, and Reichhardt would say: "Mozart." Then the sounds coming out of the mouth of the musician would become grave, and would beget sort of a pain in Quangel's heart; or he would feel brought back to the time of his childhood, when he was accompanying his mother to the church: he still had all his life in front of him, and it was to accomplish a great task: "Jean-Sébastien Bach," would say Reichhardt. (Fallada, 1947/1965/2002, pp. 476-477, my translation)

The imaginary experience occurring in one's interiority can thus be described, first, as a series of whole complex composites of embodied emotions and conduct aiming at conferring meaning to the cultural experience. Second, because this process is rooted in past experience and constantly generates new expectations, it can be seen as a progressive reconfiguration of personal experiences, present, past and therefore future: the begetting of one's temporality (Ricoeur, 1985/1988). Third, what occurs in one's interiority can be described as a complex system of processes within a bounded field, that is, as a form of dialogical process (Valsiner, 2001a, 2001b). In effect, streams of thought can be seen as diffracted, guided, and recomposed along semiotic guidance, thus bringing about new imaginary locations. The deployment of cultural experiences can also beget tensions, which will evolve through time. Such processes have been described as dialogical creations (Benson, 1993; Hermans & Kempens, 1993), fruitful ambiguities (Abbey, in press), which thus can create intrapersonal dialogue (Hermans, 1996; Ouaknin, 1994; Valsiner, 2002), or new perspective taking (Kögler, 2000).

The cultural experience enables imagining new images, bodily experiences, emotions, perspectives, and categories, general and abstract ideas; through the semiotic guidance, the person can experience herself as-if in another sphere of experience, or as-if in another position. The processes of relocating through the complex mediating enabled by the experience can be called empathy—if empathy is understood as the very movement through various positions within the architecture of the self. In some cases, during the imaginary experience, a person can enter a state of aesthetic absorption, a state of nondeployment of the self—or, more exactly, an absence of the self-consciousness that usually accompanies such internal movements (Benson, 1993, 2001).

In terms of changes in the architecture of the self, the imaginary experience enabled by participating in a semiotic configuration helps to *capture*, isolate and fix embodied conduct. It can bring to *reflect* on them. It can propose *links* (unlinking, relinking) between semiotic units, and, thus, guide possible sequences of thoughts. Cultural elements crystallize others' externalization; they thus always add a *surplus* of meanings to a person's initial experience (Gillespie, 2004). Hence a cultural experience proposes a semiotic guidance of thinking: it organizes and transforms images, thoughts, and emotions of various degrees of generality (Diriwächter, 2003; Janet, 1934/1935; Kaës, 1994, 1996).

These processes are constrained by one's skill in deciphering a given type of cultural element, by one's ability to modify the imaginary/reality status, by one's bodily possibilities,[11] by one's current readiness to mobilize emotions and memories, and to play through semiotic dynamics (see also chapter 6).

4. *Cultural experiences comport post hoc elaborations.* Minimally, after some moments of self-loss, of relocation, of modification of one's sphere of experience within a cultural experience, the person

Modeling Cultural Experiences and Symbolic Resources in Development 63

becomes aware of having had that experience. The simple movement of loss-recovery would be the basic movement of change enabled by any cultural experience (Benson, 2001). This post hoc elaboration can succeed in oscillation while engaged in the imaginary experience, or afterwards. All the previous aspects of the cultural experiences can be objects of awareness or reflection, alone or in interaction with others. When with others, people can coconstruct reflective positions and interpretations of the whole experience; they can thus transform the experience itself and social and interpersonal dynamics (Lembo, 2000; Livingstone, 1997, 1998; Tisseron, 2000). Posthoc elaboration include an awareness of the quality of the cultural element—its semiotic qualities, some linking or framing processes—and of the transformations within one's interiority: the multiple positions adopted, the felt emotions, expectations, tensions and releases. These two aspects of the experience can be reflected in their mutual relationships (e.g., this type of music has brought one to cry). Post hoc elaborations partly determine how a cultural experience will be internalized, and possibly recalled later on.

Post hoc elaborations are constrained by the modalities of the socially located interactions around these experiences, and by constraints affecting metareflection in general (Benson, 2001; Cupchik, 2002).

5. *Uses of symbolic resources.* These four aspects can become internalized as part of one's personal culture. They can then endlessly be mobilized as *symbolic resources*. A distinction is thus proposed between (1) the changes triggered by a cultural experience, as these are inherent to its realization (such as, mobilizing memories, emotions, etc.), or primary uses, and (2) changes, as they redirect that experience towards something *that exceeds itself.* Such changes hence require intentional uses of cultural elements (Brentano, 1874/1995; Searle, 1983). Such intentional uses can be called *secondary uses* of cultural elements (Zittoun, 2001, 2005a). Only secondary uses of cultural elements will here be called *symbolic resources*.[12] *Symbolic resources are cultural elements used by someone, with some intent, that is, they are used about something that does not belong to the cultural experience itself.*

An example can help clarify this distinction. Jean can be moved by the loneliness of the characters in a Thai movie (*Last Life in the Universe*, by Pen-ek Ratanaruang, 2003). She can feel the subtle tone of that feeling of absurdity: she sees an abandoned house, invaded by dust, disorder, and nature; the image is dominated by browns, greens, greys; the music is a repetitive three tones melody. The semiotic configurations thus trigger in her mnemonic traces of embodied experiences that thus compose that soft emotion. For this to happen she does not need to know where she receives these mnemonic traces from; they are just in the background of any semiotic process. However, during the film or after the very moment at which she starts to evoke, *as designated by that film*, memories of English landscapes, ideas about her own state, or a sad friend's recent story, then she is addressing that cultural experience *about* something that exceeds its own realization. The film becomes a distancing device toward other issues. It is now used as a symbolic resource intended at these thoughts.

It is such mobilizations of symbolic resources, analyzable as complex processes of semiotic mediation, which I will examine in the rest of the book.

Finally, cultural experiences and their use as symbolic resources appear as powerful means to feel and live experiences beyond the limits of the here and now. Their emotional and imaginative power, their link to socially shared reality and their strong cultural connotations in given social settings and network, constitute many of their features that might be attractive for young people. Cultural experiences such as the one offered by music channels or popular films are powerfully moving, and likely to be important as a basis of social exchange.

SEMIOTIC PROCESSES IN YOUTH DEVELOPMENT

Cultural experiences can become part of people's personal culture and can modify the architecture of the self. From a theoretical perspective, it is clear that the five aspects of cultural experience imply semiotic processes, unlinking, linking, or relinking memories and present situations, in their social and cultural aspects, with their emotional and fantasmatic prolongations (see also Boesch, 1997/1995, 2001 for an account). The five steps of cultural experiences might thus modify a person's location, identity, thinking skills, and memories. From a developmental and empirical perspective, the question that imposes itself is whether such changes are momentary reorganizations of thoughts and experiences—as the wind caresses a leaf—or if these transformations can be part of durable psychological change—as a river sculpts an old trunk.

Looking for durable changes enabled by cultural experiences, authors have privileged one or the other of the first four aspects of cultural experiences. Tisseron thus emphasizes the importance of framing and manipulating aspects of the cultural experience, as these are likely to reinforce durable and basic thinking abilities (Tisseron, 2002, 2003). Benson's answer to such a question is that it is the imaginary phase of the cultural experience, when it entails an experience of loss of I consciousness accompanied by a reflective I-redeployment, which might have developmental effects (Benson, 1993, 2001). Hermans and authors that have a dialectical understanding of change note the importance of perspective change and its subsequent synthesis (Hermans & Kempens, 1993); Cupchik (2002), Tisseron (2000) or Cottle (2001) insist on the importance of posthoc reflective stances.

It is probably the case that in some circumstances, one or the other aspect of a cultural experience might have long standing effects. Yet I am interested in their fifth aspect, *the shift that leads from having a cultural experience, to using a symbolic resource*. This action of using a symbolic resource in effect needs the deliberate, if not conscious, linking of at least two spheres of experiences (the imaginary one offered by the cultural experience, and any other).[13] Using a symbolic resource thus always requires, even if in a very elementary way, a form of learning, or transfer of skill or emotions, that is, the emergence of new intentional links, or aboutness.

Symbolic resources function like any other semiotic mediation. Thus, I would suggest that, as complex semiotic mediations, symbolic resources might help to delimit, fix, name, and transform emotional experience. Symbolic resources might enable moves from the unconscious to the conscious; they might enable semiotic mediations at the horizontal level of the semiotic hierarchy, or vertically, between levels. This is how I will explore development enabled through the use of symbolic resources.

Let me now come back to the broader picture: to approach psychological development, I have proposed consideration of ruptures, transitions, uncertainty, and the psychological work that these trigger. I have identified three interdependent processes of transition: those related to identity repositioning and definition, skill and learning acquisition, and meaning making and elaboration of emotions (chapter 1). These three processes require semiotic mediation; but, in particular, it is impossible to account for the third without explaining the semiotic work at stake. Hence, I have proposed examining semiotic elaboration enabled through the use of symbolic resources. The question we are now examining is, what is the role of symbolic resources in the work of youth transition, where people use their newly acquired symbolic responsibility? In the case of youth, I have identified two dimensions on which we might expect to see transitions be turned into qualitative changes: acquiring a time perspective, and developing a system of orientation (chapter 1). Therefore, youth development might be said to occur through uses of symbolic resources, if uses of symbolic resources support the construction of a time perspective and of a system of orientation. More exactly, the following set of arguments needs to be grounded empirically to support the idea that development is possible through symbolic resources:

1. Cultural experiences can lead to the use of the cultural element as a symbolic resource, that is, to its subsequent use *about* another sphere of experience, rather than the one enabled in the imaginary zone;
2. Such symbolic resources can be used so as to establish links between a person's past *and* her possible futures;
3. Such symbolic resources can be used in a way that enables the development and the stabilization of a system of orientation, that is, of the multiple levels of semiotic mediation of experience;
4. Symbolic resources enable processes of unlinking and relinking that might reduce uncertainty, elaborate emotional experiences, link unconscious and conscious thoughts, and thus create new positions within the architecture of the self.

Hence the following proposition: symbolic resources can be understood as playing a role in psychological development (and not only in psychological change), when they propose not only future actions, but also modify past memories; when they affect not only intrapsychic processes, but also one's relationship with others and the world; when they can affect one's apprehension of local matters, or general understanding, but also provide means to further affect local situations, and, finally, when they not only bring to repetition, but also enable the adoption of radically new positions within the architecture of self. It is these propositions that I will develop through analysis of the narratives of young persons (chapter 4 & 5), which follows after a methodological chapter (3).

NOTES

1. Fuhrer's recent attempt to combine these two triangles results in a *transactional* square model (Fuhrer, 2004), which includes axes and dimensions that are descriptive, but not functional.
2. See note 2 chapter 1: Jules and Jean are hypothetical characters; their names are used every time I invent an example for rhetoric or exploratory purposes. All the other first names mentioned in the text refer to actual empirical data.
3. Of course, some cultural experiences carefully aim at not provoking emotional answers, which will also call for meaning-making for the person who has them (i.e., some forms of contemporary art).
4. Some studies focus on emotions as cognitive apprehension of the modification of the body state; other approaches examine emotions as regulating thoughts (Kahneman, 2003; Piaget, 1954/1981). A third group of studies distinguish emotions that have propositional properties from these that have not, and consider these two variants as two moments of one unique emotional experience (Lambie & Marcel, 2002; Russell, 2003).

Modeling Cultural Experiences and Symbolic Resources in Development   67

5. *Reflective* means here a thinking-conduct that is addressing another one, otherwise done without awareness; for example, a thought about an action, about a thought, and so forth. This is a different definition than Dewey's, for whom a reflective thought is a "careful, persistent, and careful consideration of any belief or supposed form of knowledge in the light of the grounds that support it, and the further conclusions to which it tends" (1910, p. 6).

6. The difficulty with this position, if I understand it properly, is that it equates the conscious with secondary processes, the logic of emotions to the logics of the unconscious, and the unconscious to primary processes: we lose the topology of the unconscious (its closeness to the id, and to the body), as well as its dynamics (its strength to irrupt consciousness).

7. From here on, I use L for Level.

8. Emotions thus seem to have a double origin: they can be triggered by experience in the world, or by psychic events. Modifications of the field of experience in the world can provoke immediate physiological reactions and reflex conduct (Valsiner's Level 0). An emotion can also be activated through thinking or linking processes, triggered by memories and semiotic mediations. Then, these signals can be minimally apprehended (Level 1) through mnemonic traces of previous experiences, or identified as being part of a emotional configuration, thanks to the use of memorized or available semiotic means (an image, a word, someone else's facial reaction) (Level 2). These can be subsumed under more precise, or categorical representations of emotions (Level 3). Some composites of embodied emotion-thought-act patterns can be recognized as prototypical emotions (Russell, 2003); they can be labeled emotion X or Y, with the risk of losing the specificity of the experience. Such a labeling or distancing might also terminate that emotional experience (Janet, 1928; Valsiner, 2003). Fourth, at these various levels, emotional experiences can also be kept out of direct consciousness, either because of failures at Level 1 or because of higher level values, such as moral principles that would condemn some elementary pleasures (Level 4). Fifth, these various contents and mediations, conscious or not, can awake lateral mnemonic traces, secondary thoughts, and infinities of symmetrical linking. This double and mediated origin constitutes emotional composites.

9. Authors admit a distinction between nonconscious processes—automatic ones, as described by cognitive psychology—and unconscious processes, that have a dynamic and a logic independent from consciousness, as described by psychoanalysis.

10. Other researchers have traced the evolution from children's play to adult cultural experiences. Psychological studies on symbolic thinking in children have examined prolongation of play in nonludic adults' activities and in various other cognitive abilities. Most current studies are adopting a theory of mind perspective, and among them some consider adult cultural experiences through a *simulation* hypothesis (which is based on the idea that people run mental models of fiction in their mind (Byrne, 1990; László, 1999). The semiotic approach developed in this chapter does not need such a hypothesis, for it assumes thought to flow, the very processes of thinking being shaped as it is produced through semiotic means; the current state of representation is constantly modified though looping and feed-forward dynamics (Kögler, 2000; Valsiner, 2003, in press). For a thor-

ough discussion of the limits of theory of mind see Leudar and Costall (2004).
11. Benson (1993) explains how a temporary paralysis of the lower half of his body prevented him from having the experience of a familiar painting of an Irish beach: the experience of walking on the beach was unavailable during the paralysis.
12. This definition of uses of symbolic resources is more restrictive than the generally accepted sense of *cultural* or *psychological tools* (Vygotsky, 1930/1978), where there is no distinction between primary and secondary uses of a cultural element—with the consequence that if every word is a tool, then the very notion of tool—which is *intentional*—becomes trivial.
13. Hence the difficulty raised by Schütz (1945) is solved: for him, cultural experiences are bounded by their finite province of meaning, and therefore, cannot be intentional. Symbolic resources precisely enable the individual to connect various provinces of meaning; one province becomes *about* the other.

CHAPTER 3

ACCESSING PERSONAL CULTURES

There is no symbol without a beginning of interpretation; there where a human being dreams, prophesises or poeticises, another begins to interpret; interpretation belongs organically to the symbolic thought and to its double meaning.

—Paul Ricoeur, *De l'interprétation: Essai sur Freud* (1965/1991, p. 29)

The previous chapters have developed a problematic—the study of youth transitions as offering an unique access to developmental dynamics—and a theoretical framework that qualifies symbolic resources as specific semiotic mediations. In this chapter, I reflect on these constructs: What is their epistemological status? How can they be operationalized? I then discuss my methodological choices, the status of the data produced, and issues of generalization. I finally briefly present the 30 cases studies that will be discussed in the chapters that follow.

EPISTEMOLOGICAL ISSUES

The models presented in these pages are constructed on the basis of models existing in previous theoretical and empirical studies. There, they gave some visibility and structure to ideas and parts of the socially shared reality. Such models are here extended and reworked, so as to confer readability to the portion of that reality under scrutiny. Mediating the relationship

70 Transitions: Development through Symbolic Resources

between the researcher and the real, such models are part of the construction of the data; but they are also modified so as to account for the data. What is the status of the types of model proposed in the previous chapters? And how can they be evaluated?

Status of Models and Metaphors

Models give us *metaphors* for the real. As semiotic tools, metaphoric models enable us to take distance from our experience (Gillespie, 2004). Models are metaphors that can create *distinctions* in the diverse world of the given: they *organize* patterns, and thus help to differentiate variations of conduct and their *logics*. They should not be reified: there are no *semiotic prisms* in the brain or in the world. Yet, these metaphors organize the researcher's perceptions, and help him to make hypotheses about relationships between the parts of the real thus rendered visible. Ultimately, these metaphoric models aim at identifying *structures* (Valsiner, 2004d), which might correspond to some extent to the organization of the *real as it appears to us*. In the frame of our psychological enquiry, models aim at giving good descriptions, not predictions (Brentano, 1887).

Metaphorical models are assemblages of signs (or semiotic units) (Valsiner, 2004d). It follows that models can themselves be seen as taking part in semiotic dynamics. They can thus be located within two triadic relationships: the first one links earlier theories, the current model, and the data; the second links the model, the data, and the real under scrutiny. Of course, one will have to reunite these four poles, and to keep track of the dual constraints exerted on the model and the data, on one side, by past and present other theories, and on the other side, by the real.

Implications of the Chosen Metaphors

Metaphors are usually based on common-sense intuitions. They have a history, and carry with them the weight and the harmonics of their past uses (Bakhtin, 1934-1935/1981, 1979/1986) in everyday life or in the history of science. They also have their own logic, and when used may imply more than was intended by their users (Lakoff, 1987; Lakoff & Johnson, 1980). Checking for the absence of unintended consequences of a metaphor is one of the criteria through which a theoretical enterprise can be evaluated. Some implicit consequences of a metaphor enable seeing more to the real; others bring us to absurd considerations (Gillespie, 2004). Up to a certain point, a scientist can define how much of these consequences he accepts, how much they are essential, or dispensable (Thompson, 2000). In some cases he may have to renounce a metaphor because of its possessing too many nonuseful implications, or due to its destructive effect on the whole theoretical enterprise.

Let me explore some consequences of the main metaphors chosen in this book; that of *use*, and that of *interiority*. Other will be mentioned more quickly.

With the metaphor of *uses of symbolic resources*, I imply that people, agents, are doing things with certain intentions (they are *active*). The notion has a history in social and human sciences, which I will summarize here.

The metaphor of use of a symbolic object has various origins. In the French sociological tradition, Michel de Certeau (1980/1984) was interested in the distance between the logic of production of social objects, and what people indeed do with such objects. De Certeau examined people's *usage* of television or of urban space. He came to consider these usages of social objects as practices of *bricolage* after Levi-Strauss (1962/1966) (see chapter 5), before calling them *arts de faire*, arts of making. After him, Jacques Perriault (1989) developed the idea of consumers employing *logics of uses*, whereby they transform new technical inventions according to their own needs and understanding. On the British side Wittgenstein (1953/2000) proposed to consider the meaning of a word as given by its use in a given utterance, meanings thus being given by the uses of semiotic elements in *language games*. In a more developmental and emotional perspective, Winnicott (1968a) introduced the idea of the *use of an object* to describe the psychic function of *objects* of emotional investment in infants.

From these various perspectives, the notion of use in the human sciences tends to designate a consistent group of phenomenon linked to a person's capture of an object. Little attention is given to its originally intended function. The object is temporarily considered as part of a person's conduct. Its functions, although constrained by its form, are defined by the person's current needs, fantasies, intelligence, or goals. These use metaphors share an emphasis on the unique recuperation of agents, individual, or groups, that transform given social productions into unique things-for-them, in their sphere of experience. Psychoanalytical variations of the metaphor insist on the importance of a person's emotional involvement in the object, and on the fact that an emotionally charged object has the power to change the person. All in all, the objects in themselves, and the objects-as-used-by-a-person, are radically different.

Uses can be realized through physical conduct, as well as through mental, emotional, or verbal activities; uses are about something else. In that sense, an use of an object is a form of tool-mediated activity as described by the historical-cultural tradition, as discussed earlier in this book. Let me simply note that the notion of use focuses on oriented actions-by-someone, whereas the notion of *tool* in the latter tradition does not necessary specify whether an object can be a tool in itself if it is not being used by an agent. This difference grounds the choice made here to work with the metaphor of *uses of* books and so forth, rather than the alternative metaphor of books, and so forth, *as tools*.

A notion also carries the shadow of its negation (Abbey & Valsiner, 2003b). The notion of use implies the reverse notion of *nonuse*. However, put in a new meaning-field with a certain goal orientation, a given use or nonuse can become a *misuse*. A teacher who asks her students to use their dictionary to write their essay will notice students whose dictionary is still on the shelf (nonusers). Yet if she admits that the dictionary should be used to check orthographic rules, then the student that uses it to support his notebook is *misusing*. Additionally, uses can be evaluated on the basis of additional criteria—such as the (normative) rules of written English: some uses then can be qualified as *better* uses (Zittoun, Duveen, Gillespie, Ivinson, & Psaltis, 2003). If something can be used in a better way than another, it is possible that one can ameliorate uses, or develop expertise in them. These two aspects will be examined in chapter 6. Finally, various meanings of use, such as *applying one thing to another*, or to *transform* something (Oxford English Dictionary, 2004) can be accepted here: they imply temporal sequences where a subject-mean-object relationship is dynamic. Similarly, semiotic means can transform meaning and understanding, experiences and actions (Valsiner, 1998). There are other meanings of use which I ignore, such as the idea of habits and ritual, or of the exploitation of one person by another.

Most of the metaphors presented here are based on spatial and temporal concepts. Two dimensions are necessary to express relationships; three dimensions are culturally required to express time within such relationships, and the best way to represent three dimensions is spatial. The danger of spatial metaphors is their rigidity, when our aim is precisely to analyze ever-changing structures, processes, and dynamics in the flow of semiotic mediation. I can only insist on the fact that such metaphors are spatial, because time is to be seen as one of the dimensions of the model. These geometrical structures are hence to be seen within an ever-changing flow.

Interiority is originally a spatial notion. It is used as a functional, spatial, and temporal metaphor. It can be seen as *inside* the bodily boundaries of a person, thus separated from, but included in, the rest of the *outside shared world*. It can be seen as a function of the *private and not public*, of what can be hidden or disclosed through deliberate and nonconscious forms of externalization. It can also be seen as a temporal metaphor: interiority is a moment that takes place within dynamics of internalization-externalization processes (Zittoun, 2004b).

The *semiotic* prism, the *architecture of self* and the *levels of generality* are spatial metaphors of processes that are supposed to be located within interiority. This means, on one side, that they are part of the *private*, inner world of the unique person; and on the other hand, that they exist at the time-spot at which a person is addressing a particular inner or outer issue, within the moment of transacting and internalizing-externalizing.

The *semiotic prism* has already been presented as constantly moving spatial-temporal structure, whose poles might change, and whose sets of dynamics can always be modified. The metaphor of *levels of generality* is directly derived from the hierarchical understanding of semiotic activities (Toomela, 2000; Werner & Kaplan, 1963). It accepts the classical metaphor that considers some thinking processes as *higher* than others (i.e., more distanced from concrete, embodied here-and-now experience). This model has been developed following Valsiner's dynamic propositions, where achieving a certain level is only a temporary moment within the ever-going loops of semiotic dynamics. (These higher mediations are thus not necessarily better or more evolved than lower ones: they always coexist with these other types in adult life). Similarly, the *architecture of the self* suggests the organization of interiority as it is triggered when the person is engaged in a particular piece of conduct. Hence, semiotic hierarchies can be seen as included within, or constitutive of, the architecture of the self. Semiotic prisms are smaller units of analysis, and are the processes through which these two other systems are constantly produced and reshaped. We may see semiotic prisms as spinning entities, moving within the space provided by the architecture of self: the moves of the prism, and the directions of its spinning, may be due to its precise position within the lines of force of the architecture, at a given time-spot; in turn, such spinning and moving may modify both the lines and the architecture. We may compare these logics to those of Jean's organism: the yogurt Jean eats participates in the rapid changing of the cells of her skin (which are determined by her whole organism) through basic organic processes (i.e., semiotic prism dynamics); in the short term, such processes do not change the structure of her skin, but they may in the long run (i.e., through changes in the architecture of the self). Here, I choose not to consider all the implications of these metaphors (their architectural implications, the physics of light in prisms, etc.).

Evaluating Models and Metaphors

There are various criteria to exclude a relativistic understanding of such models and the data they enable us to produce. Turning back to our semiotic prism, the data can be evaluated within various relationships. They should not contradict their general theoretical framework and models; they may then be susceptible to the resistance of the real; finally, they have to be consistent with the author's intentions and must be open to the perspective of *others*.

First, the metaphors used here all come from traditions of psychology (cultural psychology, psychoanalysis, pragmatists traditions, see previous chapters) that share some basic assumptions—in particular, that development is seen as an open-ended process that works in systemic wholes, and that semiotic mediations are central to this process. Also, they do not contradict each other within the general theoretical construction. Second, reality can resist models, or fail to correspond with them. Metaphorical models can produce data that then overwhelms them. This does not necessarily sign the death sentence of the model: models, as signs, are open to revision and extension. Theory building can in effect be seen as a cyclical open-ended process, as with any other developmental dynamic (Valsiner, 1997; Valsiner & Connolly, 2003): a continual adjustment between various possibilities that operates thanks to semiotic tools which project representation unto the real, meet its resistance, and modify semiotic constructs (Peirce, 1868a, 1868b). For example, in terms of the evolution of my framework, I started analyzing data with the idea that symbolic resources are tools used *about* various things (Zittoun, 2001, 2005a). The data revealed unexpected aspects, and it is in order to account for them that I mobilized existing theories so as to develop two dimensions of analysis that turned out to be central to my whole enterprise—those of temporality and levels of generality. This book presents these dimensions as initial assumptions, when in fact they result from this interplay between data and theory. This is thus how I tried to satisfy the consistency criteria. Such constant revisions exemplify, once more, the refutability of careful qualitative research through the resistance of the real (Flyvbjerg, 2001). Third, metaphoric models have to correspond to the author's intentions when using them (Gillespie, 2004). At the minimum, an author's intention is to convey his analysis to the reader. My intentions are, first, to render visible and readable some overlooked phenomena of everyday life, and second, to extend our current understanding and theorizing of modes of thinking and developing. It is this the role of others—you as a reader, my colleagues, and my reviewers, and other people, to tell me whether these models make sense at all, and if they modify their readings of everyday life phenomena and their understanding of meaning-making dynamics.

METHODOLOGICAL ISSUES

How can we move from our theoretical assumptions, to the study of uses of symbolic resources in everyday transitions? We need to define a methodology that is consistent with those initial assumptions. In particular, two aspects of the theoretical framework have to be accounted for: a psychology that acknowledges development, that is, time-situated processes; and a psychology that acknowledges symbolic objects at the meeting of the social and the intimate. I will begin by recalling the theoretical moves accomplished in the previous chapters, and will then define their methodological counterparts.

Consistency

First, because this is a developmental enquiry, I moved away from evaluating endpoints or the achievement of phases of change, to concentrate on the work of change (*processes*) (Perret-Clermont, Carugati, & Oates, 2004; Van Geert, 2003). Also, I moved from psychosocial transitions to psychological ones, that is, transitions that follow *subjectively* perceived ruptures and which create uncertainty *for* a person, rather than transitions that are defined by their psychosocial endpoints. Second, while cultural artifacts are mostly studied as entities applied to groups of people once and for all, I consider cultural elements as they are relevant for a given person, the agent that may use one of them to address felt uncertainties. Hence, I proposed to study the single person, who perceives a rupture, has memories of cultural experiences that she may mobilize in situations that appear new to her. The object of psychological enquiry becomes the person for whom things *matter*, and who is therefore engaged in specific conduct. Without renouncing the fact that psychology examines people that are socially and culturally located, submitted to tensions and constraints, I state that the persons observed here are composed of interiority, intentions, and some degree of freedom (Zittoun, 2004b). On a theoretical level, my account aims to address a repeated warning by many psychologists: the loss of the *psychological subject* in current developmental and cultural enquiries (Grossen, 2001; Mischler, 1996; Notterman, 2004; Salomon, 1993).

Qualitative Approach

Per definition, only a qualitative methodology can give us access to the processes we aim at observing (Valsiner, 2004d). We need, in effect, to know what a given person experiences as a rupture, what dynamics of change she engages during the period that follows, and whether she finds a new balanced organization of experience. We also need to identify cultural objects and symbolic means that cross the path of that particular person, which become noticeable, relevant, part of her personal culture. We thus need to collect data in such a way that it maintains its richness and uniqueness as long as possible. Finally, we need to have some cues to the basis on which we might generate hypothesis about the processes of interiority.

What *techniques* for collecting data should we adopt? There are two main classes of techniques that can be used: reconstructive techniques, and techniques that gather data in real-time. Some *reconstructive* techniques rely on the observation of existing data—such as in historical-cultural analysis (for e.g., Gillespie, 2005; Perret-Clermont, 1997), and some are based on interviews (Bar-On, 1995; Bruner, 1990; Zittoun, 2001). Data are gathered in *real time* when techniques follow processes in the making, such as when children are observed while solving a task (Psaltis & Duveen, 2004), when an institution's changes are observed during the period of a few months (Cornish, 2004a, 2004b; Perret & Perret-Clermont, 2001), or when a person is asked to think aloud (Staudinger & Baltes, 1994).

Such options have been chosen to study people's interaction with cultural artifacts, and have included the observation of people viewing television (Lembo, 2000; Liebes & Katz, 1990/1994; Lindlof & Meyer, 1998; Pasquier, 1999), the recording of the discourse of people exposed to disturbing pictures (cf. quasi-experimental techniques used by Abbey & Valsiner, 2003b; Valsiner, 2003; Valsiner & Capezza, 2002), and diaries which are compiled by subjects *on the spot* (Csikszentmihaly, 1997/1998; Csikszentmihaly & Larson, 1984; Rossier, 1997).

Whatever choice is made, the psychologist will then form a hypothesis on invisible semiotic dynamics. What are observable are situations, people and elements that a person may be in contact with and may internalize; and some forms of externalization. Semiotic work occurs at the articulation between internalizing and externalizing (Valsiner, 1998); part of it occurs within interiority (and is not visible through an analysis of a person's activities). The researcher's interpretative work consists in producing an exploratory hypothesis about that which may have turned what has been internalized into what is externalized.

Because internalization and externalization are never-ending processes, some unifying observing principle must be defined. One possibility is to ask people to address a clear-cut symbolic task that has an ending. The externalization comprises the end-point and all that has been said or done to achieve that aim: it is the case when one has to solve a task (Abbey & Valsiner, 2003b), or name a child (Zittoun, 2001). People can also be observed around a defined strange symbolic object. Their externalization can thus be observed as they deal with memorials (Zittoun, 2004d), uncanny objects (Ivinson, 2002; Zittoun, et al., 2003), or a strange country (Gillespie, 2004). Finally, the same cultural element can be followed through the whole process, as a *marker* within thinking: when publicly available, a cultural element as it is before internalization can be compared to externalizations linked to it, so as to reveal *what has been done to it.*" This can be done at the level of the individual—where one can compare a movie with the summary someone gives of that movie (Zittoun, 2001), or at a collective level, as when Gillespie (2004) follows the migration of a guidebook quote into the discourse of tourists.

In all these procedures, there is a necessary mismatch between processes as they occur, and the analytic stance. The mismatch can be both due to the externality of the observer of a given form of conduct, and his spatial, temporal, and cultural distances, or to the distance created by the self-reflective procedure implied in most of these techniques (as in any form of introspection). The fact is that psychological enquiry *necessarily* involves a reconstructive part and a hermeneutical stance. Any psychosocial enquiry is *per definition removed from the flow of conduct as it happens.* This fact is not an obstacle to research; rather, once acknowledged, it frees the scientists from the need to stick to the *truth as it occurs. As a counterpart to this, the scientist has to account for the nature of his distance and hermeneutical position in a given enquiry.* She has to make it explicit, so that another person can imagine how the data and the analysis of it have been produced.

Reconstructive Interviews

For my part, I have opted for in-depth interviews as a reconstructive method to collect data about people's use of symbolic resources. Similar techniques have been chosen by researchers interested in the cultural experiences of young people (Fine, Mortimer, & Roberts 1990; Lembo, 2000; Pasquier, 1999; Tisseron, 2000; Zittoun, 2001). I also choose to examine externalizations that enable us to trace back the transformation of cultural elements that have been internalized. I will first describe the distance between data created on the basis of interviews, and a person's act of using a symbolic resource. This distance is due to the temporality of the use of symbolic resources, as well as to the very nature of discourse.

The spatio-temporal problem is due to the activities under scrutiny: there is not necessarily a finite moment that can be examined to catch the use of a given resource. In effect, suppose a person has an initial cultural experience in a given situation, which she may internalize. At any time distance from it, a rupture takes place; she may now mobilize mnemonic traces of that cultural experience. Women choosing first names of children can suddenly remember a radio talk happened 12 years earlier and use it as symbolic resource (Zittoun, 2001, 2005a). Also, these mobilizations do not necessarily occur at a specific time-space spot: meaning making processes can take place over a long period of time. Thus, future parents can think for months about possible first names, and mobilize symbolic resources while walking, before sleeping, when confronted by movies or novels, or within interactions.

Overall, internalized semiotic structures carry multiple temporalities, which have their own logics of duration, association, and transformation. This brings us to the fact that there is no possibility to observe the *whole* of the use of a symbolic resource. In that respect, asking people for past uses of resources can bring them to identify these nonfinite processes over a long period of time. The deformation of the initial facts due to the work of memory and reflectivity reveals only more of the ongoing transformation of internalized semiotic devices, and thus informs us about these transformations, as they are externalized and used in the present of the interview.

The second distance from the initial facts is due to the nature of discourse. The classical problem researchers are confronted with, is, how much does language give us access to *mind*? There is no direct path from thought and perception to language as it is used when addressing another (chapter 2). It requires slow transformations that modify the nature of experience, add meanings and suppress others. Yet discourse reveals something about people's experiences and how they understand them, and with it, something about the content and structure of thinking. This has been exploited by both *clinical interviews* à la Piaget, where the interviewer's intervention and contradictions aim at sketching the nature of the organization of the interviewee's understanding of the world (Duveen & Gilligan, 2004; Ginsburg, 1997; Piaget, 1926/1976), and by the psychoanalytical setting, where the modulation of voice and discourse are read as cues about unconscious processes (Green, 1992; Tisseron, 1996).

Another difficulty is that discourse is necessarily only an interpretation of memories of experiences, and that memory and interpretations are affected by situational variations (Bartlett, 1932). In research interviews, situational variations comprise the two participants, their history and their story of similar situations, the social setting in which the encounter takes place, and its wider context (Grossen, 1988; Grossen & Perret-Clermont, 1992). These components enable and constrain the meanings that the person confers on the interview situation, as they look for an *implicit* contract (e.g., Schubauer-Leoni & Grossen, 1993) (e.g., "Is it like a job talk? Is it like going to a shrink? And why am I sitting in this university office, I that might never be able to study?"). These interpretations, together with the evolving interpersonal dynamics, constitute the *thinking space* of the interviewee (Perret-Clermont, 2001, 2004). Thus, discourse that is produced in the situation of an interview is a form of externalization on the basis of the person's current understandings and feelings, informed by contents and actions of the past, within the limits of a person's memory; it carries the echoes of other discourses held by that person, and of previous situations of discourse or semiotic dynamics (Bakhtin, 1979/1986). Finally, discourse occurs within interpersonal dynamics and is thus constituted by it—it is coconstructed (Grossen & Perret-Clermont, 1994) in a way that is beyond people's intentions; it thus can reveal to or hide from a listener more than what is intended by the speaker.

Interviews are occasions for new representations and new understanding to develop. First, because the interview is a new experience, it brings *per definition* the speaker to think from a new perspective, and within the interviewer's explicit and implicit demands. Second, as an interpersonal relationship, an asymmetrical research interview can bring any of its participants to change (Baltes & Staudinger, 1996; Perret-Clermont, Carugati, & Oates, 2004), both because of the content and structure of the other's interventions, which might bring the speaker to form new representations or to adopt new perspectives on those that already exist; and because of the interpersonal dynamics, in which each participant resists or follow the other's interventions. The interviewer's interventions or expectancies can orient or canalize one's stream of thought-speech; yet the interviewee might *hear* himself thinking, and thus reflect on his own discourse and memories, as through the ears of the other. He may even create an agenda that is not shared by the researcher: for example, he might decide to use the interview to explore this or that part of his past from various perspectives. Hence, as Gillespie (2004) proposes, as with any social interaction, an interview is a social act: each person is not only reflecting on him or herself, but also reflecting on the basis of the perspective of the other on oneself, that is, the *surplus* of knowledge the other has over self. For the researcher, the challenge is to turn this surplus into a technical tool for research.

THE RECONSTRUCTIVE INTERPRETATIVE METHOD

The general exploratory hypothesis of this book is that young people use symbolic elements as resources in periods of transition. It aims at capturing people's engagement in change as enabled by their newly acquired symbolic responsibility. It was thus decided to approach young people at the beginning of their youth adulthood, that is, having acquired a symbolic responsibility, but likely to be at the beginning of a series of ruptures that would eventually lead them to a socially acknowledged adult position. This research has been done in England at the beginning of the twenty-first century, where it seemed reasonable to approach people between 18 and 25 years old.

The Participants

Because the first assumption of the project is that change is to be observed in the work of transition, the sample had to be defined so as to ensure that people had indeed experienced ruptures. It also had to be chosen so as to be sure that some contrasting uses of symbolic resources would be visible. Such sample definition is thus guided by some expectations about the information to be found (Flyvbjerg, 2001).

The notion of rupture followed by processes of transition enables us to identify very different events as theoretically equivalent (Valsiner & Sato, 2004). Theoretically constructed equivalent points can take various observable forms, and can be perceived very differently by the participants themselves. Yet their interest is that equivalent points can be compared, as can be compared the varieties of antecedents and subsequent trajectories. Here, two things had to be distinguished: ruptures theoretically *likely* to produce transitions; and theoretically defined ruptures felt *in effect* by people. The sample has been defined on the basis of the former, with the expectation of finding the latter. Criteria for choosing the participants was drawn from previous studies that showed some typical psychosocial transitions experienced as ruptures by people: entering student life (Coulon, 1997), coming back from a religious form of life to the secular world (Lawrence, Benedikt, & Valsiner, 1992), and leaving school to enter the professional world (Perret-Clermont, et al., 2004).

To ensure that the sample would include people who use symbolic resources in a sufficiently diversified way, the following observations have been considered. First, it was necessary to increase the likelihood that interviewees had access to cultural elements and were using them as resources; hence, interviewing university students was a way to ensure that the population under scrutiny were using symbolic resources at all (Flyvbjerg, 2001). (Note that students do not constitute an homogeneous population: some students come from boarding school, some are leaving their parents for the first time; some have taken a gap year, some have never stopped studying.) Second, some forms of study of biblical texts appear to encourage the development of *symbolic competencies* including hermeneutical skills, a consistent cultural system, and an ability to use these as symbolic resources to address real life problems—for example, use a biblical story to understand one's relationship to otherness (Zittoun, 1996; Zittoun & Cesari, 1998). On this basis, a group of young religious Jews were approached with the expectation that they would have developed expertise in the use of symbolic resources through their religious studies; they would constitute *extreme cases*, and analysis of their symbolic conduct might offer a grid for other cases (Flyvbjerg, 2001). Third, the use of symbolic resources does not imply formal reasoning: rather than formal syllogisms, they require metaphoric associations and analogies. Also, it is less *what* resources people use, than *how* they use them which is important. Thus, socioeconomical origins are not expected to make a difference in the use of symbolic resources (Luria, 1908/2003; Zittoun, 2001, 2004b, 2005a). On this basis, a group of school leavers were interviewed as a *critical case* for this hypothesis (Flyvbjerg, 2001), as well as for the purpose of diversifying the participating population.

In the end, 30 persons currently living in the same U.K. university town were interviewed. From now on, I will capitalize "University" when reference is made to that particular university. As with many wealthy U.K. towns, economical inequalities are high and cultural diversity important in that University town. These 30 young people are between 18 and 25; 11 are women and 19 men. Eighteen were students; six were Orthodox Jews; and six had stopped studying (see Appendix 2). The students were interviewed first, until saturation of the data in terms of modalities of uses of resources; young people from the two other groups were then contacted. Numbers of participants were not fixed *a priori*, rather, when some saturation of information was attained, I stopped contacting people. The smaller number of the last two groups is thus justified by the rapid saturation in terms of modalities of resources; the great similarity in the experience of the religious students, who were a very small and closed group; the fact that young people who stopped school had many different reasons for doing so, reasons which would not have been exhausted within the frame of these interviews. Such a sampling method excludes the strict verification of correlations between sociocultural class and the modalities of the use of resources (or any other quantitative evaluation).

Setting and Definition of the Situation

People have been contacted through three ways. A lecturer spoke about the project to his students; those who were interested gave their e-mail address and I contacted them. To approach religious students, I started attending the activities of the local Jewish community, after having informed the rabbi (here called "Chaplain"), of my intentions.[1] Finally, I met the school drops-out at the local pub, partially through a snowball effect. Each person was told that the research was on the role of cultural experience in people's lives, especially in periods of change or transitions "like the one you/we are in." Concepts such as the use of symbolic resources were not mentioned. Anonymity was guaranteed, and it was said interviews would be recorded. After confirming their interest, only one person did not come to an interview without reason.

Interviews took place in my university office at people's convenience; I picked up the nonstudents in front of the local pub. I used two seats set at an open angle (more or less 90°), the recorder being left on a third chair. Here, I again explained the topic and the anonymity of the research process, making sure I would not mention anything out of that interview setting—"especially given the fact that I know one of your teachers," or "especially given the fact that we might see each other at the pub." I said a few words about the exploratory dimension of the work; I was not expecting any *right* answer, it would be a joint effort. A consent-form was read and signed. After the interview, a short sociodemographical form was filled in.

Some participants must have felt more at ease in an university office than others, and some were more used to semiformal interview situations than others; the meaning of the situation must have varied between them. Some persons actively became research partners, using my questions to guide an introspective quest, or examining memories to see whether they had a link to the phenomena I examined. There were thus some interviewees who were clearly interested by the project, and that engaged in thinking about possible uses of resources and that realized them for the first time, while others were clearly already aware of these possibilities. Also, it may be that some resources were added during the interview; yet, if these were resources required for the rupture that the interview situation created, they are still, nevertheless, resources whose function needs to be explained. Many finished their interview with an "I hope it helps"; if they asked what would be done with the data I would explain more. The interviews lasted between 58 minutes and 1½ hour and were recorded. Only one was lost for mechanical reasons, but notes were taken immediately afterwards.

Interviewing

The general interview schedule was two-dimensional: one axis was chronological and aimed at identifying events felt as ruptures (see Appendix 2). People were first asked to describe their present situation (arrival at the University, or starting of the current professional situation), and what led them there. The interview then went backwards, exploring older experiences of ruptures; it included questions about family and relationships with grandparents, and finally turned to future plans.

The other axis, transversal, was aimed at identifying possible resources and their uses. People who had had to move were asked about the objects they had brought with them; others, about objects that they took with them on trips. In effect, such objects have an emotional or a personal valence: their being chosen indicates that they play a particular role for that person (see also Csikszentmihaly & Rochberg-Halton, 1981 on personal belongings; Habermas, 1996/1999a, 1999b; Laser, Josephs, & Fuhrer, 1999; Tisseron, 1999, 2003). Technically, starting from that repertoire of cultural elements, it is then easy to ask about other ones that might have an importance, might be thought about, or might have played a role for the person. This facilitates the exploration of the person's uses of symbolic resources, her past cultural experiences, and her personal culture.

During the reconstructive research interview, the surplus I have over the other and that the other has over me are used as tools for guiding my questions and my understanding. During the interaction, I mobilize at least three lines of representations: I have my agenda and the themes I would like to see covered; I have a knowledge of what the use of symbolic resources can be, on the basis of my own experience (on which I have been reflecting) and on the basis of previous interviews; I have the memory of what the person tells me during that interview. On this basis, I adopt a *floating attention*. This floating attention tries to be nonjudgemental regarding contents and structure of the discourse. Yet it is active, for all the information is used to construct and transform a representation of the world and the trajectory of the interviewee. Such a nonjudgemental floating attention is not emotional neutrality: On the contrary, I place myself in a state of emotional receptivity. I let emotional variations exist and I try to observe them. I thus use techniques linked to the analysis of counter-transference (Blanchet, 1991; Green, 2002; Viderman, 1970). I understand some of these emotions as linked to the content of the discourse; some as simple emotional reactions toward the speaker, such as empathy, or rejection; some emotions are linked to the associations the situation triggers in me. This emotional receptivity, first, enables the speaker to feel followed and thus allows the interaction to go on. Second, it enables me to see my biases. But more importantly, my emotional reactions indicate the points of the discourse that are of interest for me: for example, sequences that appear to me as boring, or sequences with high enthusiasms; sudden sadness or confusion, or a feeling of sudden truth. Changes, confusion, relative emotional intensity, contradictions, constitute the traces on the basis of which I will identify a rupture, what has not been thought-through, or what a given symbolic resources is used for

(Green, 1973/1999, 1992, 2002; Tisseron, 2002). Finally, although I come with the limitations of my agenda, I expect the interviewee to bring me to new perspectives or ideas (Falmagne, 2001). This can bring me to ask questions outside the agenda in order to reinforce my understanding of the other's discourse; it can also bring me to intuitive questions that might suddenly bring the person to talk about an important theme.

Producing and Analyzing Data

Discourse constitutes the data which is analyzed. Discourse is a form of semiotic externalization that testifies that there has been previous internalization and that the situation is a form of rupture demanding activity (answering the interviewer's question, finishing with it as soon as possible, or using the occasion for complaining, reflecting, or making a good impression). The discourse, which is produced within the interview situation, answers many situational demands. It informs in its contents, but also in its structure; finally, it carries traces of thoughts that are voluntarily withheld or simply not fully thought-through. Discourse can also inform about other forms of externalization on the basis of symbolic resources (such as giving a name to a baby, painting a wall, writing poems or a diary, etc.).

The interviews have been recorded and analyzed as sound files with Atlas.ti. Selected and coded sections of the discourse have then been transcribed before further analysis; the procedure enables the researcher to return easily to the recorded versions. The analysis has been constructed by alternating case studies and transversal, comparative contents analysis (Valsiner, 2004d).

Part of the analysis is intuitively done during the interview so as to orient it, and also as an effect of the action of the interviewee on the researcher; the rest is done afterwards. Here are the main analytical cues for the operationalization of the notions into categories during and after the interviews.

Transitions have been identified *a priori*, in terms of sociopsychological events. The interview tried to establish whether the person had experienced some events as rupture. Ruptures have been identified when explicitly pointed out ("I was very sad after the death of my grandmother," "It has been eye-opening"), when appearing through a sequence of things reported (a period of disarray, having been anxious or stressed, worried by newness, having engaged in new actions), or finally, through the discourse itself (change of tone, of speed, of the type of images employed, etc.).

At the time of the interview, some people are still in periods of uncertainty and engaged in *the work of transition*. Some still express their lack of orientation or distance. Elements considered as cues for such nonresolved ruptures are: signs of disruption or confusion, an absence of future oriented representations, or a great confusion between levels of discourses perceived as problematic (having some ideals that can not concretely be applied). The work of transition can also already have brought about new regularities. Such resolutions might be explicitly mentioned ("I was sad at that period (but now I am not anymore)"), but also, as a form of balanced discourse, linked to future orientations and a relatively consistent system of orientation, in contrast with what appears as a previous uncertainty.

Cultural elements have been explored through the aforementioned "what [objects] did you take with you" question; their uses were explored either indirectly ("And what do you do if you feel sad after a day at work?") or directly ("is there any film that was particularly important to you?"). Some cultural elements were thus mentioned within the discourse, while others were explicitly considered as objects of reflection. Hence, it is the case that the interview might have added some reflectivity to uses of resources.

How to identify cultural elements used as *symbolic resources*? In the extreme, symbolic resources in use are simply internalized cultural voices that have become constitutive of one's thought or speech.[2] This is where the distinction proposed in chapter 2 between primary and secondary uses finds all its importance (Zittoun, 2001, 2005a). The necessary traces and harmonics of past uses, and the shape of one's conduct on the basis of sociocultural patterns, correspond to what I call *primary uses* of cultural elements. These are transparent to their users, and methodologically difficult to identify. It is only this specific act of addressing an issue, a person, a situation, by mobilizing these harmonics, or these other voices or genre, with the intention of bringing about change, a form of transgression towards the taken for granted, that I describe as a *secondary use* of a cultural element, that is, a use of a symbolic resource.

Various cues enable the identification of a person's uses of symbolic resources. What has been helpful, relevant, or simply done after ruptures and in relationship to these, has been considered as *resource*, that is, having an *aboutness*. To be said to be used as *symbolic resources*, the cultural element must been linked to another entity, matter of fact or event—being sad *and* listening to music—or must have been linked to a form of intentionality. Such mentions might be spontaneous (having a poster on one's wall *in order to show* who one is; to listen to a song *in order to recall* past holidays); sometimes it appears in the interview, in a grasp of consciousness or as a juxtaposition.

Other resources acquire such aboutness, and are explicitly mentioned: friends, parents, grandparents, others with whom one interacts; textiles, clothes; or organized sports. These share properties: they are socially located and thus identity constitutive; they suppose material manipulation; they can be reflected on, they can be used for a novel purpose. But contrarily to symbolic resources as defined here, they are not made out of an organization of semiotic units, they have not been primarily constituted as a carrier of shared meanings (their other functions exceed their semiotic function—a scarf, even if it is a purple scarf to designate one's admiration of an *indie* singer, still has its scarf-ness function) and they do not organize imaginary experience at the level of one's interiority. Thus I do not analyze them, in contrast to authors who treat as equivalent all personal objects, whether of a semiotic nature or not (Csikszentmihaly & Rochber-Halton, 1981; Habermas, 1996/1999a, 1999b; Laser, Josephs, & Fuhrer, 1999).

Case Studies: Interpretative Analysis and Uses of Symbolic Resources

For the case studies, a close interpretative analysis developed by Zittoun (2001, 2004b), based on the theoretical assumptions explained earlier, has been used. It assumes that meanings that people develop through uses of symbolic resources cannot be reduced to meanings determined by standard discourse analysis of the cultural element (Anderson, 1998; Lembo, 2000). This interpretative analysis combines aspects of qualitative narrative or life-story analysis, and elements taken from psychoanalytical theorization on thinking processes in discourse and culture. In order to see whether and how it can be said that these elements have been used as resources, it thus includes:

1. A reconstruction of the present transition period of the person, in the context of her biographical lines (Rosenthal, 1993a, 1993b; Kraus, 1996a, 1996b; Bar-On, 1995);
2. A review of the cultural elements mentioned by the person, and a close examination of the most relevant books, songs, movies, and so forth (that have been internalized).
3. An identification of *knots* in the person's discourse: conflicting themes or unelaborated experiences.[3] When not explicitly mentioned, such knots are indicated by changes of emotional intensity in the discourse, by repetitions, contradictions, by cross-thematic common semantic fields, by phonologic recurrences, and so forth (Tisseron, 1998, 2002; Green, 1992, 1999). It is not that *identifying*

these knots is an attempt to *explain* them (which would be a real psychoanalytical work).

The analysis compares these three lines: are the cultural elements presented in some way that maps on, or resonates with, the themes or the events that compose the knot, or to the general biographical line?

Such case studies allow inferences about elements that have not been reflectively seen by the participant, and the making of hypotheses about motives, reason, or emotions, which are not verbalized (Zittoun, 2001). Case studies also allow the observation of the interplay of the identified analytical categories, and to complete the sketch of modelization.

Interviews and analysis thus constitute 29 case studies (Lina's interview has not been analyzed: it was the first interview, the framework was still unclear, and technical problems made the interview inaudible). For each of them, I try to understand the world in which the person lives, her personal culture, the problems she deals with, who are her important others and what are the symbolic objects and constructs that enable her action. I also try to get a sense of her emotional moods, how she regulates them, and what are the contradictions and blurred zones of which she is not aware. At the same time, I use the same sets of notions for each of these cases. I try to see how each case modifies my theoretical tools, and how each case is illuminated by them.[4] Of course, such an analysis of changes through uses of symbolic resources does not *explain* the whole of a person's trajectory.

Choosing Examples and Case Studies

In the next two chapters, the case studies will be presented in more detail. In chapter IV, a general model of the use of symbolic resources is given. Categories are constructed on the basis of recurrences identified through a transversal analysis; for presentational purposes, excerpts have been chosen for their clarity in supporting this or that point. These might come from interviewees who are more reflective, or more used to verbalizing their thoughts.

Various criteria have guided the choice of the cases that are presented in more detail in chapters 4 and 5. First, it was necessary to choose cases based on interviews in which a greater richness of information and engagement has been attained. Second, the cases of Lily and Julia in chapter 4 are presented as paradigmatic cases—they illustrate the various developmental uses of symbolic resources, in a purer way than many other cases. As such, they are referred to throughout the text. Third, in chapter 5, cases are presented with the aim of maximum variation (Flyvbjerg, 2001): people belong to the three initial transitions subgroups; they have very different uses of symbolic resources; and they have contrasting ways of reflecting on their uses. In the frame of this researched variation, the cases do not simply confirm initial hypothesis. Rather, these five cases are chosen to represent recurrent difficulties raised by the data, as they questioned the theoretical model and called for revisions. In such a research enterprise, case studies are the only way to accede complex, context-related data—and it is only through such cases that a theory that aims at accounting for complexity can develop (Cornish, 2004b).

Validity

As mentioned above, a cyclical approach has been adopted here. The model has been developed through a cyclical movement from case studies to the transversal analysis and reciprocally, and from the data to the theory and analysis of previous cases of uses of symbolic resources, and reciprocally. This cyclical double triangulation aims at ensuring internal consistency for theory building (Valsiner & Connolly, 2003).

Yet an additional checking of the data has been done through a third form of triangulation by multiplying data and observers. First, the interview framework has been given by a colleague to a group of students, who have been asked to interview friends about their use of symbolic resources on the basis of the objects in their room. They have been free to analyze these interviews as they wished. Comparable data has been produced on the basis of about 25 interviews; students' analytical categories overlapped with my first set of distinctions (aboutness of use, identity functions). Second, data and analysis obtained with the Jewish students have been discussed with the Chaplain of the community, whose perspective could usefully complete observations and interviews. Third, I have reflectively examined my uses of symbolic resources across years, both in order to test my model and to be aware of my biases, through my writing, in a psychoanalytical setting, and in endless informal discussions. Fourth, I did a biographical interview of a 76 year-old man; he had a long practice of self-reflection (he is a psychoanalyst) and my analysis of his use of resources in transitions have been systematically discussed (Trier, Zittoun, & Perret-Clermont, 2004; Zittoun, 2006a). Finally, many examples of the use of resources have been observed within literature, cinema, and music. This additional data and analysis have no reason to figure in the present book; yet they are in the background of the present constructions.

GENERALIZATION

The cases closely analyzed in chapter 4 have been chosen for the purpose of crystallizing most of the variations within the 29 cases. My choice of cases reflects my experience of many instances of the phenomenon under scrutiny. These cases are thus chosen for some form of typicality. Yet they are also, overall, the occasion for questioning and dialoguing with existing theories, and for developing models or categories that might easily be applied to other situations (the notion of rupture, transition, etc.). In that sense, generalization is possible through three pathways identified by Cornish (2004b): it requires *human judgement* (Flybvbjerg, 2001), that is, a form of expertise from the researcher, based on his experience of a great number of cases; it supposes *typical cases* (in a way that has to be specified); and it relies on the use of *theoretical cases*: cases studies enter into dialogue with existing theories, and are the occasion of producing useful concepts.

This model of knowledge production has been highly generative in the history of psychology—it is the model for the major enterprises of Freud, Janet, the early Piaget, Erikson, and many others. Rather than building up a model while under the illusion of a mastery of variables, these studies account for the involvement of the researchers. Even more, their involvement enables them to move through cases, to alternate between focusing on details and seeing groups of cases from afar, and thus, eventually, to challenge existing theories and produce new ones.

This romantic view raises however two issues regarding the current state of human and social sciences in our society. First, the notions developed through scientific work need to be validated by a community of researchers or users. Yet the divisions within science make such dialogue difficult, because of both the specialization of sub areas of research and the multiplication of different notions. It is already difficult for a single researcher to define a set of consistent notions; how can he then talk to his neighbor? An important work of bridging sub-areas has to be done, and an important work of translation between notions as well. These two efforts are costly, and not always well received by the scientific community. However, they are the conditions for integrating various observations and data in a generalizable body of knowledge.

Second, in our society, as a result of contrasting but flexible life trajectories, personal cultures might appear extremely fuzzy in some cases, rigid and immobile in others. Of course, it may be doubted that there has been any period in Europe or in the United States where personal cultures have been homogenous. The point that is classically addressed to our type of enquiry remains: how can the observations made on the basis

90 Transitions: Development through Symbolic Resources

of a small group of relatively wealthy British citizens pretend to be of any general interest?

The answer is twofold. On the one hand, the type of phenomenon observed here—the use of symbolic resources in development—has been active and identified for a very long time, in very many different areas of the social sciences, and in all types of population (see Zittoun, 2006a). My aim here is to single out and isolate a phenomenon which is otherwise merely observed. If this aim is achieved, this work might just help other people to identify, in their own environments, similar processes. In effect, as Cornish reminds us, a pragmatist approach conceives that "'truth' is always in the future. We have expectations and if they work, they are called 'true'" (Cornish, 2004b, p. 101). On the other hand, however, it is also true that such phenomenon can take a wide variety of forms: very different cultural elements might be used; people can be confronted with a wide range of transitions; diverse constraints are applied on their real, inner or imaginary experiences (Crapanzano, 2004). If the model is powerful enough, it should be able to account for radically different uses of resources leading to forms of change that differ from the one observed here. If it is not, we would have also learned something about the limits of its validity.

AN OVERVIEW OF 29 POSSIBLE CASE STUDIES

Within the setting of research interviews, 30 persons agreed to say something about uncertain periods in their lives, and about the people and objects that were important for them. In what follows, I briefly summarize these 30 stories; without making a strict analysis, I highlight transitions, the resources that were used, and the very general tonality of the interaction. Cases that are discussed more extensively in the next chapters are just sketched out below; some cases that I will not discuss are given more space.

Personal names and names of places are invented for purposes of anonymity; details that might enable identification have been changed.

Transcription conventions are as follow:

- *Q followed by italics* are questions or interventions by the interviewer
- *Isolated italic words* indicate a title of a cultural element
- ... indicates an interruption
- - - indicates as silence
- xxx indicates words that have not been understood

- [ab] are words added or corrected by me in the interviewee's discourse
- (ab) are comments added by me about paralinguistic events
- (...) indicates a truncation by me
- CAPITALS indicate emphasis added by the interviewee
- ::: indicates an enduring syllable

Adam took a gap year before coming to university, during which he worked in the United Kingdom and went to South America where he was involved in some charity work. Travelling was his first long experience out of home. He also discovered social inequalities both inside and outside England, which was what he calls an "eye-opener." He is an evangelical Christian, who teaches children in Sunday classes. He also reads the Bible every day, and defines his opinion in social and moral matters on this basis.

Anne has been quite shocked by the newness of life in college at University (even though she had been to boarding school). She likes to travel, and sees herself as open to various cultures. Food, music, and even novels are, for her, ways to evoke absent places, to retain memories of trips, or to make sense of what she has seen. Her parents are from different cultural origins; they converted to another religious life, to which they are strongly committed. Anne is ambivalent as to whether she should keep that religious life. Her mother used to cook food from her culture of origin.

Charles dropped out of secondary school after two attempts, and now lives from small jobs. He feels quite handicapped by earlier negative school categorization and exclusion, and has strong reactions against teachers or priests who tried to impose their views of "what is good for him." He used to read a lot in the bus during his school years, especially a series called *My Teacher is an Alien*. He did small jobs to earn money, traveled in South America with friends, and in both situations read a lot to pass the time—it is more about "sitting and reading" than about what is read. He reads at work in breaks. He has read *The Beach* many times and sees it as an "escapist" story. He would like to go back to school.

Elaine left her town after college, realizing that she did not like academic studies, having had negative social experiences (peers rejected her because her mother was known as a severe teacher). She worked for a period, moved town, and started an art program, but was hit by the hardness of living independently. She reads a lot of fiction and thinks a great deal about the characters when she is bored; she rereads books to see how her understanding changes through time. As a child she had been taken to art-galleries by her grandmother and mother, who taught her to try to understand art pieces. She used to play a lot of music as a way to make her feel better. Now art is for her a way of self-exploration. She is thinking about one more gap year before, possibly, starting to study.

Eli came from a religious Jewish family, with an open attitude to secular culture. After Yeshiva, religious high school in Israel, he studied in such a way that he could reconcile his interests with his studies. Yet coming to university was difficult; secular novels and films helped him to think about the relationship between the two spheres of experience (See chapter 4).

Esther chose to go to one of the very few women's yeshiva in Israel. Back in England, after the initial shock of adjustment, she discovered that she had to define a way to explain her singularity to others. She also realized that her religious studies had led her to find in each secular text, a form of better understanding about her life, others or the world.

Felix had been at boarding school, and so knew what to bring when coming to university: his bass guitar, music—some for the lyrics, and some groove for the energy—and many books. He does not seem to have felt any strong rupture. He reads a lot of scary thrillers, travel books, and magazines he likes for the beauty of the language and style. He also has a encyclopedia about Formula 1 (F1) that he browses through when he is stressed; he shares his F1 passion with his father. He watches TV—cool movies to help him "switch off," and the morning news to stay informed about the world. He runs regularly. He is reflective about his time and stress management—when to work, when to relax.

Greg went to a state school and did not take a gap year; he apprehended finding only public school (i.e., privately educated) people at university (and thus can be seen as feeling the rupture). Raised religiously, he is actively questioning the role of the church and claims the right to understand the Bible as he wishes. He worries about morality and the future. He reflects on the evolution of his readings: is there a logic in moving from science fiction, to political texts (e.g., "what could the world be like? What is it like? How should it be?"). Recently *The Lords of the Rings* offered him a way to think about the real world: good and evil, the cyclical nature of events, the problems of an extended democracy, and so forth. *Matrix*, also pleasurable, was in contrast much lighter. After work, he enjoys poetry, Shakespeare, or texts of the sixteenth century; he discovered these texts during his A-Levels. He plays guitar.

Gustav has been bullied at boarding school. At that time he used to write poetry; he also had a "low profile"—choosing to play viola or to be goalkeeper, rather than taking more "glorious" positions. After boarding school, he took a gap year, during which he first spent a lot of time reading "challenging" books (Sartre, Wittgenstein) without much interest. He then travelled to China and met a very extrovert young man with whom he became very close. When he finally traveled by himself he felt very lonely and stressed at not having anyone to share his experience with. Yet, he explains that the gap year changed him: it made him more open and social. He does not write poems anymore, but theatre reviews. His reading, mostly advised by his grandfather, should be useful, that is, related to his studies, or "worth mentioning" in discussions. He is engaged in the debating society (his grandfather used to debate as well).

Ilona comes from a religiously mixed family who traveled a lot, from country to country, following her parents' jobs. She has grown used to changing places and finding different groups of friends, and thus does not express a particular sense of rupture. She, for instance, just joined the Jewish group. She reads fantasy novels that she shares with her friend and her mother. She keeps thinking about characters while doing boring tasks in her lab, or here and there. For her, movies should be shared and discussed with friends.

Julia had difficulties with leaving home; she arranged her University room to be similar to her home one. Before this, she had a hard time after her grand-mother's death, after which she started listening to the *Manic Street Preachers*; she progressively discovered the texts to which the lyrics referred; she joined communities of fans and became politically aware, and finally she decided to study politics (see chapter 5).

Lev came from a religious family and spent one year in a yeshiva. His father wanted him to study and thus he had to go to university, where he engaged in a short program. However, his religious yeshiva masters disapproved of his choice, and he had not lived in a secular environment before; he thus had a very difficult first year. The rabbi and the local community played an important role in helping him to adjust to his new form of life. He still finds his studies meaningless, for most modern literature appears morally valueless, and academically authorized text analyses are not aimed at finding life-relevant meanings—which is contrary to a basic assumption held in Jewish studies. Through personal readings, he tries to transfer this moral assumption into a psychological interest; yet his attempts to read Shakespeare psychologically have not been legitimized by his supervisors (see chapter 4).

After having been to boarding school, **Lewis** came to this University, as had every member of his family. His father used to travel; he grew up in various countries. He took a gap year, did a few boring jobs and traveled in Africa, Asia, Brazil, and Europe—the "best time of his life." He chose to travel to Vietnam and Thailand partly because he had seen *The Beach* and Vietnam movies. Coming back to England has been difficult. Lewis feared the first few days of the school year: homesick, he had been unable to socialize when he arrived at boarding school. He wanted to be sure of having a better start at university, and feels his gap-year taught him social competence. He declares that he is able to recognize the people who have had a gap year. Overall he regrets not having kept a diary during his trip;

he fears the time is "lost," and wishes he could share his memories and have pictures to turn to when feeling low. He likes *Harry Potter, Lords of the Ring* and is a movie fan—*James Bond, Jackie Chan,* and scary movies (it is fun to be scared). Both traveling and movie watching should be shared with a friend. He is going to make movies with a friend, a western:

> I like westerns. (Slaps his hands) Now, westerns kind of sum up the whole idea. It is all about the kind of... it is all about coolness. It is all about zooming the camera in the eyes, you know, high moon sort of stuff, and it's all about one person - one person being extra-cool. You know what I mean, it is just so satisfying, when you see someone like, when you see Clint Eastwood shooting one guy, and the xx... Yeah, that's so classic, and this is the kind of movie we are going for. Not western, but the finesse from it. The satisfaction you get watching them. Because it is so satisfying: the good [guys] usually win, and they do it in style. So what else do you want in a good film?

Lily came from overseas to University after a long decision process. Books were important in her preparation to come to this country, and movies helped her to think through her decision. She is still a great reader (see chapter 4).

Lina also came to University from overseas, after a job experience, where she quickly had acquired a demanding managerial position. She describes her parents, siblings, and friends as offering her support when she needs it; here, she quickly made friends. Her family has brought her to appreciate arts, yet novels or music seem not to have played an important role in the difficult periods she has had to live through.

Mary stopped university for familial reasons; she then worked for many years, and it took her time to realize that she could take some interesting evening classes. She has been a heavy reader since her childhood, and reads everything. She is doing art, and has long been familiar with museums thanks to her mother and grandmother's interests (see chapter 4).

Max comes from a religious family and reacts against his parents' values. He took a gap year, during which he worked in a factory, on building sites, in pubs, and thus discovered another side to things, which has been an "eye opener." He took with him music, novels, pictures, and graphic reprints. He did some art of his own, but does not feel "driven" enough to study arts or graphics. He listens to music, that he likes to exchange with other people, and admires graphic works, especially the work of an artist who leaves posters and stencils from *André the Giant* in public spaces (see chapter 5).

Moshe's mother is head of a Jewish school; he went in and out of religious orthodoxy, and traveled here and there, with his religious texts in the back of his car. His life is told as a long story of complicated ruptures.

Moving places he also moved social groups and modes of activity. As a scientist, he is worried about questions about time and infinity, which he links with his reading of religious texts.

Olivia left home to do a short university program that she did not like (it was very far from what she thought it was); she traveled with friends. She is now working to pay back her loan. She is thinking about training for a job she heard about on the radio; she wants to travel in a country which she has heard about. She sees movies with her mother or friends; and is now reading a lot of novels, about movies she has seen, because her job is very boring.

Orson dropped out of university in his first year, as he was living in hall for the first time. Staying there and not going to class anymore, for the first time he had his "own space"; he discovered the pleasure of reading—as a way of understanding himself. *Perfume*, by Patrick Süskind, was his first experience of new forms of perception. He plans to take a gap year abroad and is looking forward to wandering and discovering towns.

Paris took a gap year after attending a private college. He worked for a while in an alienating job (and read to escape at lunch breaks), and then traveled by himself in Italy and South America. He chose to study difficult disciplines because he is looking for challenges, but wants to find a job that is useful to others. He thinks of himself as nonintellectual and sporty. He reflects on the time management studies require, knows his strength and respects his needs. During his trips and journeys he pays a lot of attention to the architecture; he also gave some importance to his flat and room (he brought plants with him). His possible future profession is linked to architecture.

Pat dropped out of secondary school after two attempts. He started a job that he disliked and that revealed itself to be alienating; after a difficult time he defined progressively his interests. He tries to meet people and hear about their experiences, and he rediscovered the value of his childhood and youth experience as a member of the Scouts. He also plays role-play games, and reads only occasionally for leisure (see chapter 5).

Randy's family has been moving from country to country and he has always been in boarding schools—coming to university was not worrying as such. He took a gap year before coming to University, during which he worked, and traveled in Europe and Asia. He became a massive movie watcher between the ages of 8 and 15; his parents offered him information about movies when he was 15, after which he started to develop an expert interest in films, guided by his father. He is into "talky" films, and films that have some tension, entwined stories, and ambivalent endings (such as *Casablanca*). His passion stopped since the gap year, because of the alienating rhythm of the work experience, and because he now prefers talking with people, although he misses the friend with whom he used to discuss films. Cinema developed his "romanticism":

> I think it just… it made me always see… relationship just having to be special. (…) It is a cliché about … movies and stuff (…) But I don't think… It is not—as it were—romantic in a love sense? I think it is in a life sense? Making me more - - less cynical, I think. And believing that things are happening, that you should pursue interests and stuff.(…) I think it just made me view, about how friendships, or relationships might be. And I think possibly, one of the reasons why… I stopped watching as many movies, because I got to enter strong a personal relationship.

Robert comes from a rather poor area; he is the first of his family to go to university. He listens to a lot of music, plays music, and reads poetry. Playing music can be "therapeutic" when he is stressed; music can be listened for its intrinsic qualities, and also because it means something to him—it is thus attached to other times and friends, which is especially important now that he is away. He admires a poet who enables him to reconnect to where he comes from (landscapes, mood), and that makes him think about social and political iniquities. His mother has introduced him to poetry and music as a child. He thinks that he has adopted "a poetic outlook" from lyrics of songs he likes. Poetic language indeed enables seeing and saying different things in normal life, in a more cheerful, optimistic way. This, for example, guides his writings in local magazines.

Ron came from a religious background and stayed 2 years in yeshiva. He keeps a very rigorous frame to his life and avoids contact with non-Jews. He thinks that it is more the act of doing religious actions and studying the Jewish legal text of Talmud that make him feel satisfied, than the content of the texts. He also uses his "legalist" modes of reasoning in his university studies.

Thomas was at boarding school and came to this University after having been encouraged by his teacher. He comes from a traditional and conservative island community, from which he had to take some distance. He took a gap year, during which he worked overseas, and got professional experience working for a MP back in the United Kingdom. He feels the gap year gave him "a future horizon." He reads the Bible daily, and political biographies of such as those of Thatcher and Major, who he sees as driven personalities (see chapter 5).

Wanda had never left home, and coming to university was difficult. She misses her family, boyfriend, and friends. She suffers from the pressure and the lack of intimacy and personal space. She also had to renounce practicing sports for time reasons, given the exigencies of her courses. She took with her books that she knows, and that make her feel better.

Accessing Personal Cultures 97

She also watches again her preferred movies—seen with her boyfriend—to feel good. When sad, she listens to sad music or eats chocolate; she has objects (songs, smells, perfumes) linked to her boyfriend that "make her happy" when she misses him. She likes *Bridget Jones*, because "it shows that life is not only of sadness, but also bits of joy." Yet before coming to university, she had to go through difficult events: the death of her younger brother, the disablement of her other brother, the life-threatening illnesses of her father. Strong family links and support from the local social and religious community were important in withstanding these difficulties. Books played also an important role: Christopher Nolan, a disabled writer from a Catholic background similar to hers, allowed her to examine her own ambivalent attitude toward her disabled brother and to recognize her dark side. Another important text was Khalil Gibran's *The Prophet*, received by her mother at the brother's death. She remembers the importance of: "The deeper the sorrow carves into your being, the more joy you can contain." Such a metaphor helped her to overcome her sadness; she also read it to her boyfriend when she was leaving home to come to university.

William started university again after having left during his first year, where he arrived directly after state school. He then read a lot of American travel literature (Beat Generation) and nonfiction as a preparation for his new studies. He traveled to New York, but overall he has been "very bored" during that year. He refuses the artistic values of his family (Mozart, etc.), and thinks of arts in terms of politics and social issues. He shares with a close friend his interest for contemporary art and music. He is also a big DVD movie watcher. For example, he repeatedly watched *Taxi Driver*, *Angel Heart* and *Blue Velvet*. Yet he denies any "identification" or connection between his moods and the movies; he analyzes them in a very formal way. He plays music and writes art criticism.

Wolf went on gap year to Russia after leaving his boarding school. He had been interested in the Russian revolution at school, and his mother had always encouraged him to read Russian literature. There, with his friend, he visited places described in the novels. He met Russians and saw their life conditions, and discussed the novels he had read with them. He likes reading the biographies of Lenin and Mao, who he defines as driven personalities. He considers himself left wing and is engaged in the debating society.

For **Xenia** it had been difficult to come to University, for she loved living at home. Going to college, where she was boarding, had been difficult as well: everything appeared surreal, as in a book or in a film. She had read novels about boarding schools, and the environment and the education system appeared familiar to her from these readings. Here, this university town appears her as if "in a bubble": seeing punting on the river is like being in a movie. She is a great reader, ever since she was a child. She loved *The Beach* which she had read on holiday, and a book her father read to her. At times, parents advise her on books to read; she shares some taste with her mother. Now, she reads diaries and novels; she re-reads anthologies and diaries, to see what happened the very same day (to another person, in another time.). The only thing she does not read is scary stories: she read one once, and it invaded her thoughts so much that she decided never to do it again. She prefers woman characters, for one can relate to them more. When she likes characters she thinks about them, here and now.

> There are a lot of things that I haven't experienced, but that I have read in novels—and this is the only reference you have. (...) When someone tells you a story, you could remember it as something else—like with the association with a story. I remember all the boarding experience with [the stories –] – sometimes it is just an image, like you are cycling along and the image just comes back.

NOTES

1. I thank here the Chaplain of the Jewish community of the University for his availability and his support.
2. Hence, for Bakhtin (1934-1935/1981, 1979/1986), some distant voices or discourses can be simply visible as harmonics or distant echoes within an utterance; they can also structure the utterance as a particular genre of discourse; they can finally appear as irruption of other voices breaking into the discourse. Baktkin is analyzing fictional characters; yet he is aware that the moulding of an utterance within this or that genre, or the inclusion of the other's voice as a form of anticipating dialog, are bounded by social constraints. First, the words or the genres which are used have their own life as such; they carry the weight of their previous uses; and they mean specific things for a given person. Second, using this word rather than another, is an act by someone who has a specific rhetoric intention towards a specific addressee, in a specific situation, that creates specific relations. Characters' uses of various genres and voices in specific utterances are thus partly the result of their past histories, and partly the result of their intentional stance and specific attempts at acting over something or someone.
3. This method has been developed, and successfully used, in research on first-name choice in the transition to adulthood. There, the identification of knots was facilitated by the semantic-phonetic games surrounding mentioned first names (Zittoun, 2001, 2004b).
4. This hides the difficulties raised, at times, by having to compare. In effect, the discourse varies from interview to interview, according to the mutual sympathy between interviewer and interviewee, my own receptivity, the need for secrecy of the interviewee, his habit of self-reflection in dialogue, or his own defence mechanism. For example, William tells me that he

watched many times *Taxi Driver*, *Blue Velvet* and *Angel Heart*. He also affirms that his attraction to these movies has nothing to do with identification and moods, and that he just appreciates their formal features (on which he comments at length). For my part, I know that these movies are powerfully crafted to bring the spectator to intense and ambivalent feelings; I also know that they belong to a group of *cool* movies for some social groups or networks. Am I authorized to consider that William is making intrapsychic and social uses of a resource, even if he says it is not the case?

CHAPTER 4

YOUNG PEOPLE'S USES OF SYMBOLIC RESOURCES

L'objet de la sublimation ce n'est pas le livre, c'est la lecture.[1]
—André Green, *Idées directrices pour une
psychanalyse contemporaine* (2002b, p. 164)

*In the day that followed I spent hours on end arranging my little library, twenty or thirty books that I dealt and shuffled like a pack of cards, rearranging them in all sorts of different ways. So I learnt from books the art of composition, not from what was in them but from the books themselves, from their physical being. They taught me about that dizzying no-man's land or twilight zone between the permitted and the forbidden, between the legitimate and the eccentric, the normative and the bizarre. This lesson has remained with me ever since. By the time I discovered love,
I was no greenhorn.*

—Amos Oz, *A Tale of Love and Darkness*, (2004, p. 24).

Interviews with 29 young people aimed at identifying transitions and the role of cultural elements in their lives (chapter 3). This chapter is based on a transversal reading of all these cases. I first give an overview of these young persons' important transitions, and I present the cultural elements —books, movies, religious beliefs, songs, and so forth—that belong to their personal cultures. Interviewees mentioned these either spontaneously, or when asked more directly. I focus on cultural elements that are not only mentioned as objects, but also when these are mentioned when

102 Transitions: Development through Symbolic Resources

talking about something else, in a secondary use. From a developmental perspective, what is important is not which cultural elements are mentioned; rather, it is how they are used. Most of this chapter will thus explore how these cultural elements are turned into symbolic resources, supporting the psychological work of transitions. This emphasis on patterns of choices, logics, and uses justifies the absence of quantitative treatment of the data (see chapter 3).

WHAT TRANSITIONS, WHAT RESOURCES?

In the first chapter, I proposed to distinguish between expected, or expectable, psychosocial transitions, and transitions following ruptures felt *as such*. Through people's discourse, overlaps between these appear: some persons perceive as ruptures events that are also culturally acknowledged as leading to processes of transition, such as coming to university (Coulon, 1997; Iannaccone, Ghodbane, & Rosciano, 2004; Park, 2003), or moving from school to work (Perret-Clermont, Carugati, & Oates, 2004). Other perceived ruptures are less typical of youth, such as coming back from a setting of religious orthodoxy (Lawrence, Benedikt, & Valsiner, 1992; Zittoun, 1996), coming back from a gap year, or the death of a brother or of a grandmother (Bagnoli, 2003). Some ruptures are thus imposed, such as the death of a close one; other are looked for and deliberately created, such as when one travels or decides to study abroad (and at times, symbolic resources are used to created that rupture, Gillespie in Zittoun, Duveen, Gillespie, Ivinson, & Psaltis, 2003). The ensuing transitions processes are sometimes extended over years, and others seem to lead to a new balance after a few weeks or months; some have a clear beginning or ending, and others have blurred boundaries.

Young people engaging in some work of transition mobilize various sorts of resources. Some people rely mostly on their own previous practical and emotional experience; some seek dialogue with others to reflect on their actions (Falmagne, 2003); and some, indeed, use symbolic resources. Yet when they do so, it is often combined with other resources, as we will see in chapter 5. Here, I examine only uses of symbolic resources.

In their leisure time, that is, out of work or study, the interviewed young people have various forms of leisure activities (see also Bruno, 2000; Hendry, Sucksmith, Love, & Glendinning, 1993). Among these, many can be considered as cultural experiences: interviewees read poetry and novels, act in plays, play role-games or music, are scouts, meditate on religious texts and pray—activities that are forms of cultural experiences as defined in chapter 2. They also engage in other interactive activities which are not strictly speaking cultural experiences: they study, engage in sports, program their computers, interact with their families, do charity work, drink, and dance, travel and go out with their boy and girlfriends. However *each interviewed person*, whatever his or her financial means and sociocultural background were, *had cultural experiences*.

Interviewed young people had thus cultural experiences based on interactions with and around films (mainstream, classical, and experimental), music and songs (from hip-hop to English neo-classic minimalism), poetry, theatre-plays, novels (classics, bestsellers, biographies, fantasy, science-fiction, thrillers, psychological dramas), Biblical and religious texts, paintings (classical and modern), graphics and architecture. Some of these cultural elements were repeatedly mentioned: George Orwell's *1984* is often described as an "eye-opener," *The Beach* by Alex Garland is mentioned as important for most people having travelled (see also Gillespie, 2004), and novels by Tolstoy are frequently included in personal cultures. These recurrences reveal sociocultural constraints: some of these novels are part of secondary school programs; some have been commercial successes; some might have been targeted at the interviewees' specific age group. In their studies of youth leisure, Fine, Mortimer, and Roberts (1990) similarly observe that gender, social, and cultural factors, mutually interdependent, canalize cultural choices.

Yet choices of cultural experiences do not strictly reflect sociocultural predictions (also Buchmann, 2001): a working person from a modest family can live in a world of books and paintings; an academic, child of intellectual upper-middle class parents, can barely consider cultural elements as personally relevant outside of his studies. Also, listing privileged cultural experiences and examining how much time is invested in these cannot explain the meaning that these experiences acquire for a person, and what she will do with them. A person can watch TV everyday, but without involvement (Bruno, 2000); she might rarely go to the cinema, but highly enjoy each film she sees, think about it in the following weeks, and turn it into a symbolic resource.

In the remaining of this chapter, I examine cultural elements chosen by young people—cultural elements that matter to them. I show *what* can be done with these when used as symbolic resources. Following the theoretical categories defined in chapters 1 and 2, I will examine three dimensions of uses of symbolic resources. First, I will explore *what* these cultural experiences are *used about*. Second, I will examine the uses of symbolic resources in the construction of a *time perspective*. Third, I will show how symbolic resources can be used to mediate experiences at *various levels of generality*. Each section will be constructed on the same model: first, different modalities of uses of symbolic resources will be distinguished within each of these three dimensions; second, the relationships and dynamics unifying these modalities will be shown.

THE *ABOUTNESS* OF CULTURAL ELEMENTS

Symbolic resources are cultural elements that persons *use*. As semiotic mediations, that is, as representational acts, we have seen that uses of symbolic resources are by definition intentional, even if not necessarily conscious. The interest of such uses is that they mediate changes, beyond the sphere of imaginary or esthetical experience enabled by the cultural element (chapter 2). They can thus become *cultural tools*, as described by Vygotsky and neo-Vygotskian authors (Blandin, 2002; Cole, 1996; Rabardel, 1999; Valsiner, 2002), that can enable thinking or acting. As others cultural or psychical tools, semiotic mediation can be used in various directions, *about* the social or the material world, about interpersonal relationship or about oneself. Semiotic objects can also be oriented to confer meaning to other symbolic means, as in the case of intertextuality (Ricoeur, 1969/1974, 1976; Ouaknin, 1994, 1986/1995)—which I will not consider here.

People can easily express the *aboutness* of their uses, and doing so, they often are or become aware of such uses. In this section, three main directions of uses of symbolic resources are explored separately: uses about the social world, about other persons, and about oneself. You might note that these various aboutnesses correspond to possible poles of the semiotic prism. Therefore, even if these three directions can be observed by themselves, they are in fact structurally always interdependent, as I will suggest at the end of this section.

Uses About the Socially Shared Reality

The socially shared reality about which symbolic resources can be used first includes the societal milieu in which a person lives, which has an historical past and a collective future. Second, it includes a person's direct and indirect spheres of experiences. Third, it includes the concrete objects and situations that she might meet. *Uses of symbolic resources can here have two functions: a performative one—where uses of symbolic resources can change one's location in the social reality—and a semiotic function—where uses of symbolic resources support meaning constructions.*

The societal world and each possible sphere of experience are structured by, made out of, and are constrained by streams of human and symbolic relationships, that allocate positions to people on symbolic, social, or material grounds. Within such fabric are created zones, or groups, defined by the easiness with which people can have access to some, rather than other, symbolic or material goods. It might be said that people's position in these networks are fixed by their possible access to cultural elements. Social mobility, that is relocation within the societal world, often across spheres of experience, becomes dependent on the modifications of one's access to cultural elements, and on one's uses of symbolic resources (Moscovici, 1973; Pedler & Ethis, 1999). Choosing or using a symbolic resource thus *performs* the persons' location in a matrix of relationships within the social world, by *expressing* it, or by *modifying* it through the complex interplay of legitimization. Hence, using a given symbolic resource expresses one's position on that social symbolic fabric and one's possible spheres of experience; it also indicates one's distance to other zones or groups. Having read Orwell's *1984* positions a young person as having been to an English high school in the twenty-first century. Being a reader of Kerouac constitutes a person as a member of a particular group, either in a direct way, by sharing that interest with friends, or in an indirect way, through online exchanges or through affiliation to imaginary communities of readers. Others, here, validate the person's use of that resource and therefore her position. Such phenomena have been widely studied by social and cultural sciences interested in the circulation of knowledge and its social functions (Duveen, 1997, 2001; Moscovici, 1973). From such a perspective, symbolic resources are reduced to their value of indicating social positions; their contents—the actual literary quality of Orwell or Kerouac's text, or what these designate—are not directly relevant.

The *semiotic function* of uses of symbolic resources suppose a link between the meaning content of these resources, and aspects of the socially shared reality. This link can be based on similarities of semantic contents, structure, emotional qualities, or any other characteristics of the semiotic configuration or its meanings that can move or trigger the person. Having this or that cultural experience can inform a person about these aspects, or give templates to read and organize them. Symbolic resources can thus *participate in the making of meanings* that the person confers on her human, symbolic and material spheres of experience (Bruner, 1990). Tales, mythical, and religious texts might be seen as collective crystallizations of shared understanding of the world. These have been and are still used for their explicative or didactic functions. Contemporary uses of the Bible appear as paradigmatic uses of symbolic resources as means to decipher a given sphere of experience. Here, Adam, a Christian, explains "connections" he sees between biblical texts and political matters:

> Q *Can you give an example of one of those connections?* xx I just got to... I just got into Exodus. I haven't been far, so far. But, we are looking at the Israelites' flight from Egypt, from the Plague. So I guess, the main thing that I could

connect is that. (…) these Israelites had a lot of confidence in their leader Moses. Because I think it is so easy to sort of criticise your judge, criticise anything they are doing. And the Israelites, even though they didn't understand [the rules], they were ready to follow him, risk their lives and follow him there. And so… one practical thing is that there is no sense to criticise our leaders all the time, because they are probably closer to God than we are, and they probably most of the time, know best. So that obviously this applies for archbishop X, who is someone I personally disagree, strongly disagree with some of the views that he said or expressed. But at the end of the day, he is our judge, if not representative of the whole country, he is our judge, (…) even if he has dodgy opinions here and there. (Adam)

For Adam, if the Israelites were able to trust Moses' authority beyond what seems reasonable, a *fortiori* he should be able to trust the "dodgy opinion" of the archbishop. His discourse reveals his contradictory views. The proposition "it is easy to criticize," an impersonal form that might reveal an internalized rule, contradicts the opinion expressed in the first person: "I strongly disagree with." The symbolic resource itself seems to enable the young man to represent tensions between internalized rules and personal opinions: in the text, the Hebrews were dealing with a contradiction between the rule (following Moses) and their own opinion (to resist), and they overcame it. The biblical story offers a space to think this tension, legitimize it (it is OK to be stiff-necked) and bring it to a resolution (the Hebrews finally followed their leader). The resource can be seen as functioning on an analogy which is both structural (what the archbishop is to rebel Christians, is equivalent to what Moses is to rebel Hebrews) and emotional (both the young man and the Hebrews are facing uncertainty; both place a deep hope in the divine; and both fight against their doubts, so as to be able to maintain their trust in a leader who is close to the divine). As a result of that use, Adam finds an imaginary space to legitimize his doubts towards the archbishop, and reflect on the lack of clarity of his discourse. Additionally, this use reassesses positions: Adam, who questioned his subordination to his religious leader, finally reassesses his obedience to the archbishop. This interestingly shows that symbolic resources are part of the constant negotiation of consensual meaning and positions.

The performative and semiotic functions of uses of symbolic resources within spheres of experiences are thus deeply interdependent. On one side, young people can find a position, a voice and a form of discourse in using symbolic resources such as hip-hop songs or political propaganda; these discourses, that provoke others' reactions, can reinforce their own position (Hundeide, 2004; Lightfoot, 1997a). Julia (chapter 5) reports singing political songs in public spaces, being sure to be heard; the content of these songs is shared; the associations these trigger in listeners will necessarily bring them and Julia to be mutually repositioned in their current spheres of experience. On the other side, symbolic resources can at the same time promote some moves and repositioning, and confer meaning to that displacement or to the new sphere of experience hence generated. Tourists develop the goal to visit Ladakh using movies, *National Geographic* photographs and *Lonely Planet* guides (Gillespie, 2004). Young people read novels about the places or the countries that they are going to visit. Once within that new sphere of experience, mobilizing these same symbolic resources enables them to confer meaning to the unknown: tourists in Ladakh organize their experience by distinguishing *authentic* inhabitants from others. A young man's experience of Russia was organized and canalized through his novel reading:

> I had a friend who was reading [*War and Peace*] at the same time. So we went to see to the Tolstoy's house, and we went to see, there are a few streets where the families lived, and there is I think there is the Battle of Borodino where the battles were... we went to see the sort of military sort of stuff, so let's see that, it, I think people are quite keen on that, there is a Web page we looked at, with all the places of *War and Peace* that you can trace around Moscow and XXX that was quite interesting. (Wolf)

Hence, as other forms of social knowledge—such as social representations (Duveen, 1997, 2000; Moscovici, 1973)—uses of symbolic resources allow the unfamiliar to be turned into something familiar, the meaningless into the meaningful, the disorganized into events that flow towards a consistent ending; they enable actions and thinking, and promote social and personal identities. However, unlike the majority of the studies of other forms of social knowledge, the study of uses of symbolic resources emphasize a person's particular use of a cultural element, engaged in a particular conduct, with a particular intent (Zittoun, et al., 2003). At the minimum, the intentional use can aim at overcoming the feelings linked to the rupture, but it can also be broader, such as when it becomes the project of achieving a new goal. Uses of symbolic resources can thus enable the restoration of a person's sense of continuity, after a rupture caused by changes in her spheres of experiences. Such uses of symbolic resources enable change in a person's ability to apprehend a given sphere of experience, or the way through which that sphere appears to her.

Uses About Interpersonal Relationships

Studies of interactions in children at home or at school have largely explored interpersonal communications taking place around symbolic actions, or symbolically mediated activities (Grossen, Liengme Bessire, & Perret-Clermont, 1997; Perret-Clermont & Carugati, 2001; Valsiner,

2000; Vygotsky, 1933; Werstch, 1999). In effect, in learning and teaching situations, the interpersonal relationships create the symbolic object of knowledge, which in turn justifies and modifies the relationship. In some situations, the interpersonal relation becomes salient, and in others, the relations to the object are more relevant (of course, various researchers also emphasize one or the other).

Similarly, uses of symbolic resources within relationship can be examined with an emphasis on the person, or on the object. Again, uses can be largely performative—they enable the creation of a relationship—or semiotic, by enabling interpersonal understanding—which may participate in the maintenance of the relationship.

Cultural elements can be used to create relationships in various ways. They can be used to meet other people, and thus, to expand one's social world. A person can talk about her repertoire of symbolic resources to someone else (Zittoun & Cesari, 1998), or confront her use of a symbolic resource with another person's use. Hence, Wolf, the young man who travelled to Russia after having read Tolstoy, met Russians who had read the same books. This first facilitated the possibility of creating a dialogue. But then, it appeared that their perspective had brought them to confer different meanings on these books. Discussing the aboutness of these novels in their lives and sociohistorical contexts, the young man and the Russians could explicate their mutual differences. Similarly, while doing charity work in South America, Adam had to discuss his interpretation of the Bible with local people. The Bible first enabled the dialogue to take place, and then highlighted resemblances and divergences. In such cases, the symbolic resource mediates relationships at two levels: it facilitates the creation of the relationship, and through the expression of the different meanings that it acquires within different personal cultures, it enables individuals to explicate their positions and to access the standpoint of the other, that is, to understand their mutual spheres of experience. In turn, it is rather likely that this modifies the relationship of a person to that cultural element and its further value as a resource; the relationship is finally reconstructing the object.

Cultural elements can be used to *maintain or transform* interpersonal relationships. A book or CD can be used as a gift to mark or maintain a relationship. The gift is also offered because the giver thinks that the content might speak to, or be suitable for the receiver. The gift becomes an indirect way of communicating with the other, about the giver, the receiver, the relationship, or their mutual positions. This is stronger when the two persons can discuss their mutual expectations and reactions. Relationships can develop through sharing, discussing, enjoying, and expanding on a given type of resource. A young man hence spent a gap year reading literature classics and discussing his reading with his best friend. A woman read the books recommended by her boyfriend:

> But with my friend I would talk about that (...) like, you know, whether I agreed, you know, that person should have done that, you know, usually if someone gives me a book I try to report that of them if I liked it, what I thought about that. (Ilona)

Some relationships are constructed around the sharing and the discussion of books or movies, as mutual ways to explore emotions or memories; such relationships obviously modify each person's relationship to herself, the other and the cultural elements. Interpersonal relationships, as well as these within groups of friends, can develop thanks to a passion for a given cultural element, sharing both the fact of having chosen it, the imaginary experiences it creates, and their link to the socially shared reality:

> A lot of these movies, a lot of my friends here have also seen... I don't know, may be it is people I have associated with... . But it seems that a lot of them have seen these movies and can talk about them. *Q So you meet people and you talk about movies?* Yes, yes. May be you can say, "so you remember when in *Harry meets Sally* they did that," or stuff like that, or "this reminds of when they did this"... *Q Yes.... It's reminds me... Could this start in an everyday situation?* Yes, yes! - You know, "Oh, I've done"... you are doing something -" Oh, this really reminds me of this movie; Have you seen that?" "Oh yes, I've seen that." "Isn't it so funny when this or that." And you start talking... . Yes, it could be completely everyday situations... *Q This happens often?* Yes. I guess I watch a lot of movies. (Ilona)

Some pairs or groups of people deliberately engage in shared readings of cultural experiences to deepen their mutual knowledge and to strengthen their relationships. Social sharing of cultural experiences can also change relationships and groups through the constitution of a shared memory of past common experiences, which might become part of a joined identity and project (see Heath, 1996 on groups' symbolic memory).

Hence, interpersonal uses of symbolic resources participate in the transformation of the ongoing architecture of intersubjectivity (Gillespie, 2004): people multiply positions toward the cultural experience and others while sharing or discussing their possible meaning. Through such exchanges, each person is likely to be brought to consider the other's perspective, and at times, to modify her previous understanding of the cultural element, either through the exchange or by herself (Perret-Clermont, et al., 2004; Tisseron, 2000). This may in turn modify the social relationship, and the relation of the person to the world. Eventually,

110 *Transitions: Development through Symbolic Resources*

through such dynamics, the person may internalize these positions and thus transform the architecture of her self.

Intrapsychic Uses

Symbolic resources can be deliberately used to transform one's relationship to oneself. Various modalities of intrapsychic uses of symbolic resources can be identified. These correspond to various emotional needs and the modulation of a person's thinking abilities and are usually not deliberate choices. They are part of the tension between the need to maintain a sense of continuity while dealing with change in the work of transition. Some intrapsychic uses acquire rather a soothing function, and others an explorative or playful function. Some persons use symbolic resources to reflect on their own experiences, while others seem rather to use them to avoid thinking about their experience.

Hence, *soothing* uses can maintain a sense of continuity and security beyond a rupture. Psychologically, they offer a form of safe and containing space, a resting zone out of the reality of the struggle for newness (Winnicott, 1971/2001). Hence, many first year university students bring their preferred, known-by-heart books to their new residence. When they feel a little lost or depressed, they read their favorite section of a poem or of a novel, which will reassure them and make them feel better:

> I brought the [text] books because I thought it would be useful to the course. And the poetry, because I think it just—and I don't know, because I think it connects me more with me, than novels do. There is something in poetry... a poem can suggest in a short space. (Robert)

Multiple readings of or listenings to a cultural element appear to be used for their soothing effect, or their power to create comforting feelings attached to well known absent places and friends (Habermas, 1996, 1999; Haskell, Valsiner, & McHale, 2003; Tisseron, 1999). They can also be seen as forms of repetition of patterns of experiences or emotion that reaffirm one's sense of self, at a time when it is threatened by the rupture.

Uses of symbolic resources can also be turned to the unknown; they are used to create new emotions and thoughts, and thus become part of self-explorations that will *reveal* new aspects of oneself (Alvarez, 1992).

> It seems to me very sane to engage... So I engage., and I engage completely while I am sitting there, and I'm - and because I am very interested in - I don't know when it started, but I have been interested with cultural artefacts like films (...) - I tried very hard to immerse myself, some real movie, or some home videos like a real blockbuster, and I tried really strong that it was

me... (...) Just to feel the sensations... Now that I am a bit older (...) I will just see what it does to me. (Lily)

Some uses of resources can thus primarily aim at exploring one's interiority: the person, like Lily, can be willing to be taken by the movement of empathy to travel within imaginary zones, created and guided by the cultural experience. In effect, empathy is a process of relocating within interiority, that goes along with the internalization of new voices (see chapter 2).

A third type of use of symbolic resources appears primarily for the purpose of *escaping* a present situation, for example reading novels when one is bored at work or during a bus journey (as Charles did).

Whether such repetitive, and soothing uses can later turn into uses that enable exploration of alternative lives, depends on whether they enable to reinforce sufficiently the person's sense of self or her semiotic abilities, in such a way that she becomes ready to apprehend newness. Escapist uses can be turned into resources as well, if a person reflects on her experiences.

The Historicity of Semiotic Dynamics

In this section we have so far seen what symbolic resources could be about: about the social shared reality in various spheres of experience, about other persons, about oneself. Seen through the semiotic prism, each of these relationships is necessary attached to another. Uses about positions within shared spheres of experience are mostly dependent on people who legitimize such uses and positions. In Adam's example, we could thus trace a prism linking Adam (*person*), the Bible as *symbolic object*, the issue of dodgy opinions as *meaning for person* and the archbishop as *other*. Uses about others also create meanings oriented toward the socially shared reality (Ilona and her friend link everyday situations and films they share). Hence, if this section has separated various directions of uses of symbolic resources for analysis's sake, we now need to rearticulate these aspects in their mutual dependency.

Once we do so, we also bring back the historicity of semiotic dynamics represented in semiotic prisms. Uses of symbolic resources keep traces of their conditions of internalization; when this trace is linked to a personal relationship we have called it the *shadow of the other* in conduct (Zittoun, et al., 2003). Also, at a given moment of use, one side of the prism might stay in the background (e.g., a memory of a previous use); yet this aspect might add a special coloration to a situation (Bakhtin, 1979/1986). As a consequence of this historicity and foregrounding dynamics, personal uses of symbolic resources in the present might carry traces of their inscriptions in past situations.

An example will show the stability and the evolution of these semiotic dynamics. Mary left home to study in a remote town; because her family was in crisis, she quickly quit her studies and came back to her hometown; she then had to earn a salary. It seems that these two rapid ruptures did not give her enough time to work through the transitions; Mary had to engage in new conduct, without considering the meaning of these changes. In effect, she started to work as a shop assistant; being talented, and before realizing what was happening, she had been appointed as shop manager. Having to endorse increasing responsibilities, she soon found herself exhausted, without understanding how she got there or how to modify the situation—that is, she was alienated from herself because of her social repositioning. However, one day, she met by chance her former drawing teacher, who, remembering Mary's color skills, encouraged her to try to enroll in evening art classes. This meeting with a former teacher was enough to enable Mary to move out of her situation. She quit her job and found less demanding part-time work, started an evening program in arts, and thus engaged in a process of learning and personal change.

How can such a short intervention become so meaningful? I suggest that it enabled Mary to use *arts* as an important symbolic resource, because art experience had a long story for her, which can be analyzed as an evolution and slow migration of semiotic prisms. We might say that thanks to that woman recalling her talent (*other*), Mary (*person*) rediscovered pieces of art (*symbolic object*) that offered resources that enabled her to define a project for her future conduct (*meaning for person*). The genealogy of this *art-prism* appears in Mary's description of her childhood:

> I was looking at illustrations in books. *Q Like?* There was one particular book when I was very little, that I still have got now - *Cinderella* was my favourite tale, like probably most of the girls, and I found it really, really beautiful - it was only a 50 pence paperback - and I was... for years I was obsessed with the designs, because they were so intricate in these pictures; I was... I used to draw seventeenth century dresses for years and years! I tried so hard. [I was about 8] And Mum... also I remember Mum taking us to see the Degas exhibition at the [museum]; and they had the *ballet dancers*. And - I loved ballet anyway; my granny would love ballet and I'd have picked on her anyway. And I have been obsessed with that! You know... I was painting these dancers - ballet dancers! Tutus! This is just where... I am terrible at drawing buildings. But I can do people fine.

For Mary, painting and arts appear as anchored in significant interpersonal relationships. From this quote, we can identify a prism such as *Cinderella-Mum-Mary-her dreams about tutus*, becoming a prism *Degas-Mum-*

Mary-her-dreams about tutus, itself reinforced by a prism *ballet-granny-Mary-her dreams about tutus*. Important relationships seem to have allowed Mary to invest in books and painting; these were resources for the relationships with significant elder women (mother and grandmother). Mary developed a passion for tutus and dancing bodies, and committed herself in painting tutus—first under the mother's eyes, then with friends, and alone. Eventually, painting bodies and tutus allowed her to develop serious painting skills, which were acknowledged by another significant person (teacher), in a prism now transformed into *colors-teacher-Mary-her possible future*. Her teacher's idea that she should start studying appears thus loaded with all the additional meanings due to that genealogy. From this point on, Mary also defines herself as becoming artist, going to galleries and seeing artwork form her new position. One could say, it is in the shadow of these women and of *Cinderella* that Mary now appreciates arts and sees herself as able to create.

After having seen the changing nature of semiotic dynamics at the heart of uses of symbolic resources, we will now concentrate on the two aspects of the work of youth transition highlighted in the first chapter: the development of a time perspective, and the construction of a system of orientation.

TIME ORIENTATION

Psychological ruptures as defined in the first chapter can impose a suspension of a person's sense of continuity. Consequently, the psychological work of transition requires microgenetic processes that allow its restoration, while letting new forms of regularity emerge. We have also seen that one of the qualitative changes expected in youth is the construction of a future oriented time-perspective.

Signs in general can be seen as distancing and linking devices (chapter 2) that can have three main time-orientations. As Valsiner (2000, p. 13) suggests, they can *re-present* "facets of already lived-through experience," *co-present* something currently being lived, and *pre-present* possible future experiences. Cultural elements used as symbolic resources are complex organizations of signs; as such, they can be expected to be oriented toward the same three directions.

In this section, these three directions of uses are first examined separately, and then brought together. It will be important to examine the interplay of these time orientations: as we have seen in chapter 1 and 2, if cultural elements simply offer resources for *change*, they should support processes that allow the person to keep a sense of continuity through change, that is, they have primarily representing and copresenting functions. If cultural elements are also resources for *development*, they must be used as resources enabling the construction of a future orientation. It must thus be shown that symbolic resource can have retrospective, as well as prospective uses.

Retrospective Uses

We have seen above that reading a known passage of a text can have a self-maintaining or soothing function, as can have bedtime stories or games in childhood (Haskell, Valsiner, & McHale, 2003). Let us come back to uses oriented toward the past, as with this young woman who brought back Spanish music from her last trip:

> For example, when I came back from Madrid I was quite in a Latino mood, [I would go to Spanish evenings]. I think when you come back from somewhere, when I come back I try to RETAIN something, when I tend to integrate quite quickly to the English culture. [Q *did you bring only music, or other things as well?*] Yes, postcards, pictures newspapers... something to hold on. Q *So if you listen... would you go back in memory?* Yes, I think there is a strong connection when you hear, or listen to something, a cassette or so, there is the whole..(...) For example, a particular song might be, it was when I was in the bar with such and such. Q *If you listen to Spanish, Turkish music [as you said] is it for the music or for the memory?* A bit of both... Depends of my mood... if I feel particularly bored of being in England... I can put a music on to REMIND me the place... but it depends on my mood. (Anne)

Here, cultural elements such as postcards, newspapers, or songs are sometimes used as resources that point to, or designate past events. More exactly, the resource is experienced for its embodied, emotional qualities; these are similar to what had been experienced in the past, in another sphere of experience. When listening again and again to a song, Anne is reactualizing her past. In the quote, verbs are creating a particular semantic field: resources are used *to retain, to hold on, to remind*. The resource appears to be used in a *retrospective orientation*, to maintain some past experience, that is, a sense of personal continuity; it also seems to turn the hostile present into something known and comfortable, if not comforting.

In this example, the retrospective use is independent from the semiotic properties and contents of the cultural element itself. Thus a smell or a taste, that do not contain shared meanings, can have the same function as music that is used as a soothing symbolic resource—an embodied point of anchorage to the past. Anne thus also uses spices and dishes for the same retrospective purposes. The difference between positioning effects and retrospective uses of symbolic resources, is that the former are still based on socially acknowledged meanings, while the latter are very idiosyncratic.

However, retrospective uses are not necessarily only simple, nonsemiotic ones. Thus, Elaine likes rereading novels after years, to confront her present reading with the one she once had, and through that confrontation, to understand how much she has changed. Here, the semiotic resources is used in a retrospective orientation, yet is deployed in all its semiotic complexity.

Finally, one might wonder whether retrospective uses need to be oriented toward the self. In fact, many people engage in cultural experiences to reconnect with the past of their family, or their group, or the past of a whole society; hence, visiting churches, listening to ancient music, or participating in historical reconstructions (Zagórska & Tarnowski, 2004). Yet in the case of uses of symbolic resources during youth transition, past-oriented uses of symbolic resources are mostly about oneself—which would tend to indicate that these are indeed, foremost, used to maintain as sense of continuity beyond the rupture.

Microgenetic Uses

In situations where a person meets a new and changing present, uses of symbolic resources might imply constant bridging of the immediate past and the immediate future. For example, the rather picturesque town in which this study has been done has been widely represented in movies, novels, and paintings. As expected, many students said that they recalled movies and novels when visiting it for the first time, as this woman:

> When I came with my friend [to find a place to live], we went for a walk in town (...) and we kept thinking, and we kept walking, and looking at the swans, in the river, and we kept thinking about things we had read, and these things, which are so stupid to read, but are so true, and things in painting, and literature (...) and we thought about everything. (...) Like people having picnic under tree? We just kept naming thing. (Lily)

Here, a person in a given situation mobilizes resources to confer meanings on what has just been seen (the trees, strange persons walking around), or to anticipate the next moment to come (if there is such a river, some romantic boat will be visible). Thus, uses of symbolic resources, which involve oscillation between past memories of cultural experiences and the future to come (Cole, 1996), enable a *microgenetic binding of the changing present*, which mediates self-continuity through unpredictable events (Valsiner, 2003). Similarly, when Julia's uses her favorite songs to support her own continuity through a period of mourning, she is using resources to support an enduring present (chapter 5).

Prospective Uses

Beyond such microgenetic processes, symbolic resources can also support the exploration of possibilities, and the emergence of newness in more distant futures.

> When I thought I was going to France, and I didn't actually go, but when I was picking up the books I wanted to take with me - I realised afterwards I didn't do it on purpose, but they were all French, (laughs) and some of them were, you know, academic, some were just novels. For some reason, unconsciously I just choose books like that. And I think, you know, before coming here I've picked up more British things (laughs). For whatever reason, yes? I mean if I read more Virginia Woolf, xx than somebody else - that's partly, you know, that's partly to give me a sense of where I am? You know, if I would go to [Italy] I would probably read more [Italian] fiction - or [Mediterranean] fiction. (Lily)

The cultural experience of reading a book—say, a Virginia Woolf novel —supposes the construction of an imaginary sphere of experience (a colorful Britain), that enables imaginary exploration of England and the future, *as-if* it might occur (Josephs, 1997, 1998). Like play for children, the use of symbolic resources opens an imaginary zone: it enables the creation and trying out of possibilities, engaging real emotions, without the risks involved in a real experience. It thus participates in the proximal zone of development in which the future will *in effect* take place (chapter 2). Such uses of symbolic resources can be called *prospective*: they enable populating a blurred world to come with possible representations, envisaging likely-to-be experiences, anticipating related emotions and guiding possible conduct. As such, uses of symbolic resources might be important for youth transitions.

Binding Times in Transitions

These dynamics might seem to occur on a different time scale. On one side, retrospective uses, which reinforce what is already known, seem to support the maintenance of a personal sense of continuity and to provide soothing techniques, while prospective uses, turned toward the unknown, support future orientation and the definition of possible new conduct. On the other side, microgenetic uses of symbolic resources seem to participate in the constant work of maintenance and change of a person. Yet these microgenetic dynamics are not independent from these longer prospective and retrospective dynamics; these are in fact deeply connected.

Looking closer at the three examples just mentioned—music to retain the past, a novel to create the future, and multiple images to accompany the constant microcreation of the present—it is easy to show that connection. These three types of use always occur in the present of the person. This present might be experienced as more or less satisfactory, and the person might have intentions of modifying it. Hence, in the case of the retrospective, mnemonic uses of music, Anne was slightly depressed; she used the resource to call on happy memories. For this she had to draw on her memories of the cultural experience and its transformative effects: she knows that it had *worked* to calm her and modify her mood. She thus appears to use the resource with the intention of recreating a past mood in the present, in order to modify it—that is, with the intention of creating a known mood (be more cheerful) *in the next future*. In the example of the prospective use of novels, Lily creates an imaginary experience that might help her to comprehend realities to come. However, as seen in chapter 2, the experience of reading is itself enabled by the mobilization of *past memories* (imagination is reconfiguration: one cannot imagine an English village described in a novel without having had some experiences of houses, villages, trees, colors, smells, etc.). Hence, these prospective and retrospective uses are *both together* prospective and retrospective; they appear to require oscillation between past and future, and thus are based on the very same dynamic as microgenetic creations (the town-visit example).

An important difference between retrospective and prospective uses subsists: in the music case, the future is *expected*—the uncertainty of the next moment is reduced by a hope to repeat a past experience; in the novel example, *uncertainty* of the future is emphasized and populated with new possibilities. From a developmental perspective, in the long run, we might think that the first type of use, closer to repetition (see chapter 2), does provide support for one's sense of continuity, but opens fewer possibilities for change; the second, while not necessarily providing this continuity, creates new pathways—and is potentially more generative. Retrospective and prospective uses can thus be seen as variations of different balances between assimilation-accommodation (Piaget, 1964/1967): in retrospective uses, assimilation of the unknown into a preexisting structure of understanding is stronger; in prospective uses, accommodation of the structure of understanding to the new given is dominant.

Thus, for these elementary processes, both are necessary, and thus can be seen as mutually enabling. This observation might in fact reveal deeper structures of change. Discussing the acquisition of language, as the progressive construction of the ability to use signs as tools, Vygotsky indicates the following progression: language might first enable the child to reflect on his action post hoc; language then accompanies and reflects on current tasks; finally, it can become involved in future planning (Vygotsky & Luria, 1994, p. 120). Similarly, Winnicott (1968a, 1971/2001) observes that uses of objects need first to ensure some present emotional security, before being used to play with possible futures.

If there is such a genetic sequence, it might thus be that, in adults as in children, it might at times be more important to reinforce one's sense of continuity than to create change. Retrospective uses can thus be seen as occasions to reconsider memories and emotions, or to re-elaborate, reconfigure them, in a way that makes them less strange, painful, or more understandable—and forgettable. Going towards the future indeed requires *forgetting* (and not forgetting stops one's development, Luria, 1969). Forgetting is not cleaving or erasing the past; it is to relink its images and emotions in new ways (Bion, 1977; Kaës, 1996; Matte-Blanco, 1975) (chapter 2). Uses oriented toward the past might thus be part of the movement of working towards the future. Similarly, uses turned toward the past always imply the mobilization and reconfiguration of past memories and emotions, which might prepare the ground for the future. Present, past, and future are always part of the use of symbolic resources.

Finally, because of the historicity of semiotic dynamics (section 1), uses of symbolic resources always imply the interplay of multiple temporalities. For example, one might imagine that Jean's experience of reading a French historical saga supposes the encounter of: first, the historical temporality of the referent in an imaginary world (France's eighteenth century); second, the flow of her present experience (reading in her room with broken heating and noisy neighbors); and third, personal memories mobilized to make the experience alive (images of countryside and castles, impressions of velvet, emotions of betrayal, genre-literacy enabling the anticipation of the return of the good character). A cultural experience necessarily involves the interplay between these three experienced temporalities. It can be assumed that each of these temporalities is slightly reworked by the others (not radically: there are strong psychic regulations that allow us to know that what affects the hero of the French saga in an imaginary past does not affect one's own memory). Other temporalities can be added: the cultural element has its own historicity (for example, that manuscript brought its author to be decapitated); smaller semiotic units can have a history of past social uses (certain words become outdated), or can have a story of its personal uses (the word *azure* remembers Jean of how Jules used to say it). Through such vertical and horizontal linking the use of a symbolic resource involves much more than the meaning-content of the cultural element, but an infinity of undertones, overtones, and echoes. These multiple layers of memories, inscribed in different temporalities, might modify each other, and thus uses of symbolic resources are likely to modify semiotic configuration and the architecture of self.

LEVELS OF SEMIOTIC MEDIATION

In chapter 2, we have seen that semiotic mediation can occur at various levels of generality, various distances from the here and now of the experience. In the interests of clarity, four levels have been distinguished: the level of immediate embodied perception (L1), that of local conduct (L2), of stable categories or self-properties, or rules (L3), and that of commitments and long-standing beliefs (L4). It has been suggested that, as organized forms of semiotic units, symbolic resources might produce psychological change at any of these levels of generality. I will very shortly illustrate uses of symbolic resources at each of these levels; I will then examine the interdependence of these mediations at various levels. In effect, what is more interesting from a developmental perspective is the fact that because of their internal organization, symbolic resources can *transform the level of semiotic mediation* at which an experience is apprehended. I will propose that one of the most important contributions of symbolic resources in transition lays in these transforming properties. These transforming effects can go in two directions: uses of symbolic resources can help to redefine a practical problem in terms of general commitments; they can also help to reconnect issues thought about in abstract terms with practical and located conduct.

Uses of Symbolic Resources at Various Level of Mediation

Uses of symbolic resources can mediate conduct at various levels of generality within semiotic hierarchies. They offer semiotic mediations for first level processes (the given of the experience here-and-now). A symbolic resource can directly re-present simple bodily states or emotions—for example, Julia can discover her grief when listening to music whose melody and harmonics contain and reflect her emotional state (L1). Second level mediation (labeling a situation) can be done through symbolic resources. For example, Adam, while walking in the street, meets a beggar; he immediately visualizes the biblical image of Jesus giving money to poor people. The image, a symbolic resource, organizes the situation into one of *charity*, and enables the student's next action—to give money (L2). At a third level (categories of the world or of the self), symbolic resources can also be used to mediate thinking and action: Ilona explains that she uses movies to learn about types of persons that she would never meet otherwise; she sees this as a preparation for possible real encounters with such people (L3). Finally, symbolic resources can operate at the fourth level of mediations (standing beliefs). Randy explains that he acquired his romanticism through movies; this general attitude towards life supports his commitments in everyday conduct (L4).

Using a Resource to Elevate the Level of Elaboration

The logic of a cultural experience can enable a person to create new links and distancing processes, progressively bringing an uncertain present to be elaborated in terms of higher-level mediations, which can then bring her to envisage new possible actions.

For example, Lily arrived in her university town after a difficult decision process; she had been facing various possibilities of places to live and courses to take, and was still not sure about her decision. At some point, I asked her if any movies had recently been important for her:

> Something is a movie I watched (...) I think it was called the *After Life*—it is a Japanese movie (...) they end up... it is like an immigration office, and they have to pick up a memory... and it is all about the selection process. So you have young people, you have old people, and all kinds of people. And it is all about this process, you know, about going, choosing, and being able or not able to choose, and these people who are unable to choose, xx so they are stuck there, for centuries. I always think of that - I think about that often for a reason or another. I've thought about it the other day, just a couple of days ago - but I can't remember xxx. It is interesting, because when I watched that movie, I didn't think automatically what would I choose. But the people I was watching the movie with, just asked me xxxx - what would I choose, I really don't know - it would be sort of logical, but I didn't ask myself xxx (...) *Q You choose that example because...* I think about it because - when death comes in memory... xx I think about it when I think about sorts of life... about relative happiness, and the difference between being content, and not, or having lots of energy, or not much energy. I mean all these things I have been thinking [about] for a long time, it is a schedule for life. So every time these things come out, and because I am thinking about the future quite a lot right now, and about people, whether they are staying in my life or not staying in my life. xxx Because how people choose their memories, has a lot to do with how people choose their lives.

In order to analyze this quote I will expand on its content, before highlighting the semiotic dynamics at stake. The cultural experience of watching the film *After Life* has been shared with friends; it had a strong effect on

Lily—she was participating emotionally, not just reflecting on it. The story of *After Life*, by Hirokazu Koreeda (1998), is located in a strange school that seems out of time; people are there in brown uniforms. We see people sitting in front of a desk behind which is a clerk, trying to answer to a difficult question; we very slowly understand that these people are dead, and are being asked to choose their best memories—the one that will be recreated for them and in which they will stay for all eternity. The strangeness of the situation appears only through the content of the dialogue and the difficulty people have in choosing—nothing apart from the title explains the surrealistic situation. After seeing the movie, still unable to take distance towards her emotional participation, it is through her friend's question that Lily is pushed to reflect on her experience. Then only can Lily think about what she had memorized, elaborate her experience through the shared discussion, and use it as a way to think about her own real-life situation. Lately, Lily said, she came to think often about the movie, especially when wondering about her future; the film hence appears to have become a symbolic resource to think about decisions she has to take.

How might this have worked? At a first level, we can imagine that the colors, décor, childhood, and dream-like qualities of the film, might have found some resonance in her memories (L1), awakening a complex and very vivid network of feelings and impressions. Such personal resonances make this movie a good candidate for further uses, for it stays in memory. At a second level, the embarrassment, confusion, and uncertainties of the characters who have to choose a unique memory might have accurately captured and reflected her own apprehension about the decisions she had to take (L2). After seeing the movie, the question asked by another person enables distancing from that here-and-now experience and reflecting on her experience. Thanks to that other perspective, she is brought to transform the cultural experience into something that might be used to think *about* her own life, that is, into a symbolic resource. Lily thus realized that the film framed small decisions (choose a memory) in terms of important and general scope (eternity). Lily thus retains the very general principle at L4: *choosing one's memories is choosing one's life* (note that this externalization is already a transformation of what has been internalized: the movie shows that choosing one's memories is choosing one's death). It is then with this L4 principle in mind that Lily seems to come back to her problems of decision, this time operating through defined sets of conduct at L3—what is being content, what is being happy or tired. From there, she seems able to address local decisions—to move or not, whether to keep someone in one's life (L2).

Thus, through the use of the movie as a resource, Lily comes to see her reflection on studies choices not only as here-and-now, isolated decisions (L2), but as linked to general worldviews (L4), which help define which

Lily and « After Life »

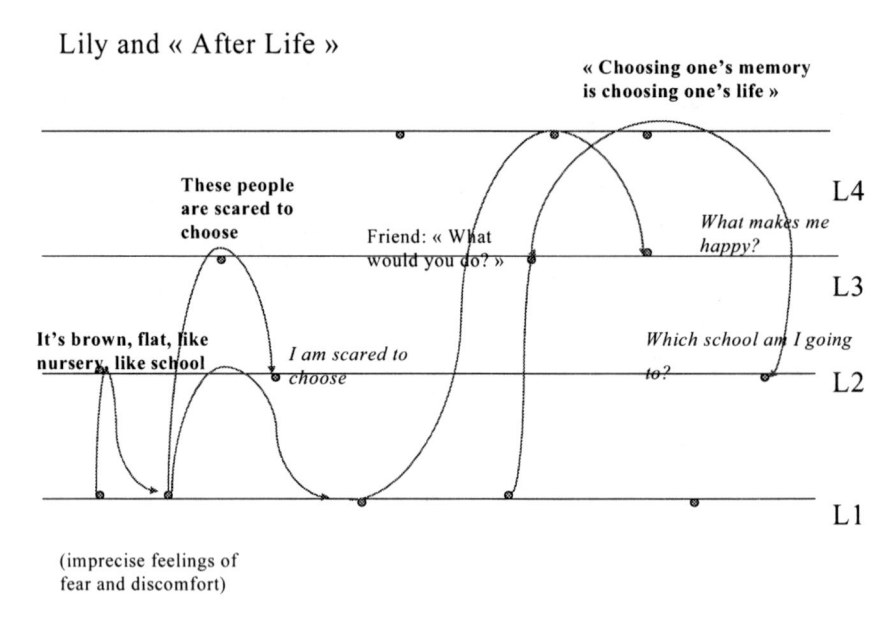

Figure 4.1. Elevation of the level of mediation.

class of conduct to consider when taking a decision (L3). Through this higher-level mediation, the temporality of issues changes as well: for Lily the decision is no longer only an immediate problem, it is now to be seen as part of a longer time-scale-narrative—how to be sure that when she looks back at her actions in the future she will be happy with what she will have done?

In that reading, the use of the symbolic resource is both retrospective and prospective, and implies various fields of experience. It seems to enable the work of transition by supporting the elaboration of confused impressions into possible options, by allowing the rereading of past experiences in terms of possible futures, and by enabling the definition of criteria to guide choices.

Using a Symbolic Resource to Lower the Level of Mediation

In the last example, the use of an available symbolic resource enabled a person to work through a rupture by raising the level of mediation of a problem, from a local choice to a higher-level principle. However, the opposite difficulty can occur: a person might use symbolic resources to think about situations in general and abstract terms, without knowing how to guide local conduct. In the following example, a symbolic resource is used so as to create links between higher-level commitments and particular actions.

Lev is one of the interviewees who came from a religious background (see also chapter 5). He spent a year in yeshiva, a rabbinic, very religious college, where all aspects of everyday life are highly regulated, and he experienced returning to a secular life as a rupture. In the religious environment, all quotidian conduct (eating, having religious friends, sleeping, studying religious texts, L2) is regulated by a religious rule (what to eat when, and under what conditions, L3); these rules depend on a general set of religious beliefs and commitments (e.g., following the rules about eating are the way to actualize one's respect for the divine, L4). Among these, daily study of religious texts is a very important way to actualize one's relationship to God, to improve both oneself and one's relationship to the world as divine creation. When Lev came back to a secular life, everyday situations in which he had to take decisions (what to eat, when, with whom) had to be radically redefined (new food, noisy secular people to interact with, etc.), and religious rules—keeping kosher, studying religious texts—seemed difficult to apply. The rupture causes a problem that can be seen as a transfer of knowledge into a new sphere of experience. High-level rules have to remain as they were; yet the specific forms of conduct on which these might apply have to be redefined on the basis of the opportunities given by a new sphere of experience. Additionally, Lev comes from a yeshiva in which teachers judged negatively his attempt to study in a secular university: if internalized, such significant *others'* perspectives would de-legitimize attempts to apply religious rules on a secular sphere of experience. It is what seems to happen: Lev is very critical towards student life and habits and secular studies. He complains that students seem to approach their class-readings without any overarching commitment—that is, they do not expect to improve themselves through these readings, or to aim at improving their understanding of the world. He criticizes students for their very dissolute lives (going out, drinking) which are incompatible with his own commitments. He thus radically avoids interactions with non-Jews or public places.

The rupture he feels can be articulated as *how to reconcile a religious life with the requirements of secular studies*? In other words, how to apply longstanding beliefs (L4) and religious rules (L3) in a sphere of experience that incites conduct radically different to the sphere on the basis of which these rules have been developed? Among resources that helped him, Lev mentions his use of a symbolic resource: a metaphor found in a book by Berne on transactional analysis (not strictly an imaginary cultural experience, though):

> The author says, in terms of structuring time, we all should learn to function like the heart - because the heart, the way it works, is one third of the time physically pumping, and two third of the time resting; so the way you should may be structure a day, 8 hours you're doing your work, 8 hours your due - for yourself, whatever it is, and 8 hours a day sleeping. So:: you know, that has been a quite useful model, that I try to integrate.

It thus seems that Lev used that metaphor as a symbolic resource to organize his time, or to split his everyday life into various spheres of experiences. In one third of his life, his previous system of orientation can apply, and he can dedicate his time to Jewish study and practices; in a second third, he can tolerate engaging in secular activities; the last third is dedicated to rest. Turned into a symbolic resource, the heart metaphor enables him to legitimate his need to maintain his previous system of orientation, while making the necessary compromises to adjust to the new situation. The work of transition is thus actualized through a reorganization of his sphere of experience within a new set of constraints. It might thus be said that the resource enables him to create a new area of concrete validity for his higher-level rules. The symbolic resource canalizes ways of applying previous abstract knowledge (L4) to new situations, by enabling him to recognize patterns for possible conduct (L3) within the given (L2). In that sense, using symbolic resources becomes a way to lower the level of mediation of these rules.

In this chapter, we have analyzed and reassembled a tri-dimensional model to apprehend the use of symbolic resources in transitions. Periods of transition confront a person with unknown situations and possibly anxious feelings; but for the work of transition to take place, these should not be overwhelming. In our societies, young people have to elaborate projects to turn their commitments into actions. Distancing processes are required to link past memories to future-oriented ideas, regulated by more general systems of orientation, necessary for a person to choose the conduct she might engage in as a symbolically responsible person.

Thanks to their semiotic organization, symbolic resources can be used to mediate embodied experiences and emotions, or thoughts about oneself, the world, and others. These mediations might be turned toward the past, the present or the future. Symbolic resources can also enable further elaborations through the modification of the levels of generality at which the experience is symbolized. They might help distancing from situations, so as to address issues in more general terms, with a wider time-scale and more generality; they might also facilitate reconnecting existing higher-level principles to the local given, thus enabling the person to live in her new sphere of experience.

But the model we have analyzed and then reassembled is theoretical. How does it apply when applied to a singular life? We now need to examine individual cases of people who have gone through a rupture and transition processes. What resources have they used? What is the role played by symbolic resources? How did the use of symbolic resources enable processes of transition, and the attainment of new, generative regularities? What has facilitated or constrained observable uses?

NOTE

1. "The object of sublimation is not the book, it is reading."

CHAPTER 5

SYMBOLIC RESOURCES IN DEVELOPMENTAL TRANSITIONS

And in our times the 'bricoleur' is still someone who works with his hands and uses devious means compared to those of the craftsman. (...). The set of the 'bricoleur's' means (...) is to be defined only by its potential use or, putting this another way in the language of the 'bricoleur' himself, because the elements are collected or retained on the principle that "they may always come in handy." Such elements are specialised up to a certain point, sufficiently for the 'bricoleur' not to need the equipment and knowledge of all trades and professions, but not enough for each of them to have only one definite and determinate use. They each represent a set of actual and possible relations; they are 'operators' but they can be used for any operations of the same type. The elements of mythical thought similarly lie halfway between precepts and concepts (...) there is an intermediary between images and concepts, namely, signs (...). The elements which the 'bricoleur' collects and uses are 'pre-constrained' like the constitutive units of myths, the possible combinations of which are restricted by the fact that they are drawn from the language where they already possess a sense which sets a limit on the freedom of manoeuvre. (...) And the decision as to what to put in each place also depends on the possibility of putting a different element there instead, so that each choice which is made will involve a complete reorganisation of the structure, which will never be the same as the one vaguely imagined nor as some other which might have been preferred to it.

—Claude Levis-Strauss, *The Savage Mind* (1962/1966, pp. 16-19).

Levi-Strauss proposed the metaphor of "bricolage," do-it-yourself, to define the *pensée sauvage*, a "savage thinking" that he contrasted with a scientific, logico-deductive occidental mode of reasoning. Bricolage designates both the action of amassing potential material that might once become useful, and of drawing from this repertoire to address a certain demand. There is no preexisting plan to the construction thus made; the material has its own limits, and each of its steps enables and constrains the next one. Bricolage implies object-embezzlement, and with it, impertinence and playfulness. Children do bricolage when they construct a colored stuff with matchboxes and toilet rolls and call it a train. *Art Brut*, produced by persons considered as marginal and mentally disabled, with no artistic goals (rather, mystical or fantastical ones) can be seen as an art of bricolage: see for example *Picassiette's* house constructed with bits of broken plates (cf. Figure 5.1).[1] Bricolage has also been used as a metaphor by sociologists of religion to describe new forms of religiosity in modern societies, that aim at satisfying people's craving for existential meaning (Campiche, 1997).

The use of symbolic resources can be seen as a form of symbolic bricolage. A user of a symbolic resource is someone who has collected cultural elements without a clear intention, and constitutes a certain repertoire, his personal culture. As the *bricoleur*, or the handyman, the user has to destroy existing meanings and construct new ones with bits of cultural elements. Like in *pensée sauvage*, the use of symbolic resources implies the manipulation of units that are not pure perceptions, images, or concepts: they are signs, or for us, semiotic units. As in bricolage, the use of symbolic resources is both constrained and constraining.[2] In mythical societies, bricolage might be limited by taboos; here, symbolic resources are bounded by internalized social norms and by others' legitimization.

This comparison leads to the following questions. Levi-Strauss draws a clear distinction between the bricoleur, the mythical thinker, who uses signs and has no project, and the *engineer*, who uses concepts and is goal-directed. Eventually, science has to replace bricolage, based on ignorance and mythical beliefs. Such a replacement hypothesis holds only if one accepts that mythical thinking and science have the same function, that is, to confer intelligibility to the universe and answer to *how does it work?* questions. However, one might hold that mythical thinking has another major function: that of addressing the question *why does it work as it works?* Mythical thinking addresses such questions, because it aims at *meanings*—unlike science (Bruner, 1990, 1996). If it is so, an exclusive division between mythical versus scientific modes of thinking does not hold; as much as science, forms of mythical or symbolic thinking are required in modern societies.

Figure 5.1. Maison Piccassiette.

What is exactly this symbolic thinking? My assumption is that it is what operates within uses of symbolic resources; it is likely to be based on combinations of elementary horizontal and vertical forms of linking, and is not necessarily verbal or narrative (chapter 2). To understand how it functions, we need to document it at work. This is what this chapter does by examining five cases of the use of symbolic resources.

The bricolage metaphor raises a second question. For Levi-Strauss, the expert version of the mythological bricoleur is an engineer. If we admit that symbolic bricolage answers to questions not addressed by science, what is the *expertise* of a modern symbolic bricoleur? In other words, is there a form of expertise in using symbolic resources, which is not based on the scientific model of higher-level abstractions? What would it be, and how is it developed and transmitted? These questions will be addressed in the next chapter.

130 *Transitions: Development through Symbolic Resources*

In this chapter, I present five cases of young people's use of symbolic resources in transitions. As the 15 others that have been interviewed, they had to face an event or a number of events perceived as ruptures. According to our theoretical constructs, they are thus in an equivalent point in their trajectories (Valsiner & Sato, 2004). These five cases illustrate a variety of transitions, and the resources that people might mobilize. They are both constitutive of the theoretical propositions examined here, and exemplars. Each of these five cases concentrates modalities of uses of resources present in all the other cases; yet their uses are more clear, more extreme, or put the model at stake. Taken together, they highlight similarities and differences in possible uses of symbolic resources in transitions (see chapter 3).

For each of the cases, the situation from which the person comes, as well as what has been perceived as a rupture, is identified. The various forms of resources mentioned by the person, and how they combine, are examined. How symbolic resources have been used is highlighted: in the shadow of whom, what *about*, and with what implications? How does it affect time perspective and system of orientation? Did the use of symbolic resources support changes in terms of relocation and identity change, learning and meaning construction?

The first analysis is done in quite great detail, following the levels of mediation, tracing back possible semiotic prisms, observing the slow transformation of the architecture of self. To facilitate reading, the other cases are analyzed with less explicit mention of these terms; the processes at stake will be discussed and synthesized in the last section and in next chapter.

POP LYRICS FOR GRIEVING AND CHANGING SCHOOL: JULIA

Pop culture has an ambivalent status for social scientists. It is acknowledged as an important component of young people's lives, but often seen as mostly answering their need to define identities and lifestyle, affiliation and recognition. As a consequence, young people tend to be studied as members of particular groups or subgroups (Heath, 1996, 2000; Hundeide, 2004; Kamberelis & Dimitriadis, 1998; Pasquier, 1999). Adopting a developmental perspective focused on the person enables to see that immersing herself in a given subculture can be a self-piloted enterprise, satisfying a broader range of needs.

Julia, presented in this first case study, is very able to speak reflectively about her path into the cultural nebula associated with a pop band. She reflects on how their songs supported her development, soothing her in bad days, or helping to define professional projects. This example illustrates most of the modalities of the use of resources identified in chapter 4, as well as transformations through the use of resources. In this example, the work of transition is clearly developmental. The case is very exemplary, yet it is not unique; independent interviewers, who ignored my hypothesis, have gathered similar cases.[3]

A Transition Might Hide Another One

Julia is a first year student in politics; she experienced going to university as a strong rupture. From a former mining area and a low middle class family, she has neither been to boarding school, nor has she taken a gap year. She had always lived with her family, and coming to university:

> That was, that was, quite a big event. I am very close to my parents, and I am very close to both the sides of my grandparents especially on my mum's side... It was very... The longest time I had been away from my parents it was like 10 days in a school trip. The longest time I had been away from my house, from my town, was 2½ weeks. I've never been away more than that. xxx (...) And me and my parents were very quite worried about it. And also because I am 18, I am very young, xxx I am the first one to go away, I didn't know what to expect, and I can't cook, I can't clean, I am not so domesticated.

This perceived rupture corresponds to a psychosocial change, implying both a geographical move and a symbolic relocation, which could be called *young college girl enters university life*. The rupture is personally felt, but also acknowledged and reflected by Julia's close relatives. In effect, her departure seems to disrupt the familial transgenerational story: never had a member of the family been to University, and it would not have been expected in her sociocultural context. The strength of the rupture for the whole family can be inferred from various signs. Julia's self-description is a description in terms of lack of skills or of capacities to take care of herself. The rupture itself is expressed as precipitant: although the family had probably had enough time to prepare for the change, Julia describes the time-acceleration that occurred just before her move to the University town. The contrast is obvious when compared to young people that have been to boarding school and are used to move to a new school—for them, starting university just means buying a few clothes. Thus, it can be inferred that, in contrast to families where parents and siblings have been to higher education, no elder can offer guidance to Julia. She cannot rely on the resources that are offered by social support, and she feels exposed.

However, she is not totally powerless. Feeling that her move was a significant rupture, Julia anticipated her need to find some comfort by creating a *homely* room in her new University accommodation:

> I used various things... to cover my entire wall (laughs)... It is just white and boring! It doesn't have purple.... I really like purple. Because my room at home is purple. I really like purple. My mum has got me a vase of purple iris [I put everything possible purple on the wall, using bits of magazine]. I was just, "Go away, white!"

She also has a kind of memento: pictures of her mother, father, brother, friends, grandmother, that she had framed before coming to University. This strategy allows her to use various resources for their *containing* function (Tisseron, 1999): the purple textiles and objects transform her foreign room into a motherly holding space. The framed pictures also offer containing spaces for specific memories. Operating in a very embodied manner, these resources that can be touched and manipulated can be seen as maintaining a link with the family and her childhood, and sustain Julia's sense of continuity beyond the rupture.

Asked about other objects she brought with her, Julia mentions books and CDs, like most other young people. Among the CDs are those of a popular band, the *Manic Street Preachers*. That band, she immediately adds, influenced her very much. Her encounter with that band is linked to a *previous* rupture in Julia's life: the death of her grandmother. Julia was raised by the latter, as her mother used to work. The grandmother's death, when Julia became adolescent, was felt as a major rupture. According to Julia's narrative, it is after this rupture that she started to go through a long period of transition, resulting in many changes: coming from a religious, conservative family, Julia now presents herself as an agnostic, active left-wing person. The band is presented as having played a major role in the changes that brought Julia to university. I will thus focus my analysis on that first rupture, and the turning of the songs of the *Manic Street Preachers* into various symbolic resources, linked to her developmental moves.

Turning a Pop Album Into a Resource for First Aid Uses

The death of a close relative can be felt as a major rupture during adolescence (Bagnoli, 2003). In young people's narratives, some strong investment in a cultural element many times follows a close relative's death, or a mother's psychological breakdown. Death or close affective losses, which trigger conscious and unconscious questions, particularly call for emotional elaboration and meaning making. Traditionally, religion has framed and conferred sense to grief (chapter 1). When without religion, people still need to support their mourning processes; mourning has been shown to be a very dialogical process that needs to be semiotically mediated (Josephs, 1997 1998; Zittoun, 2004d). It is in this perspective that we can read the particular significance of Julia's encounter with the songs of the *Manic Street Preachers*: "The time when I got into the *Manics* was about the time my grand mum's burial, and just after she died." The *Manic Street Preachers* seem to have been suddenly available to support such a mourning process.

In effect, the story of Julia's encounter with that band is narrated in a particular genre. A few years earlier, a first encounter turned out to be inconclusive: she had bought an album, listened to it, and hated it, regretting having spent 10 pounds on it. Later, during the holidays—probably after the buria—Julia found herself with a group of peers, and the discussion was about the band. This is, in Julia's narration, when things suddenly started to change:

> Then someone says the story of the singer who had vanished, and nobody knows what happened to him, and I found on the web this story - and I said, "Oh this is quite interesting," and then I bought another album, and I knew I was going to end up with all the albums.

It is here not possible to know why the figure of the disappeared singer has been so striking—it might be that, at the time of Julia's grandmother's death, or in unhappy teenager years, the singer's ultimate escape reflected the feeling of loss of an important part of oneself. But still, one might ask, how can a hated album be turned into a loved one? The contrast might be a rhetoric effect of the interview; however, this can also be interpreted differently. When represented to Julia after the grandmother's death, the album is taken in a new semiotic dynamic. It might be that the songs were more apt to reflect Julia's grieving mood than her lighter feelings a few years earlier. Also, as in Lily's case (chapter 4), it is the mediation of others (a group of friends) that enables Julia to look closer at what the cultural experiences has provoked in her.

Thus, at that time, a rewarding semiotic prism is created: the album (*symbolic object*) enables bonding with a group of young persons that share one's experience (*others*). The story of the lost singer might have enabled Julia (*person*) to find a personal meaning in the album, linked to feelings of loss: the loss of the singer resonates with the loss of the grandmother, of the loss of part of herself (*meaning for person*). Additionally, Julia had known that cultural element before; it might also have bridged that new period of her life with her past (historicity of the prism). This semiotic dynamic seems to have enabled Julia to turn that music album into a symbolic resource. After that meeting, Julia went to buy other albums, and started to find a real comfort in that music—that is, she started to use the music as a resource, first directed toward herself:

> I was not especially well at that time. And therefore the music kind of s... I don't exactly now how it worked, but it was as a kind of companion. xxx it kind of articulated... xxxx It is not a particularly happy music. It just kind of kept me a company when I was not particularly happy. It was not a very happy time of my life. It kind of articulates how I was feeling as well.

It is for the physical experience or presence that Julia first likes the music. At this point, the meaning of the lyrics does not seem relevant; music is rather used for its soothing and emotional wrapping, as a container allowing Julia to be *held*. It is also, by its very presence —or possibly, because of the imaginary presence of the dead singer—a *companion*. Finally, the songs "articulate how [she] was feeling": they seem to delimit and fix the emotions, that is, they support a first level of mediation of the confused field-like feelings of loss and grief (L1); they then enable Julia to distance herself from these emotions which are then represented to her, mediating her reflection (L2):

> I think I am not a poet, I am not a writer. It is very difficult for me to - put down on paper how, how I would be feeling. Especially about thinking my mum or my grand mum's death, xxx it is very difficult for me to write it down. xxxxx But then if you hear it, in a song, you hear words, yea, xxx ... it kind of... it kind of... it means something to me. When I say it articulates, it kind of represents what I'm feeling, what I can't, I can't actually articulate it with a bit of paper. If you find what you're feeling by being strongly identifying with that song, you identify with that song and what you are up to.

The song thus gives words to feelings in Julia. They thus support processes of thirdness (chapter 2): her own emotions are given a space; a language is offered, and a position is provided—that of the singer. These new linking are both horizontal and vertical, as Julia nicely formulates: her "feelings identify with the song," becomes she identifies with the song," becomes her projects are identified with the song. In effect, these progressive extensions of links are based on similarities and symmetric thinking; yet they will lead to very concrete changes.

Uses That Open the World

Entering into the Manic is, in Julia's case, more than finding a containing space for her depressive moods and a way to reflect on them. Becoming a *Manic Street Preacher* is for her to enter a complex nexus of meaning, a network of people, dates, places, books, and ideas, through which she will be brought elsewhere. As Julia states in a very reflective way, having been *recognized* in one's feeling allows one to trust one's guide (L3):

> There must be some kind of... something... I feel, you know, I recognise in myself something that I understand what they are saying, that means actually something to me.... It has to be something like that. Or if they think something I have been thinking as well. (...) Or: they seem to have articulated something through their music that I was thinking as well. That's why I do listen to them that much, that's why I trust them and they can guide you through books and things like that.

Feeling acknowledged in her feelings and experiences, Julia can acknowledge the presence of an intentional power behind the songs. There is someone to understand her—the members of the band—who can show her something, and bring her somewhere else; she feels close to them, as if she knew what they were thinking. Hence, the semiotic prism now links Julia to the (imaginary) singers (*others*), and through the songs (*symbolic objects*), constructs meaning about them (*meaning for self*). From now on, the songs are used as cues to the existence of the group itself.

Yet the existence of the group is also diffracted and distributed through various other cultural elements. This will canalize Julia's choice of other cultural experiences (L2). She thus starts to watch TV programs about the band, read the biographies of the musicians and explore their Web pages.

Also, she explains, the music is not an easy one, and she has been incited to read the lyrics. These are sometimes in Welsh, and need to be worked out to be understood. Online resources are discovered: beyond the official band Web page, fan's Web pages create what Julia perceives as a "kind of community, with dates, meeting.... You have to sit, and [read the] interviews." Such a Web site informs her about the lyrics, and about the background reference to these lyrics:

> There is actually... the front page is compiled like a - reading list. What books, you know, they read... there is a whole range... Keats, Albert Camus, Sartre, erm, soviets. They'll tell (...), it is books that they have read themselves and have enjoyed...(...). There is actually... there is a song called Patrick Eightmen. (...) referring to the character of *American Psycho*, and

because xxxx so I went and read it. Or a song called xxxx referring to *One Flew Over the Cuckoo's Nest* - so, you read that. (...) Sometimes its very explicit, sometimes it is not... you have to figure out.

A complex form of intertextuality is thus created: the figures of the singers (*others*) accompany fans in their explorations of texts (*objects*) and in their acquisition of knowledge about the events inspiring these lyrics (*meaning for person*). In her enquiry to understand the message of these songs, Julia came to read Marx and Orwell, and started to get herself informed about the Spanish civil war. Through this spider's web of references, the fan slowly constructs a new thinking sphere of experience:

It entered all different areas of your life, (...) like political views... not because of them, but because of this stuff I've read in *Manic*, it makes you think. It challenges the way you think, it contested my own views, that I had whatever by my parents, or whatever by the institution.

In the case of Julia, this "influence" is indeed multilayered, and seems to touch her political and religious commitments at L4, which, in turn, will change her possible conduct.

Generative Uses of Manic Street Preacher's

In what follows, I highlight a few of the various changes enabled through Julia's use of resources attached to the band. Entering in the *Manic's* nebula corresponds to a social relocation and an identity transformation. When changing school, Julia looked for people who shared her interest in the *Manic* as well as the worldview they articulate. A person that likes the *Manic* would be likely to share her political views. Clothes and other external cues signal that one is a fan of the band. To find her peers, Julia changed her style of clothing and became acquainted with people who recognized these signs, and recognized her as a fan of the *Manic*. Other forms of affirmation of her position are then possible: in everyday discussion, triggered by this or that word, Julia might recall *Manic Streets Preachers* lyrics, she will thus start to sing or talk about the lyrics. These are used as resources in interpersonal relationships, mediating the modalities of the exchange: quoting is a symbolic cue (an externalization) about her own location and possible recognition by the other, as much as clothes are visual cues. The resource is used at the level of particular actions in the world (L2), but also, contribute to defining Julia to herself (L3).

The songs are resources that allow her to widen her musical knowledge. Julia starts to listen to the bands and read the texts that have inspired the *Manic Street Preachers*, that is, the resource is used about other resources (intertextuality).

> I read Orwell - Orwell is my preferred author now. I read *1984*, because that was a thing they mentioned, and then because I enjoyed that and I went on and I read *Animal farm* and xxx which wasn't explicitly mentioned. I took myself from that... it's not particularly... it is not that I read because they tell that; I read it and if I enjoyed it I read something else. You now, like Camus, they mentioned *l'Etranger*, and then I went on and read the *Plague* and I enjoyed that more - I dreamed of that, I studied French because of that.

These also allow the exploration of the material world and symbolic world. Through her research about the lyrics, Julia learns the geography of Wales, visits the area, and goes to the cafes which the band went to. Also, the songs awaken, sustain and orient Julia's interest in history and politics, in various ways: through the references indicated in the lyrics or their backgrounds, through allusions to specific events, national and international that invite Julia to document herself, and watch specific historical programs. The uses are here about specific events, at L2.

> *Manic Street Preachers* have a song called "If you tolerate this your children will be next," which is about the Spanish civil war, so I went to read about the Spanish civil war. I do think that is one of the reasons why I did history A-level, why I got into politics (...) and all contributes to why I am in [this university] now. It's not only the music, it's what makes you go for the meaning, and it teaches you.

Julia reflects on her reading choices: she reads suggested texts, but also follows her own, newly developed interest. She adds:

> It is just a CATALYST, just to different aspects. You know, they lead you somewhere, and then you go in your direction from that, which is a bit like a guide, that give you a sense of direction.

In effect, if specific choices are still guided (L2), Julia is starting to internalize a direction which will be hers (L3-4). Exploring the singers' references, she became familiar with their historical and political analysis of the Welsh situation. Now, she can use her knowledge and analytical skills to reflect on her region of origin and its historical and social situation (L3):

> I'm not from Wales. (...). But in saying that, I think that the area where I come from has a lot of similarities with the area where they come from. It is not about Wales, it is about an ex-mining town. There are a lot of similarities. Not to the same extent. The town is very detached, (...) you feel very

distanciated from London. You feel quite isolated, not exactly, because they grew up in the eighties... but you feel kind of... slight similarities.

In other words, semiotic dynamics have been displaced again. Julia is now using various texts and films (*symbolic objects*) within a semiotic prism relating her (*person*) to the imaginary presence of the group and authors (*generalized other*), in order to address issues from the social world (Wales and her mining area) (*meaning for self, about* the social world).

She thus defines new political and religious stances (L4). At this point, the transformation of her whole system of orientation is completed. At 14 years, Julia was a discrete religious young girl, attached to her family, liking sciences; through the explorations allowed by the encounter with the *Manic Street Preachers*, she re-redefined her whole system of commitments, orientations and interests (see also Valsiner & Lawrence, 1997 on modifications of trajectories). She is now a left-wing person who requires more justice and social rights. Recursively, this change in higher-level forces her to reflect on other levels of experience and commitments, and thus modifies them.

> I used to truly believe in god, you know, truly believe in god, and then, until I was fifteen or sixteen, then it changed. I don't know why it changed. Looking back, I don't quite know why it changed. Because my grandmother died, or because the music - (xxxx) Not because it is so anti-code... (...) But there was a definite change - I use not to believe in god for quite a while. Not so much because of the music, but because of the literature. It brought me through the music (...) It challenged... Not only my political views, that where challenged, but my religious views as well.

This new system of orientation has, in turn, opened new possible trajectories where Julia's values can be translated into possible conduct. One of the actualizations of that system, is her new will to study history and to apply to this University (L3):

> And eventually I ended up here because of my approach... when I was at GSCE, I was in science (xx) and then I got into that, and I decided I wanted to do history and I did a history GSCE. And then I did a History A-levels just because of the lyrics, and I started to read history and politics (...). You know, I was always interested in politics, but because of that I started to read everything in politics and... that they mention, and I read xx at A-levels, and I came here to do politics. I was probably going to study biology somewhere, in Manchester or so - but I came here.

The funny event is that she seemed to have been accepted by the University thanks to the symbolic resources provided by the *Manic Street*

Preachers, which she mobilized as knowledge during the very serious admission interview, to answer historical questions (L2):

> And also when I had my interview here - Also at my interview here... I talked about Avenin Bevon (...) - He is a famous politician (...); the reason I knew about him is because there is one of the albums [which] is called (---) that is a quote from him. And I started to talk about that.

Now, as a student, Julia still holds strong political positions (L4), on the basis of which she commits herself into actions—such as supporting the firemen's strikes (L2).

Drawing on the same system of values and positions, she also starts to give a shape to her future, that she wants to be committed in politics and education. In effect, the whole political-historical guidance taken from the *Manic Street Preachers* makes her aware of the needs of her region of origin; her reflectivity on her own transformations (through the band and its network of related cultural element) makes her define the project of bringing education to people in her area:

> [I am] not particularly ambitious. All my family is from [that area] and my aunt lives next door. [My family has always been around - I couldn't imagine myself moving away]. That restricts a bit what I can be doing. I have benefited so much from learning about politics and it has enriched my life so much - Also, you know, the books, I've read so many of my books, and through the music I've listened, it has open my eyes so much, so many history, so many things I've learned, so many things I've gained. I want to bring it to other people...[Music is a very good way to educate people..]. Because it has enriched my life so much I want to bring it to others.

To sum up, Julia uses a set of cultural experiences for all the basic requirements of youth: to support and extend her time perspective, to develop her system of orientation, and, to give to it a very consistent shape. These uses of symbolic resources have also enabled Julia to support the transitions required by the rupture of coming to University: it supports her identity redefinition, it provides some social skills and knowledge (such as the interview ones!), and enables her to give meaning to the changes she is experiencing.

These uses of symbolic resources are directed first toward the past, before becoming prospective. They apply first to Julia's inner life, before being applied to her relationships to others, the cultural environment, the material world, and the social and political shared reality. These uses enable the redefinition of local meanings, and enable progressive distancing, so as to define general life commitments.

Hence Julia's use of symbolic resources has progressively changed level of generality. First, they have a soothing function, semiotic mediations regulating emotions (L1); the meanings of these first mediations awoke lateral resources (the novels) enabling mediators to acquire a more generalized scope, enabling representing events (L2). Songs, novels, and political beliefs then guide conduct, and lead to the definition of values and identity (L3) and then, higher-level values (L4). These can in turn be guided into actual commitments, promoting specific conduct (such as supporting the firemen's strike) (L2). Hence, these uses of resources enable the development of a time perspective and the transformation of a system of orientation. The elements entering in the semiotic prism also progressively acquire a wider scope: elements used as symbolic resources are first one song, then a set of lyrics, and a group of texts; the *other* of the prism slowly becomes more abstract: the friends, are replaced by the imaginary presence of the singer, of the whole band, of a whole imaginary community of authors generalized into a political perspective. There is thus, step by step, a slow transformation of the initial powerful semiotic prism (organized around the grandmother's death) into a prism open to the world. This transformation is accompanied by a slow displacement through the architecture of the self, which also transforms the latter. Hence, it is the whole architecture of the self that is changed: having internalized and integrated new possible perspectives, having new means to think, to feel, and to act, Julia lives in a new sphere of experience. Finally, these uses of resources do not interrupt Julia's feeling of continuity, and do not bring her to be rejected by her social world (luckily, it is acceptable to be a pop fan during adolescence).

A question must be raised: do the processes described here not strongly resemble those of a conversion process? In effect, the sequence we just described could be read in a different way: after a first shaking event, a symbolic system offered Julia its soothing effect; the system is itself guarded by a strongly trusted leading character and a "brotherhood"; progressively, thanks to the "good" action of some charismatic figure, the person's high-level values are replaced, and bring the person to define new commitments in action (Campiche, 1997; Hundeide, 2004; Nathan, 1992).

However, when talking about group-belonging, one of the main differences between sect-like and open groups is the directionality of the transformation processes they enable: do they aim at the survival of the group itself, or do they allow the person to orient her transformation in a way that might bring her to take her distance from the group (Zittoun, 2004a)? What can one say about the fuzzy *Manic* nebula? Here, the symbolic system created around the band has no coercive power (even allowing for marketing strategies); it is the user that confers on it its closeness or openness—and in Julia's case, it is obviously not for the sake of maintaining her fascination in the band. On the contrary: it is precisely the very generativity of Julia's use of symbolic resources that is to be highlighted: each step of that transformation has enabled her to open new options. For some of them, a general external symbolic system—the *Manic*'s virtual community—has provided resources that support further changes; but for the later steps of her transformation, Julia has become an autonomous chooser and user of resources—her readings have been chosen out of her own symbolic responsibility. In that sense, according to our discussion in chapter 1, Julia's uses of resources install a generative dynamic and are developmental: they give access to new spheres of experience, and open new options for further changes, rather than limiting these. They do so, because they admit complex dynamics of linking, containing and transformation of pasts and future, of the social and of interiority.

Finally, one might ask: could Julia have used the resources provided by the *Manic Street Preachers* to elaborate high-level commitments, if she had not had a previous sense of these higher-values (she came from a religious family)? More generally, can the use of symbolic resources bring one to think and feel in a qualitatively different manner? Can the use of symbolic resources really develop more complex structures of understanding? These questions will remain open until the next chapter.

HESSE TO COME BACK: ELI

Eli is, like Lev (chapter 4), one of the young people interviewed because of their belonging to a group of religious Jews. Like Julia, he went through a rupture and he seems to have engaged in an important work of transition. Like Julia, he had various cultural elements at his disposal. In contrast with her, however, he did not have to invent his repertoire of resources out of pop culture's offerings; rather, he had access to cultural elements and skills transmitted from generation to generation and to which he has been socialized.

Religious Jews are given an education that gives a central place to the scriptures (the Bible and the books of the traditional law) and their interpretation. Their practices of study comprise complex forms of interpretation, on the basis of which they should be able to identify any new situation in the light of a previous one, so as to know what their meaning is and what conduct they require. This form of hermeneutics is explicitly transmitted, and the various ways of using a text to illuminate a new situation are named and theorized (Steinsaltz, 1996; Zittoun, 1999). Therefore, I thought that young Jews were taught an expertise in using symbolic resources. I also thought that they would thus be able to use religious texts as symbolic resources to confer meaning on personal, interpersonal, or worldly situations. The analysis of the trajectories of young Jews who come back to secular life reveals something different (Zittoun, 2004e). Although they use symbolic resources, the ones that are used to address issues linked to the transitions are not taken from their religious system. Eli's use of resources will thus appear as much as a bricolage as Julia's, although part of his personal culture is strongly consistent and linked to an existing cultural system.

Transition: Coming Back From Yeshiva

Eli has a fluent, well-articulated discourse. He is open, witty, and happy to engage in the interviews' explorations. Eli grew up religiously in a middle class family, that he presents as having a comprehensive lifestyle, combining religious commitment and an interest in secular culture (arts and theatre). After religious primary school, Eli chose a secular high school, promising his parents that he would pursue his Jewish studies. And hence, between high school and University, he spent a year in a yeshiva in Israel, an orthodox, rabbinic school. Going to yeshiva for 1 or 2 gap-years is expected of young men in this religious milieu, and most of them enjoy this immersion in a yeshiva and could be willing to stay longer. In Eli's case, after 1 happy year there, he had been asked by his parents to get a university degree to ensure his access to a remunerated profession. Eli has been through a trajectory shared by most religious Jews from this milieu; and as with most of them, coming back to a secular life when entering University is perceived as an important rupture (Lawrence, Benedikt, & Valsiner, 1992).

Before examining how the rupture is expressed and dealt with in Eli's discourse, it is important to have a broader view of the life in Yeshiva that will be lost when coming back (e.g., Ouaknin, 1986/1995; Potoh, 1962). A Yeshiva is a full time, Jewish study school, where most of the day is organized around prayer, both collective and individual (religious Jews pray 3 times a day), study, with study partners and individually, and a few domestic tasks. A Yeshiva offers a sphere of experience which is framed in time and space, isolated from other sociocultural influences, with its own regulation, and its *warden* of the frame (Grossen & Perret-Clermont, 1992) (the rabbis, the head of the yeshiva, etc.). That frame allows the achievement of a life that conforms to religious commitments:[4] life in yeshiva is inclusive and predictable, every concrete action undertaken being consistent with a set of systematic rules and beliefs structuring a religious Jewish faith. For example, for religious Jews, the study of the scriptures, the laws and the traditions they gave birth to[5] (L2), is one of the main ways through which one actualizes his or her reverence of God (L4), and achieves the duty of becoming a good person and improving the world in general (L3). The duty to teach is discussed widely within rabbinic and mystic literature, philosophy and tales and is expressed in the everyday prayers. Young people who willingly go to yeshiva can experience a world where the rules followed in everyday actions, which define their identity, are isomorphic to the shared social rules. They also are provided with a social arena, where young people with similar interests, backgrounds, and aspirations can meet; time and study and effort are shared with peers; a very particular emotional and social atmosphere develops within the collective study and prayer. Young men also meet rabbis that can acquire an immense value to them. Finally, here might be, thanks to its highly structured and ritualized routine, space for some type of intellectual and spiritual explorations.

As this description suggests, a year in yeshiva creates a reality in itself. A sense of being out of the world is not only naturally created, but also cultivated. Although a lot of young people go to Yeshiva for a limited period, their rabbis strongly encourage them to stay and to become eminent Talmudists, rather than going back to the secular world. The study of the texts is done for the sake of the study of the texts, not to address external, real-life issues (although that is their original *raison d'être*). For these reasons, Yeshiva life creates a space which is closed, and which does not seem to help to anticipate or support transitions leading to other possible spheres of experience. It thus does not help students to anticipate or prepare for their life out of yeshiva and their possible return to a secular life.

Given the inclusive nature of life in yeshiva, leaving it implies the loss of various things: the every-moment conformity with high-level values, a strongly framed sphere of experience, and a social network. Rupture is felt and expressed by orthodox students propelled into a secular university town in terms of a split between two worlds—their religious life and the secular world. Some of them go through long and rather depressing periods of disenchantment, loss and alienation, which worsen when they have been forced to leave yeshiva.

Talking retrospectively about that rupture, Eli explained how, over the years, he established a new balance, suggesting a long transition process that includes learning to organize time and space, to choose friends, and to decide what is good for oneself. At the time of the interview, the transitions seem to have enabled him to overcome the split; the worlds of religious experience and of academic requirements seem integrated in a consistent sphere of experience. Eli had hence chosen an advanced research topic that required him, in an academic frame, to read a lot of old Hebraic literature.

Social Resources and Practices

The rupture of coming back to secular life breaks down young people's everyday life structure, their social life and the meanings that organize them. The transitions required will imply the reconstruction of one's world: one's position and identity, the range of possible conduct, and the meaning of all this.

When engaged in these transitions, *social resources* appear important for these young persons. Asked about what helped him to find a balance, Eli mentions having asked other people about their experiences. Yet he eventually discovered that other's experiences were not helpful and that he had to find his own way. But more importantly for Eli, the local rabbi, here called chaplain, and the Jewish society helped him to settle down in the local community. Interviews with orthodox students and their Chaplain more generally indicate that the community life created in the town fosters the establishment of a strong social network and the sharing of daily ritual activities. Jewish students can indeed meet for all the daily prayers, for lunch and for weekly dinners with the Chaplain, and for studying religious texts with a *Haver* (study friend). Hence, even if these meetings have to be combined with a regular academic life—which implies numerous furious biking through the town—the local community creates a supporting social network, organizing time, meetings, social life, and interactions with a leading figure, thus reconstituting important aspects of the yeshiva life.

Religious practices seem to offer resources for the processes of transition: identity maintenance, emotional regulation, and the construction of new forms of knowledge. Some young people realize that religious, embodied practices have an importance for maintaining a sense of who they are. In effect, they are aware that their daily rituals (binding and unbinding the phylacteries for morning prayers; ritual hand washing; benedictions before and after food, etc.) and studying practices constitute them as religious Jews—as the religious discourse says. These enacted practices can thus be seen as resources used to support identity continuity. Also, because they guide bodily actions, they might have a soothing effect and participate in emotional regulation. Those used are only oriented toward the past, and do not open space for possible futures.

Some other persons use religious practices as resources for their university studies. They thus discover that the specific modes of reasoning and epistemological attitudes developed in religious studies can be used in their arts studies: it gives to Ron's approach a "legalistic" preciseness; or it supports Esther's readings thanks to the (religious) assumption that there is always something to learn from a text (chapter 3). Yet these uses of heuristics are more intratextual, rather than oriented toward oneself or the world.

But can the cultural elements offered by a religious system offer resources for meaning making, to orient oneself in the real-life, or to open possible futures? Against my expectations, it seems that religious texts are not seen as offering such resources. Hence, asked directly about the use of religious text to deal with life-choices, Eli gives an amused answer:

> Decisions taken from this - (...) I am not going to open a book to decide where I am going to live, but definitely I will decide to live where there is a synagogue, kosher food, etc.

If the religious studies, that have such a powerful guiding and explanatory force for everyday life conduct, fail to guide in situations of newness or to account for the violent rupture experienced by that orthodox students, what will do?

Uses of Novels as Symbolic Resources

Eli maintains the comprehensive lifestyle to which he had been socialized in his family. And it is in secular literature that he finds symbolic resources to think about coming back to a secular life. Questioned about his literary choices, he spontaneously develops:

> Now, I was talking about this sort of... difficulty somehow in getting a balance between all the aspects of life. *The Glass Bead Game* [by Herman Hesse] - do you know the book at all? - Ok, I have not read it for a while. But - erm - basically, there is a sort of college on a hill, completely isolated from everything else, where the people there are very involved in a sort of esoteric learning, which is difficult to understand what it is and what sort of impact it has on anything else, and then again on the outside world obviously. And there is one character in it, who is really firmly in one world, and he feels the tension between the one world and the other world. (...) And that, I mean I could really, I really read that, in terms of having been to Yeshiva and coming to University, obviously there weren't exact parallels, but I could relate to that very strongly. Erm - and, I don't think the book actually helped to resolve the conflict, the actual conflict, it didn't really help, it sort of more... it demonstrated the differences, I think - - but it helped. It is nice to know that other people are thinking the same things you are. *Narcissus and*

146 *Transitions: Development through Symbolic Resources*

Goldmund is also, has also similar themes. Two sorts of sides, and trying to fit them together.

The novel seems to have given Eli the means to think his coming back experience. The novel represents a young scholar's sense of exception and remoteness, carrying a precious experience that keeps him apart from normal life. The novel seems to have offered forms to reflect on his feelings and tension (L1). But also, a link between two worlds is symbolized by their inscription in the same plotline: the main character moves from one to the other. One might think that this enables Eli to think the passage from one sphere of experience to the other, and the relations that link these two (L2, L3). This might also enable thinking the character to have a complex identity, bringing particular values (L4) to the secular world.

Eli also mentions resources used in real life, to think about himself, and his relationship to his family, and to his fiancée. Here is another version of the issue of coming back of home after growing up elsewhere, and then questioning one's relationship to adults:

And I read *the Graduate* when I was - I think when I was back from Israel? Or just about to go to Israel? Something like that. And I was really, I really connected with the... *Q What is* the Graduate? It's a film with Dustin Hoffman and Ann Bancroft and all sorts of people. The basic plotline is... a very successful graduate student has been very good in his studies, in sports whatsoever, he comes home, and he is sort of very stifled by his parents, by society, and by people expecting him to do certain things. He ends up having an affair with the wife of one of his... of his parents' friend, Ms Robinson. Erm, and it's not really that he loves her, and he is not really doing it for the sex, but... I don't know, he does that, and at the end he gets together with her daughter, who he does love (...).... Ok. I didn't have any affair with any of my parent's friend's wife, and you know, I didn't feel stamped by my parents, but I felt, I definitely felt... I think I identified with sort of being at a turning point in your life, and having all sorts of social expectations on so on... and the feeling the need to... I don't know (...) the rules being quite worked (?) the... There is a line of films that goes something like that: here you are again, and someone else is making the rules, and something like that.

Another cultural experience enables Eli to share the thoughts linked to his engagement with his fiancée. Here the resource enters in a semiotic dynamic uniting Eli, the novel, the fiancée, and their shared construction of their experience:

I just read Anna Karenina.(...) *Q Did you like* A. Karenina? Fantastic, yeah, fantastic. Oh yeah... You know, it was written, you know 150 years ago, by someone in Russia. And there were things.... I mean it could of course apply to all our lives, marriage, death, everything, so there were things that I hadn't experienced, obviously, but the things that I have experienced, I really... sometimes, I really... For example I got engaged recently. And someone get engaged in the book. It wasn't the same exactly. But something was revealing similar it was great. amazing book (...) [*Q Do you know what is the connection between* A. Karenina *and the engagement –?*] No, yes, I think that. ... Yes the way... the way they fall in love, the way they talk to each other when they are falling in love, the way they look at each other, the things they think about how their parents behave (...), I mean obviously it's a completely different society, it's not the same. But there were certain things which were really funny, there were some things I read to my fiancée, because it was just nice. And the history... all sort of stuff was going on, obviously, and obviously there were and all sort of questions that people would discuss about, the West and Russia, liberalism and whatever else. So, because I knew a bit about it, it was nice to put it in that context.

Through the interview, thinking about cultural experiences that were important to him, Eli comes to express a reflective understanding of his use of symbolic resources. Literature affects someone, he says, when the text is appropriate to a person at a given moment of his or her life.

Also the film, *The Graduate*. (...) You know I figured that certain pieces ... certain books or films or whatever can really affect you if you see them at the right time. I read Catherine LeRye when I was much younger; it wasn't really great for me, even if people said it had an impact on them. And I figure may be I read it too young. And I read then I read (xx) and it didn't had an impact on me and everyone said it was so great. (...) I think that if I had seen it when I was fifteen, it wouldn't have that impact.

Giving Meaning to Uses of Resources

Are these uses of secular symbolic resources contradictory with Eli's faith and religious commitment? It appears not to be the case; even more, Eli seems to realize that his use of secular symbolic resources about everyday problems, to solve concrete situations (L1 and L2) or to reflect on more stable categories or identity matters (L3), can be seen as applications of his *higher-level religious rules* (L4). For instance, during the interview, after having mentioned his use of Hesse's novels to reflect on coming back from a secluded life, Eli comes to realize that

I guess that's part of the point of the Jewish study. It is quite... it would be quite easy to go and sit in a room -not easy but - easy to be sitting in a room on your own and learn all the stuff all day. But part of it, is very strongly, being... you know, making it part of your own life in your relationship to people.

Jewish studies might offer the temptation of a protected, quasi-monastic life, which is promoted by yeshiva rabbis. Here, Eli's use of a literary symbolic resource allows the exhumation of a set of traditional rules, which then become resources for reinterpreting the transition back to secular life: entering the secular world becomes one way to achieve ethical principles, such as knowing oneself, the world and the other (rules at L3), which are forms of devotion to God.[6] Note that this complex and high-level guiding principle supports Eli's family life, which was described as maintaining a comprehensive way of life. In this bricolage, the use of novels as resources reinvigorate religious texts, grounding an idea of integration already rooted in the texture of his past everyday life. And thus, they open space for a future.

A Comprehensive Lifestyle as Future

For Eli, literature, religion, and life are clearly entwined. None of these harm the other, for they are integrated in a comprehensive system of orientation. It authorizes the resolution of most of the difficulties of the rupture Eli had experienced, without renouncing their complexity. In effect, Eli's utterances are extremely structured, dialogical, and finely shaded, avoiding simplifications and stereotypical conclusions. Past in yeshiva and present life are also entwined in Eli's future project: being just engaged, he took a decision about his career, while also planning one more stay in yeshiva as a preparation for his future married life. Hence, his identity has been reworked alongside his repositioning; he has engaged in skill acquisition, among which he has developed a reflective use of symbolic resources; and he has developed the meaning he confers on the changes he has lived through.

What appears through Eli and Lev's stories is that it is not enough to have an expert access to cultural elements, and to have acquired heuristic of interpretation in a formal setting, to be able to use them in everyday, personally meaningful situations. Yeshivas tend to condemn their students' move out to other spheres of experience. As the idea of the historicity of semiotic dynamics suggests, cultural experiences are internalized with traces of social relationships (semiotic prism) and symbolic positions characterizing the settings in which they take place. These traces, as well as the higher-level values intrinsically linked to them, constrain their uses as resources in new spheres of experiences. To overcome such constraints, which prevent Jewish students from finding applications for higher-level rules in new situations, and from using their personal culture as symbolic resources, other strategies have to be found. Eli thus excavates the semiotic device that one could achieve a comprehensive way of life from his past experience in his family (internalized through earlier semiotic dynamics). Students seem to have to find symbolic resources outside of their Jewish sphere of experience to address these issues, as if these would not be loaded by the same interdictions (other *others* of semiotic prisms). In some conditions, these external symbolic resources can be grafted into a person's system of orientation, and thus create bridges and patches so as to expand its realm of validity.

SCOUT FOR DEFINING A JOB: PAT

Unlike Julia and Eli, Pat is not a student; he is working in an outdoors shop and, in the evenings, in a bar. Yet like them he went through an important rupture—he left secondary school—that was followed by a long period of changes, which eventually took quite a generative shape. At the time of the interview, Pat is articulate, sociable, easy going, reflective, and he has defined possible plans for his future.

The Rupture of Quitting School

After what seem to have been an easy GSCE (General Certificate of Secondary Education, taken at age 5-16), Pat left formal education when he dropped out of his second sixth-form program in computing and maths. The first of these programs was given by what Pat describes as a very good school, yet it quickly went "over his head." The second, on the contrary, was so vocational that Pat felt insufficiently challenged.

> So I thought, stop this, I want to go and get a job. So that I can sort of put things in perspective, and really see what I want to do with my life.

Pat was in a situation of failure; yet he narrates the rupture as if it resulted from a personal choice. However, the feeling of rupture is visible in his description of facing a vertiginous field of possible pathways and futures, contrasting with a more ancient pattern of trajectories where one was told what to do:

> Because in those days all what you could do, was going to factory, or join the army!! But in these days: I mean the world is your Oyster! Especially if you are an English person! ! But it is actually a minefield. Too many choices.

These images might suggests how Pat feels—only master on board of a little boat on an oily ocean that could turn into a hurricane (the oyster, the minefield). "Those days" can be heard as an echo of his parental discourse; elsewhere, Pat says that his parents are ready to support him in whatever his choices are. Put together, these externalizations might indicate that Pat feels not much supported, by parents who seem out of their depth.

The feeling of rupture experienced by Pat also appears through his active attempt at making sense of his dropping out of school. He is quite disabused and critical about the system and his own behavior. On one hand, he describes the school system as requiring too much from young people at an early age, before having the required maturity. On the other hand, he is critical about his own lack of commitment, his difficulty to "put his head down" and his absorption in nonscholar activities. On the whole, Pat seems to have turned his feeling of failure into an acknowledgment of his need to mature and to explore possibilities before stabilizing his choices.

Agency, autonomy, and responsibility for oneself are difficult things to achieve for everybody. Yet for someone who quits school after a failure, like Pat, it is more difficult, but also more an immediate necessity. First, a common identity defence is to attribute the responsibility of failure to external causes (Dubois & Trognon, 1989); taking responsibility means also assuming the consequences of one's action (social exclusion, etc.). But it is the only way for someone to become actively engaged in explorations and the search for good professional solutions outside the structure of school. Second, school dropouts need to become responsible for their actions much younger than students. Students live in a highly structured institutional frame that organizes their life for 3 or 4 years, and confers on them a social legitimacy and an identity. The only choices for which they are responsible are topics of study; otherwise, the frame offers a protected space where students can explore various forms of life, ideas, and possible value—there is an institutionalized *moratorium* (Erikson, 1975). School dropouts have to be responsible and explorative, but they are also very much exposed, for there is no frame that legitimizes their explorations (Zittoun, 2004a).

The interview covered the period of transitions that, after the rupture, led Pat through two job-changes, leaving and returning to the parental home, to his present situation. Pat seems to have also progressively come to realize what system of orientation was guiding his conduct, and to turn a sense of loss of his past into a possible plan, progressively recovering a sense of integrity and agency. Now, Pat speaks about the "road" he found; he makes plans for possible training, and possible further schooling.

Entering in the Job Market, Moving Out of Alienation

After having left school, capitalizing on his previous facility in technical and computing disciplines, Pat quickly found work in a big computer shop. The first job he had there was a job as a sales person; yet he had to have it changed into a position in customer-service:

> Originally, when I started that job I went as a seller person, which is sort of commission based, and you have to sell fairly expensive equipment. - And to be quite honest, I was not particularly good at it. I don't really have the pattern, you know, I was not, I am not a natural-born seller-man. Because they are not a particularly good place to buy computers. And the... some of the policies they have on the customers are not... particularly ethical. And it is difficult because I... I suppose I have fairly good morals. So it is difficult to sell someone a PC, you know knows nothing about PCs, which is fairly... which is not a high standard, and that will go wrong at some point, and they will be stuck at some point (...). And they are going to have to pay in the future. So what I actually did, is I was transferred to the customers' service of the company. So I felt that if anything would go wrong, I know I can do something for them. So I did that instead. Q *You asked for that.* Yes, I asked for that. The money was not quite good, but...

Pat's first job experience is a difficult one: he is asked to do a job that clearly hurts his values ("not ethical policies"—"I suppose I have fairly good morals"), for he is supposed to earn money (commissions) by exploiting people's credulity. Not willing to feel responsible for people's problems, he changes his job to work at the customer service and repair the mistakes of the sellers and the company, where "if anything would go wrong [for the client], I know I can do something for them." However, he develops an increasing sense of alienation, both from himself (because of his Sisyphean work, and his powerlessness facing the company and the clients), and from others, since he neither does find support from his coworkers, nor can develop interesting exchanges with clients. That sense of alienation is indeed revealed by a long period of heavy marijuana consumption:

> But it used to be a sort of continuous, and it just stopped me functioning like a normal human being. But I used to get out of job - get stoned - go to bed - and go to work again.

Eventually—and for a reason we do not know—Pat came to realize the nature of his work and of the company. The nature of his difficulties and his sense of alienation are reflected in Pat's vivid depiction of his discovery of the injustices he was forced to be an accomplice of:

152 Transitions: Development through Symbolic Resources

> I found out... then I found out, how the company was not actually great. Because you get there Saturday morning at half past eight. And the store opens at 9. And between about quarter to nine, nine o'clock, you will see all these people that start gathering with their PCs or their laptop under their arms. And they have very stern expressions on their faces... And you think, "Ooh No," you try to hide behind the corner at this point, "I have been out drinking last night, and the last thing I want to do is be faced with all these people!" And that's the thing! People put their entire life on these PCs. Their businesses, or their diaries, or all their homework. And the things on these PCs really matter to these people. So when they go wrong, and I don't know what to do, then they become very emotional about it. And they can become very angry at you. Or they can go, "Oh I really, really need your help, whatever you can do, it would be great!" but some people can be not nice, very heated. (...) And the systems they put in place to deal with the customers is also very bad, so you end up turning away customers that have a pretty... in my opinion, that have a valid point! And you just have to tell them, "Sorry, look I can't do anything for you." And once again, it makes my moral rights, and so on and so forth. So it was not the ideal job, it was not the ideal job. *Q And was there a way where you could talk to the managers?* Well, it is so rooted in politics. Because it is a massive company (...) So there is NO WAY that somebody down here could affect anything... above them. Your role is not to question, just to do what the company wants you to do. So I became completely disenchanted. So after a year, I decided to move on, and to do something else. (...) Yes, because of the way they treated customers. And you were not a person, you [the employees] were a number.

After one year, Pat came across a job offer posted at a local outdoor shop, for which he applied, and was hired. Pat used to be a client there, as some of his leisure time was spent in hiking and mountain climbing. The job offer rang a deeper bell:

> *Q You knew that shop because you had used it; but what about your skills?* No no, it was not a complete change in my skill set, because I've always... I mean, I was a scout, in fact I have been in the scout movement... or I had been, because I am no longer in the scout movement, since I was about 5, so I have always enjoyed this type of outdoor activities. Going off to the hills, and climbing, and all that sort of things... So I was thinking: So what are my two main interests: computers, and I have done that, and the outdoors—so let's do that. And I knew that, because I would read the catalogues, I knew the stuff. So it was really another side of my interests.

Pat interpreted the job as a second option for capitalizing on his skills, among which his counts his past scout experience. This job is for Pat quite satisfying, and enables him to make a new project.

At this point, I must mention a few striking points in this interview. First, it does not reveal what conditions enabled Pat to find the strength to realize his alienation at the computer-shop and to decide to quit. It might be just chance, or linked to the fact that he had to return to his parental home (housing arrangements changed and became too expensive). What is more likely is that Pat used his discussions with others to come to such a realization. In effect, the major resource that Pat explicitly sees as supporting his transition is given by "talking with people"—social resources— which I will examine below.

Second, a strong value system seems to sustain Pat's conduct. On one side, we have seen his explicit mention of high morals to justify his decisions to quit a relatively well-paid job; the mobilization of such a rule is quite unique in the interview group. On the other side, Pat became quite close to a rather marginal fringe of the local youth, but remained a clean young man himself, developing a growing sense of certitude in creating a personal path corresponding to his needs. I thus would interpret these two elements as externalizations of a deeper value system partly developed through Pat's former belonging to the scout movement, mentioned as the decisive argument for changing job; hence, I suggest, the scout movement is here a symbolic system out of which Pat draws his main symbolic resources. In effect, scout-belonging experiences can be seen as cultural experiences as defined in chapter 2. Scouting can be understood as a cultural element—an organized system of meaning, relying on people, a corpus of rules of references, symbolic objects, some guardians of the system. More than in other cultural-historical contexts, being a scout in contemporary society can be seen as an "imaginary" experience—as Pat puts it: it is not really military, nor religious; it is a serious role playing, but people outside of it do not see how. Here, I therefore examine Pat's uses of social and symbolic resources.

Social Resources and Perspective Taking

Deliberately meeting people that have a wide range of life experiences appears to be the main strategy used by Pat when looking for resources to orient himself through uncertainty. Pat mentions his use of others' perspectives spontaneously, and when asked for clarification. Additionally, as I came to know him, Pat had easily become acquainted with older scientists, members of the alternative scene, and a group of college boys of his age. Resources to think about his experience and possibilities are

> Just talking to my parents, friends, and my parents' friends, and I mean for instance - when I had my housemates I had people over. And you can sort of talk people over on a personal level, about what they do, and that sort of thing. Because that is the problem I was having, not knowing what I wanted

to do. So I found that if I asked people about what THEY do, it would possibly give me an idea of what I wanted to do. Because there are so many options out there!!! (...) I have a faculty to meet people - and (...) it is just about meeting people who are interesting, and it is just about looking about things from a different point of view, and basically just expanding my knowledge.

Talking to people is for Pat not only a gratifying social experience; it is guided by an implicit theory on using dialogue as a mean to acquire knowledge from a diversity of perspectives—which scientists are eager to confirm. In effect, it allows the use of their testimonies and experiences as resources, as stories would be used (Harris, 2002). Talking to people is a way to work through incidents and the unexpected (Ochs & Capps, 2001), and it supports perspective taking, internalizing these other perspectives together with the surplus they bring on one's own experience (Gillespie, 2004), developing patterns of dialogic thinking (Hermans, 1996; Josephs, 1997, 1998; Vygotsky, 1931/1994), and thus, eventually extending the range of internalized positions within the architecture of self. Through Pat's discourse, it appears for example that talking to others and using their experiences and perspectives as resources helped him to realize that he might have chosen to study the wrong discipline for him (IT). Talking with mountaineering professionals, he also explored the possibilities and implications of becoming a mountain guide, thus giving a thinkable shape to his future. Talking to people is not a science, though; what are the criteria to orient oneself in the forest of opinions and experiences?

The Scout Experience as Symbolic Resource

Pat's high morals and sense of integrity are striking, and call for a closer look. The hypothesis developed here is that his socialization within the scout culture from 5 years of age, up to young adulthood, enabled him to elaborate a strong system of orientation. First reluctant to reveal this part of his experience, once questioned, Pat engaged into an enthusiastic discourse about scouts:

> The last group I was in, it was excellent. I was there, since I was 11. (...) And it was very good. We went everywhere. We went to Holland with them, we went to Slovenia together, we went all around the UK, we would have 2 weeks holidays everywhere. We had a minibus, tents (...), canoe and everything. We were a very well funded group, which I think helped a lot, because it helped me go to places and do things that I would have not been able to do otherwise. And everybody there was very cool. And I sort of worked my way through the ranks, so to speak. (...) So it was a very well run group, I was proud to be part of it. (...) Q *And the group you were with, you sort of grew up*

with them? Yes, yes, this was one of the main reasons to be in it. Because most of the things I did was sort of with them. And I made lots of friends there. And I did... I even ended up making a theatre production, with all the guides and scouts from around [the county] - came together and did this huge theatre production. It was such fun, I did that twice. (...) It was such good fun, it was fantastic fun! It was a very polished production (...) I mean, I don't want really to go into theatre or anything like that. But at the time, it was one of the best things I could have done! It was really exhausting, because I was going to school at the same time, and I was doing that production, and we would get home by 11-12, and I was 13 or 14 at the time. But it was just amazing. Because of the rush you get from doing that sort of things. I think it was very big issue for my development. *Q How?* – (Blushes) Because it stopped me going around nicking cars.

The experience of having being a scout seems to have been a very constructive one. It gave Pat a sense of belonging and participation in a group. As he progressed within the group, Pat came to take a leader role for which he was trained in management skills and first aid. Through this leading role, as well as through the theatre creation, Pat acquired skills, learned to follow rules, to take risks, but also to take responsibility, among which were to insure the smooth course of groups actions and their security. That frame must also have enabled more creative, playful experiences, like that with the theatre. Hence Pat had the experience of his competence and recognition from the in and the out-group (Heath, 1996, 2004). The scout experience is also described as what allowed him to escape from more delinquent lifestyles, mostly in terms of occupation of free time—but also probably in terms of identity consistency (Hundeide, 2004). At that time, however, Pat had to hide that experience from his peers:

A lot of people would - I mean, usually if you are in the scouts, you wouldn't say at school that you are in the scouts. *Q Yes?* Yes, because it is all a bit... you don't tell people that sort of thing. Because... Well, I had a great time. *Q Wait, wait: why wouldn't you say that sort of things?* Well, I don't know how it is in the country where you come from, but in this country, it is a bit... it's not cool, at all.

As he explains cautiously, scouts are strongly associated to a devaluated army; during the interview itself, Pat carefully explains the differences.

Pat's present job satisfaction is attached to these experiences; this enables him to reread his past with a feeling of gratitude, and to make generative projects—in the Eriksonian sense of transmitting it to others:

Yes, it was really enjoyable, but unfortunately it ended up when I was a bit too old. I might go back in a bit, and become a leader, and do that sort of thing. I think that might be fair, if I consider how much it has given me as a person. Because if I wouldn't be scout, I wouldn't be doing what I am doing, that outdoor thing. Because, I mean, my mum and dad don't really do that sort of thing. So... So it was really the scouts that opened that whole horizon to me. So I suppose it would be sort of right for me to give back some of the things I get out of that, and become a leader.

In summary, Pat had a very strong, enduring, committed, and rewarding experience within the scout movement. Its values and symbolic system might hence easily have been deeply internalized. Additionally, the fact that he had to hide that part of himself from other children might have even reinforced his fidelity to these values, as belonging to secret groups or to minority groups might produce (Deconchy, 1973, 2003). That feeling of exclusivity might also have helped him to keep some inner distance towards other lifestyles. Hence, Pat's high morals as well as his ability to explore possible ways without losing himself might reflect his use of resources that come from that cultural system.

I would thus propose that the mobilization of the scout experience offers resources for Pat's transitions in various ways. First, it allows him to resist the alienating first job: Pat discovers that he has high morals (L4) mediation, and it gives him a criteria to interpret some class of actions at L3 and L2 as contradictory with these morals, and thus to interpret his negative feelings (L1). Hence, the scout system offers the structure of Pat's sense of orientation and protects his sense of self-integrity (what sort of person he is and can be). Second, the experiences provides him with the skills and the experience of outdoor sports, that enables him to get his second job (L2, L3), and become a resource for his outdoor identity (L3). Third, Pat reconnects his present experience with positive experiences of his childhood, and transforms them into a horizon of a possible future. At the time of our meeting, he was indeed very excited to go to an outdoor fair, and seriously thinking about training as a mountain guide.

A Professional Project

Pat has not entered higher education, and has not learned formal metareflection. Asked about his cultural experiences, Pat describes watching various movies, a bit of science fiction and thriller reading. These do not play a major role in his decision and actions, and seem to stay authentic imaginary experiences enjoyed as ludic leisure, not *about* anything else. This does not preclude Pat from using relevant resources for the work of transition, as I have tried to show. Also, it does not prevent him from acquiring an important degree of reflectivity on his action. Hence, in these two last sequences, we see Pat distancing himself from the here and now, and elaborating on his position:

I mean... in getting that job, it also expanded my horizon a huge amount. Because now I am thinking what I want to do in the future, I realised, through working in that shop, that computer really isn't it. Because you realise, looking at the stock market, that IT is going down. So I realise that this was probably a good thing. (...) And getting some experience... Because I think since—over the last couple of years I have grown up more - more in that couple of years that I had before. Because I have actually - erm, got myself a job, and I moved out of my parents' house. And it sort of opened up all these avenues. And you end up looking at things differently, and studying things, seeing... and it just helps when you have got a bit of maturity behind you, and you kind sort of think about what you want to do. But I am still in that sort of phase, I am still not completely sure about what I want to do.

Through his interactions with others and his experience of being a scout, Pat appears to have developed distancing semiotic means, and a reflective stance (note the "I think," "I realise"). Pat has developed a time perspective, linking his past to a future orientation that tolerates uncertainty: he might become a mountain guide, but might start to study again when ready to commit himself enough, or, in the longer term, he might become a scout leader. Also, we see Pat engaged in meaning bricolage: linking various forms of information, provided by the media, his own or other people's experiences. His choices are not defined in the here and now, but as part of a multileveled system of orientation (for example, integrating *my experience with IT—the role of these companies—IT in the world*). Hence, Pat has turned scouting and discussing with others as into social and symbolic resources through which he could transform leaving-school transitions into developmental changes, actualized in his professional choices that comprise identity changes and skill acquisition.

BIBLE AND BIOGRAPHIES TO SKETCH A LIFE: THOMAS

Julia, Eli, and Pat are extreme cases of users of resources: their transitions are clearly identified, and they have some reflective understanding of the resources they used. Beyond the variety of ruptures—loss of a close relationship, or changes of sphere of experience and of possible identities—each of these trajectories is shaped by generative uses of symbolic resources. In other cases—and in most of the cases—ruptures and resources are less easy to identify, partly as an effect of the alchemy of interviews, partly because of the less reflective stance of interviewees, and partly because they are still in the blurred zone of trying to define their work of transition. The two next cases are chosen for their less clear-cut boundaries.

Leaving the Old World

Thomas left his little island to go to boarding school; there, encouraged by his schoolteachers, he applied to University. Before starting his studies, he took a gap year abroad, during which he worked as a teacher in a school in a remote country. Appearing shy at first, Thomas however talks a lot, quite freely, but in a very modulated way.

In psychosocial terms, Thomas has experienced a geographical relocation and thus a change of his sphere of experience. Looking at his discourse, it seems that it is not so much the departure from his island for boarding school, or his arrival at University that he experienced as a rupture. Rather, it seems, the transition work in which Thomas is engaged is the whole process of distancing himself from the form of life developed on his island, in order to define his own system of orientation. In effect, through the interview is pictured an opposition between the island and its inclusive, religious, traditional form of life, and Thomas' new values and commitments. His narration is that of a one-way departure process, starting with boarding school: he does not intend to "bury his cross there" (in his island).

Thomas describes the life in his island. Although he tries to give a fine-shaded account, avoiding simplification, the life on the island appears conservative and rigorous. While he was living there, his actions seem to have been permanently limited by strict rules (more or less explicit), and permanently made visible and sanctioned by others and the community.[7] He would for instance have to abstain from playing football on Sunday to avoid hurting his grandparents. The village life appeared him as hypocritical—people's deeds do not correspond to their discourse; it indicates that he developed some critical distance, while also complying with its rules. As a result he had the feeling of living a double life. Leaving the island, in contrast, enables Thomas to define his own codes of conduct, for which he has to account to himself only.

> Yeah, I mean - - I mean the older I come - - become, the more I exercise my will over as such over - - it is very easy to live somewhere like [the island] and have a lot of attitudes (...). And I think it is important to challenge these attitudes - and trying to - well, trying to reason at least anyway. - I would say - - - went I away to [boarding school], and especially as a result of my gap year, I was - I am more open-minded overall. (...) I wouldn't say travelling in a place particularly opens my eyes to new people's lives, I would just say, I was never ignorant to how other people live, I was never such a va—I would just

say, - it enables you to - - to experience of other degrees of openness. I feel more... --- while I'm here, I am never thinking well if I do so and so it will offend so and so. I am very comfortable, - I am confident about what I do, when I am at home or when I'm here, but here I feel comfortable because nobody will disapprove of what I do, whereas at home I would always feel uncomfortable—I mean, I would worry that people would disapprove. This is what I mean.

But if it is so, on what criteria will Thomas define his line of conduct and exert his will? Asked about what he brought to university, Thomas lists his sound-system and music, books, pictures, and objects from his trip, and two flags: the Union Jack (the UK flag) and a flag linked to his island. Among the books are political biographies (Margaret Thatcher, John Major, Alan Clark) and the Bible's daily-readings. Like any other personal objects, these can be seen as markers of identity, as having memorial functions, and as supporting one's sense of self (e.g., Habermas, 1996/1999a, 1999b). Rather than examining the flags and their role in identity construction and social positioning, I will concentrate on the role of political biographies and bible-reading, and their uses as symbolic resources. My focus here will be less on their use for emotional elaborations—which they probably aid in—than on their role in supporting a project and mediating higher-level values.

The Bible to Guide Everyday Conduct

Thomas explains having been raised religiously; he defines himself as a believer. His present religious affirmation is said to result from a conscious choice made as a teenager:

> I guess, when you are 13, 14, 15, you have to decide whether you're going to continue this kind of beliefs, or go away from that. And I decided to go on. *Q And it is a conscious decision?* Yes, I wouldn't say it is a particular moment, it is difficult to keep a middle ground.

He presents his commitment based on his relationship to God rather than to the church (L4). He says that he tries to organize his life on this basis: you should live "in accordance to your faith." He receives a journal with daily-readings of the Bible sent from the island by his grandmother. Hence, Thomas' religious life appears partly as a result of an act of personal agency, and partly as a strong means to maintain a link to his family and his island, beyond the rupture he seeks. In terms of practices, he tries to read the biblical texts every night. From these readings, he deduces values to guide his life (L3). In turn, it seems to enable him to reflect on his daily actions (L1 and L2):

› Things like forgiveness, compassion, y -yes, inner conviction, you know - - - - this guides, so, yes, I find it very useful. (...) I think that there have been times, not just here, but also elsewhere, that I - probably got quite often - in different places - feel stressed academically or whatever. And – I think, you know - it (...) it helps you to put in perspective, it says - you know, God - if you worry or so, will take care of you - gives you what you need – and - if you trust in him, you - you will - he will take care about your needs, don't worry about things, then you don't need to worry about things - hum - just trust, I suppose. Or an example you know, as an enticement, at times, there have been times where - - I - had arguments with people, sometimes in the evening - yeah - and then you go back, and it says, you know - forgiveness is important - even - it would say, I suppose you know, - Jesus has died on the cross for you. So it was like, compared to that, to forgive somebody who you just called... to whom you have said something stupid or so, is very small –

Bible readings are used for emotional regulation (stress), for the general principles they convey (forgiveness), but also, because they offer vignettes of the life of Christ as resources. Thinking about Jesus on the cross is a powerful mediation to reflect on one's conduct: it promotes a range of possible conduct, and indicates which ones have to be excluded (Valsiner, 2004c). These images can also be seen as a way to evaluate one's applications of rules in everyday life.

› I suppose - I guess, as a Christian, I would look to - the life of Jesus on this earth. And - I suppose in any situation you are in, if you say, "what would have Jesus done in this situation?," then, I would say, you, you know what the right thing to do is – and it might end up in other questions.

Thomas uses such religious resources to think about his daily actions and his relationship to others, but also about political and worldly events, or about the way in which the media report them. His high level values (L4), as well as his identity definition as a believer (L3), facilitate his positioning and guide his judgements (L2).

Political Biographies and Setting Commitments

If religion can orient Thomas' decisions and help him to trust them, it does not give the content of his commitments. Asked about his future plans, he answers in a surprisingly straightforward way (compared to the rest of his discourse):

› Well - I have - - - I have kind of political ambitions. I like politics. I would like to get involved in politics - - (...) I would quite like to be an MP.

Such strong assertion appears as a powerful organizer of his system of orientation, time perspective, and actions. Politics and religion are deeply intermeshed in that system, and to sustain that combination, Thomas uses political biographies of conservative party politicians as symbolic resources. In these biographies, politicians are religiously committed, and appear as deeply *driven* toward their aims.[8] Other interviewees mention similar admiration for Mao or Lenin as driven figures; here, it is Thatcher that offers such a driven figure:

> Thatcher I find her more - - I enjoy reading for example the *Downing Street Years*, more than the John Major's autobiography, because there is a bit more construct, I find, a bit more conviction. A bit more a sense of xxxx, whatever one might say - she was somebody of hard drive, an inner conviction. I mean she is someone to admire for a lot of reasons. She was Britain's first woman prime minister. - - And I find reading the Miner's strike, the xxx - such things, - you might not agree with her, but at the same time, you can't help but admire her - - her conviction. I think - - she is ... she is always ... from what she writes, you will get the impression that she never really loses her faith as it were in her ss... in her beliefs (..) *Q Did you read this biography before you came to University?* (...) Yes, I used to read them at school. So I particularly liked Mrs Thatcher's biography. It sort of lightens the way. But I admire her, I don't know, perhaps because she was part of my childhood, but I was young, I didn't really engage with that. *Q You heard about it* xx Yes, you probably raise your interests for things in your childhood that you don't really... you were not fully aware of. xxx Quite interested in what happen in the 90 xxxx up until to now, some people think it's good, some people think it's terrible, but whatever you say, it changed.

First, Thomas has heard of Margaret Thatcher in his childhood, when she might have been the object of adults' discussions; he took it in early semiotic dynamics. Using Thatcher now, is to use a resource that, like the Bible, offers a bridge to a childhood that has been put at a distance, both geographically, and probably through the departure to boarding school.

Thatcher is presented as someone who "lightens the way": she is a figure indicating the possibility of walking towards one's aim, beyond social disapproval and difficulties, supported by one's straight convictions. Biographies can indeed embody basic cultural narrative forms (Bakhtin, 1937-1938/1981; Gillespie, 2005). John Mayor's biography is clearly an ascensional narrative, the continuing metaphor through the chapter's title being that of climbing the ladder. Margaret Thatcher's is different: she represents her leading position as having mathematical evidence for its existence, and her life as a series of problem-solving, all addressed with the same convictions, hard work, and sense of justice (Thatcher, 1993).

The model of the narrative might be that of a driven person, against the incomprehension of others, supported by her faith, working for her vision of a better world (see also Mc Adams & Bowman, 2001, on genres of biographical narratives).

As an illustration, see how Miss Thatcher grounded her political activities in an early realization as a young politician: "I could not help noticing a curious discrepancy in the behavior of my colleagues. What they said and what they did seemed to exist in two separate compartments" (Thatcher, 1993, p. 13); she thus decided to develop her conservative intuitions "either into a coherent framework or a set of practical policies for the government" (p. 14), and she chose the latter. She also makes frequent allusion to the Bible in her discourses, finding illustrative parables, and positioning herself as a Christian (that is, driven by morality).

We might see similarities between that figure and the little we know about Thomas: an early realization of the hypocritical nature of his sphere of experience, where people claim some values but act inconsistently, as he finds in his island; the need to reinvent oneself; a strong will; the Bible as a resource. Hence, the biography might offer points to anchor empathy, and create a resonance between Thomas and Thatcher's stories. By extension, her leading figure might, through identification, help Thomas to maintain his trust in his goal and values; the narrative might offer a symbolic support to coordinate his ideas and conduct, and orient these toward his political goal (becoming an MP). Biographies might thus give, as Thomas says, "templates for the future." Additionally, such current symbolic resources as modern biographies—which are historically and factually based, and which reveal some of the intricacies of the nation's politics—also help to understand the social and political world in which Thomas wants to play a role.

Templates for the Future, but What About the Past?

In Thomas' case, the Bible and political stories can be seen as orienting his uses of other resources. Hence, asked whether other texts might be used as templates as well, Thomas proposes an example of a narrative used as a moral tale (or as a Biblical parable):

> Last time I finished the *Remains of the Day*, I suppose it might teach you, that it might ... that some opportunities might be offered one time, and if you don't take the opportunity, that might have as a consequences to be wrecked for a long time, in terms of different levels, in terms of personal life, in terms of academic, of personal ambitions (...) (Thomas narrates the story)- he blindly follows his employer, so on one hand he is obsessed

with his personal dignity, and on the other hand, because of his dignity he never takes the opportunity [... to address this woman]; and he never faced up what his [pro-Nazi] employer was indeed doing. I suppose there are two levels, yes.

After which, in the interview, Thomas reflects on his use of symbolic resources:

I think you can only ever take information as templates for the future. (...) No point in going over and over [the past]. You're encouraged to change what can be changed. (...).

Thomas' use of symbolic resources is resolutely turned toward the future. That might indicate the wish to break from his past, possibly because its memory is painful. One interpretation of this rejection of the past might be linked to village life. Another one might be connected to Thomas' departure to boarding school, which might have imposed a strong rupture and promoted success-oriented values (as suggested by Duffell, 2000; Mc Gowan, 2001).

Thomas' choices and use of symbolic resources thus seem to correspond to two parallel, if not contradictory, streams of thought: on one side, Thatcher' biography externally supports the type of values and orientations that Thomas wants to achieve, possibly as a result of schooling, and the Bible supports the system of orientation he is defining as a template for the future; on the other side, Thatcher and the Bible have an anchorage in Thomas' childhood. Hence, even though it might not be compatible with the self-made narrative that Thomas explicitly promotes, his future-oriented use of resources is grounded in the past. This is two sided. First, this past-anchorage seems to offer some depth to these resources—they are deeply internalized and structure one's personal culture; because they are solid, they might offer some space for exploration beyond the known, as is required to create possible futures (Winnicott, 1971/2001). Second, because of their anchorage in Thomas' childhood, these future plans do not threaten, even if they do not support, his sense of continuity beyond the transition. Such an anchorage would be a gage of efficiency. Through such semiotic process, thus, Thomas has reinforced his identity in a new position, from which he now engages in learning.

In contrast, let me mention the case of Adam, another active Christian young man, also engaged in daily Bible readings, teaching religion, and concerned with political and social injustice. Yet his sensibility to social inequalities finds no way to be associated with his Biblical discourse: religious experience and political concerns appear as disjointed fields of experience. Additionally, as a cause or as a result, or by lack of supportive symbolic resources, neither religion nor politics lead to projects for the future. One might suggest that Thomas succeeded in combining these spheres of experience, internalized early on, reflected on and consciously maintained, into a coherent project and high-level values, by having used as symbolic resources political narratives that represent religion and politics as entwined, and personified by strong figures, who guide possible ways of conduct.

THE AMBIGUITIES OF PROPAGANDA: MAX

Like Julia and Thomas, Max comes from a distant area of the United Kingdom and is surprised to have the opportunity to come to University. After high school, Max took a gap year, but unlike Thomas or Eli, did not spend it in a formal setting to learn or to teach. Rather, he chose to work in a pub, a factory and on construction sites, and to travel. Max's language is fluid, funny, in forms of short vignettes or anecdotes, concluded by "this was good fun." In this interview, both the use of symbolic resources and the experience of rupture are less explicit than in the previous ones. It might indicate one limit of the method used here, or the fact that Max is less reflective on the specific points explored here, or more likely, that some work of transition is still in the making. Anyway, one or two of the stories he narrates lose their light tone at times, and I see these change as cues that indicate more painful, or less elaborated aspects of Max's experience (Zittoun, 2001).

Coming to University—Soothing and Linking Resources

Max experienced the psychosocial transition that is to move town, to quit the parental house and to enter a University lifestyle. That psychosocial transition does not seem to have been perceived as a strong rupture. Max deals with it by reinstalling his room around him, and by using his social skills to create a social network. The first use of symbolic resources is about himself, as we have seen with Julia:

> Yes. I brought quite a lot of my stuff here. My room is pretty full. Like I hold quite a lot of things and I love having them. My room is covered with posters and photographs and stuff. It is quite clothed. I like quite a lot of tissue and I clothed that, I guess. So yes, I brought a lot of things. *Q What did you bring?* Mh? *Q What did you bring?* Oh, I brought a lot of photos that I've just taken over the past years or so, photos of my friends and stuff, erm posters of bands, art prints, art... like stencils... lots... some - like... things I've made. Lots of stuff like that. All my CDs, books etcetera. *Q What kind of posters - you*

said your stuff and? Erm. Yes, erm, some like just original posters of like bands or something. And then a couple I got in France, like billposters that I took out, things that have a kind of half sentimental value (xxx). Stuff like that. Then one print that I bought, for some 20 quid or like that. Some of American artist guy - who did sort of nice stuff. (...) I think partly the reason I brought a lot of stuff, it is because it is like, because I like to have lots of stuff, but it is also a bit of who you are. So like when people come in your room, they sort of see different stuff... and I guess they can put you in little box.... So it's useful..(...) No, because some rooms you go in, are pretty like sparkling... and... It is quite interesting. People who are obsessively tidy... I always tend to be slightly suspicious of people who have too tidy rooms. (Laughs..) yes – don't write that.... - No, not totally serious, but but when you see rooms which are just kind of bare, (...) It might be more conducive to work, but for me I don't think it would be good for general - sanity ... cause my walls are knitted of like sketches, because you can read something on. If I get the blues I can stick onto it. (...) *Q Do you have reasons to go back to your art books?* I don't know, I guess it somehow it is out of boredom, or if I get procrastinated and all... - - Some of it, I guess might be is nostalgic, [some might be to look back to see] what I was thinking one year ago or so. - But ... I can't think of any major reason.

Clothes, posters, pictures have a resource value taken as a whole. As in Julia's case, they offer an external envelop, a soothing and comforting space ("If I get the blues," "If I get procrastinated") that reconnects to oneself ("who you are," "what I was thinking"), as one was before coming (verbs such as *holding*, *sticking* emphasize these retrospective uses, see chapter 4). This first use addresses feeling and impressions at L1, but Max seems to have, like Julia, an implicit understanding of his need to use such resources as self-regulating means.

In his new life environment, where one of the first challenges is to meet people, Max's room and objects are also used to support identity work, as means to position himself and establish new interpersonal relationships. They appear as a form of externalization; the room shows others who you are, helps people he meets to "put you in a little box." It also enables to maintain new relationships, for example through swapping CDs that Max presents as a socializing technique. Such uses, that enable conduct at L2, still do not require us to take into consideration the content of the resources.

If Max's use of some of his objects is about himself and his new social network, his interest in art and graphics seem to have a particular status. He does not share such interests; they do not appear to be used for social aims. They are also not directly self-regulating; yet these seem to coincide with various aspects of his experience, as we will see.

The Rupture: Seeing the "Other" World

If coming to university seems to be easily dealt with, is there no other rupture felt as such? Let us turn back to the gap year experience. During that period, Max worked in pubs with friends; this brought him to discover another face of the town: the world of workers and alcoholics. Working in a meat factory, meeting a young worker, he had a disquieting experience—and this is where we see more signs of a rupture:

> Yes. I don't know, working in a factory was quite interesting, because... There were like guys, like my age, no, like yeah, I was 18, and they were like 19-20. At work night shift, that is from half-five, to half-three in the morning, and then get like 4.20 an hour, which is not good, right? And they would get up in the morning to have the school run, because a lot of them had kids. And this is kind of weird, because it is a totally different world to what I know?, and what I am used to. And that was an eye-opener. And just how really boring the work is. It is like, ten hours and then you have your break, breaks that you are not paid for, and you have your coffee and smoke fags, and - - eat, I guess. But - it's (hm) pretty crap work, and it's kind of weird, because they had like kids, and not so much older than me. - - There is no way... there is no way I'd trust me with a kid like... I don't know it's just a different world. (Tone changes) But it's quite cool to see people doing that.

In Max's heavy tone of discourse,[9] appears a sense of shock and of loss: the factory experience, that has been very hard, seem to have hurt his feeling of what is a normal life, what is given and taken for granted. He discovers another possible life—it is "an eye-opener." Through his friendship with another worker, he also enters into a dynamic where he can adopt the perspective of another—see himself as that other, or as the other sees him ("it's kind of weird, because they had like kids, and not so much older than me. - - there is no way ... there is no way I'd trust me with a kid"). For this experience of radical displacement, I would call this a rupture. It has been a distressing one: Max speaks at length of the smell of the chemicals on himself, the impossibility to take it away hours after leaving the factory, the way it covers the taste of food, modifying all his life and free time out of the factory, a form of alienation.

Yet it is not that Max had never thought of the factory or the worker's life before; but if, it might have been through a more romantic version, through what he presents as his preferred novels—*Animal Farm, Les Misérables, 1984*, or readings about the Russian revolution (some of which recommended by his brother). The rupture can thus be seen both as resulting from a change of social sphere of experience, and on a more intrapsychological plane, from a clash between imaginary, idealized fact, and plain reality.

Art as Resource for Playing With Ambivalence

Max's feeling of alienation in the factory joins another recurrent semantic field in his discourse: that of coercion, fascination, and propaganda. On one side, he notes the power of the coercion imposed by his family about the church. Max explains that his parents are committed Catholics, and that he was asked to go to church until he was about 17 years of age. His older brother distanced himself from the church, which helped him to do so as well. Although nonpracticing, Catholicism is present in his identity and easily triggered—for example, he says, it became very salient when his class discussed *Protestant ethics*. He has an ambivalent position: he acknowledges "the moral value" of religion, and the fact that his father has respectable religious commitments; yet he also displays his confusion and revolt about questions such as sex before marriage. On the other side, he describes his fascination for propaganda and advertising, but his simultaneous rejection of it. For instance, talking about his choice of studies, Max mentions his pleasure of having spent one year on an art foundation course; yet he decided not to pursue arts. It does not offer enough safety for future employment, and he might not be "driven enough" to succeed as an artist. Additionally, comes this reason:

> One of the main problem with arts - I mean I am in kind of graphics, and graphic design, and a lot ... well, the main focus in graphics is advertising... And - that was something I didn't want to do. *Q Why?* Because ... I don't know... It FASCINATES, advertising fascinates, but some... I get a bit annoyed, and irritated by it. Cause... it is intrusive, and a lot of it is such crap. *[Q You mean on the wall, printed adverts etc?].* Yes. Because I don't see many adverts because - OH yeah, I don't have TV, so printed averts. And at the end, I kind of admire... I kind of admire the tricks they use to, kind of manufacture the kind of needs, like all the things like repetition and that stuff, and - making you think about stuff. But... it's quite good. But But I don't think it is -- it's not- - it's not safe, it's not moral, some of it is a bit dodgy.

Max expresses his ambivalence: graphics fascinate and are admirable, and they are also intrusive and coercive. As a result, they are irritants and nonsafe. To take distance from them, Max has to call for higher-level principles: these are dodgy and not moral (this point is not developed, but the morals might reasonably be related to self-determination, etc.). Max seems to find a cultural experience that enables him to explore all the ambivalence and contradictions he is struggling with: the work of the artist Shepard Fairey, who has diffused stickers of *André the Giant*, and of whom he bought a print:

> He did a lot of - he did a lot of stickers, and basically, he made, he did this picture of a wrestler, and so he learns how to make stencils, and so (...) (Max explains how these stencils are made, and how the artist used to spray around skates places) he made a lot of stickers, and people saw this picture that had no apparent meaning, everyone knew *André the Giant*. He kind of created a brand without any thing, and it kind of spiralled. - You can see stickers of *André the Giant* in London, or in New York... I've seen some stickers of *André the Giant* in London, and now everyone knows. And now he does also posters as well. Kind of... a bit like old Russian propaganda posters. But - he seems quite fascinating that guy, how he just created his own... - - (he did some advertising, and used the same principle as it is used in the VW campaign). You see one, and then you ask what it is. It builds up. You keep asking What is it, what is it... you know you are being manipulated, but you keep going.

Shepard Fairey is an American artist, and comes from the skating scene. Looking for new motives to spray, he came to the idea of using the image of *André the Giant*, a forgotten wrestler champion—and thus turning it from *not cool* into *cool* (Sugar Skateboard Magazine, 2000) (see figure: the face on the screen is *André the Giant*). Eventually, he developed billboards, stickers, and stencils, that were to be seen everywhere in the urban space, and that are available for others to spray. He is now an acknowledged artist, and the author of a *Manifesto* where he explicates the function of his stickers, that

> attempt to stimulate curiosity and bring people to question both the sticker and their relationship with their surroundings. Because people are not used to seeing advertisements or propaganda for which the product or motive is not obvious, frequent and novel encounters with the sticker provoke thought and possible frustration, nevertheless revitalizing the viewer's perception and attention to detail. (Fairey, 1990)

Fairey thus gives a moral frame behind a fun practice. Although Max does not refer to that *Manifesto*, he admires the artist, and explains his legend to me; his language echoes it (he speaks about propaganda), and so do his practices (having a notebook where he notes down funny sentences heard around him). This suggests that Max is aware of the whole frame of experience proposed by Fairey.

André the Giant's stencils are to be seen everywhere; yet there is only a small community of people who know what they mean. Seeing these

Symbolic Resources in Developmental Transitions 169

Figure 5.2 Shepard Fairey: Computer.

stencils is mediated by, or mediates, a feeling of belonging to that invisible community; and this is itself mediated by the rules proposed by Fairey. The whole semiotic prism enables one to enter a regulated space for transgression and inversion: wrestler becomes cool, the slogan "obey!" means "be aware!", the aesthetic is that of communist or fascist propaganda but the portraits are of rappers, and so forth. Hence, the art expressed in the stickers of *André the Giant* offers a cultural experience as such, and it is linked to a specific symbolic system. Within this well-defined frame, Max accepts engagement in a ludic, playful, and gratuitous cultural experience (Koepping, 1997). Such an art escapes the seriousness of both religion and the coercive forms of advertising, and enables experimentation with some of the feelings they promote—being fascinated and manipulated, knowingly—which is pleasurable.

This art appears to work in parallel with Max's preferred reading—the whole of Orwell's work, *Les Misérables* and on the Russian revolution: all offer imaginary zones for experience and reflect on the fascination and danger of coercion and propaganda. Max seems at ease with such a ludic space. His interest in village gossip while working in pub go in the same direction. During the interview, as well, Max interrupted the dialogue to note down a small sentence heard through the window and coming from the street nearby; it gave him obvious pleasure, and he said he liked to collect such things. All these cultural experiences, offered by the environment or created by himself, enable him to play with spying and controlling, being manipulated and surprised—but in a safe, pretend mode. There, one need not to decide whether it is good or bad to be played by other's discourses or to play with them; it has no consequences, and does not need to be regulated by higher rules or norms.

The *André the Giant* art and the narrative that promotes it offer an extended imaginary zone to symbolize the contradictions Max experiences. *André the Giant* gives a form to feelings of distress and ambivalence (L1); as a cultural element, it can be shared with others, and explored in the material and social space (L2-L3). Max sees everyday an *André the Giant* poster in his room, and looks for the stickers in towns; he thus keeps himself thinking about these issues that are now symbolized outside of him, thus represented to him. It is likely that this will give him some distancing toward these feelings and worries, as his invested discourse on advertising suggests. In link with these interests, Max seems to cultivate an arty outlook and conduct which define an identity position, towards himself and others. However, it is difficult for me to clearly identify higher-level values (L4) affirmed through that resource; rather, scepticism or ambivalence about possible commitments might be externalized.

At the end, Max deals with ruptures at various levels of generality. Some of the immediate aspects of moving to the university town are dealt with in such a way that he can maintain a sense of continuity with his past, while creating opportunities to meet new people. In the broader picture, though, things are more complicated.

Having renounced a religious system of orientation that did not satisfy his needs and curiosity, yet keeping some principles (what is morally good or bad), Max is in a floating situation. His temporary acceptance of his choice of study is based on resignation rather than supported by a more general project: as he says, everyone who can write a good essay can succeed reasonably well at university, whereas only driven artists can chose that more difficult path. In parallel, Max finds symbolic resources to play with questions not yet solved: commitment and coercion, freedom and moral consistency. His use of symbolic resources might be said to offer a *poetic space* of ambiguities, where meanings and values do not need to be fixed (Abbey, in press). Although Max is engaged in identity repositioning and learning, he is still engaged in meaning making processes. At this point, it is impossible to know how this semiotic work might turn these issues into a more sustainable and invested project for his future: the transition work still seems going on.

A DISCUSSION OF FIVE CASE STUDIES

These five cases studies open a little window on youth transitions. These five life trajectories are treated as equivalent, for the analysis is focused on points of equifinality—a rupture perceived as such. Given a particular rupture, people find in their environment or in their memories possible ways to handle uncertainty and newness. They do so by mobilizing their own past experiences, their memories of other's experiences, or internal-

Table 5.1. Five Transitions, Synthetic View

Person	Main Ruptures	Main Symbolic Resources (SyRe)	Used for*	Significant Others Real/ imaginary	Change Through SyRe?
Julia	Death grandma (interpersonal)	Manic St. Preachers Orwell, Sartre	L1, L2, L3 L4;* Slf; social.* PF	Peer group Singer	Grief → Educational project
Eli	Back to secular life (frame change)	Religious texts Hesse, *Graduate*	L1-3(link L4) Slf; intepers; P-Pr. -F	Parents, rabbi,	Split → Comprehensive life
Pat	Leaving school (frame change)	Scouts (& talking with others)	L1-L4 idty, interpers; social P-Pr-F	Scouts, acquaintance	Dropout → Mountain guide project
Thomas	Leaves an island (value change)	The Bible Political biographies	L4, L3, L2 Social (P) F	Grandma, pol. figures	Isolated margin →MP project
Max	Factory shock (frame change)	Graphics Orwell, *Misérables*	L1-4? Social (Poetic space, timeless)	Father, Brother André G.	Ambivalence: Coercion Û Art?

Notes: * Levels of mediation
Aboutness: Slf = Self; Interpers. = interpersonal; Social = social environment; Aboutness:
Time perspective: P = Past; Pr. = Present; F = Future

172 *Transitions: Development through Symbolic Resources*

ized cultural experiences. They also find in their environment people to interact and discuss with, and look for new cultural elements that might provide resources.

Hence, because cultural elements are accessible to all of these young persons, our approach renders visible streams of symbolic work: a cultural element or system is available, interacted with, internalized, mobilized and somehow used as a resource, and eventually externalized. Studying symbolic resources offers a traceability to processes that are always engaged in thinking. In turn, such an analysis does not pretend to reveal what really happened to young people.

The analysis, focused on ruptures, transitions, and uses of symbolic resources, can be summarized as shown Table 5.1.

In this last section, these five cases will be discussed synthetically, and will be used to reflect on the notions of rupture, transition, and construction of a time perspective. On this basis, chapter 6 will be addressing the question of development through symbolic resources.

Contextually and Historically Bounded Ruptures

Interview participants were chosen for their likelihood of being in processes of transition after having experienced a rupture—a genuine disquieting feeling. However, the analysis reveals that even ruptures are shaped and enabled within sociocultural, psychic, and historical constraints.

The five young people from the case studies experienced a rupture, clearly expressed by some, less by Max or Thomas. However, young people were also interviewed who seemed even less to express a rupture, like Felix or Orson (chapter 3). Both have been to boarding school, and are very aware of their needs: they balance sports, hard working, and leisure. In the interview setting, they answer politely, but disclose little emotional or imaginary life. They also do exhibit a limited use of symbolic resources. It is strange, for these young men, as all other interviewees, have lived through major objective changes: they took gap years, travelled around the world, started university. So how to explain the fact that they neither explicitly nor implicitly express a sense of felt rupture?

It might be that these students are shy or introvert, or that they have been socialized not to disclose their interiority in the frame of an interview. Another interpretation might be tried out: according to Dufell's (2000) analysis, British private boarding school students are confronted with early major ruptures, and have to develop efficient coping strategies. Early ruptures might explain why later ruptures are not perceived as so important. Also, Duffell's analysis is that these schools do not encourage—if not forbid—emotional life, fantasy, and self-knowledge. This might suggest that some boarding school students are encouraged to develop self-regulation techniques based on body management (e.g., sports) rather than on symbolic mediations (a process which might be not so specific to boarding schools).

At any rate, such hypotheses suggest that some social constraints can bring people *not to* experience ruptures, or *not to* use symbolic resources. It might be that some social settings encourage tension discharge rather than reflection, do not legitimize attention given to emotions, ambivalence, and fantasy. Such settings might not prevent people from changing —but they would not encourage a generative development integrating identity, learning, and meaning construction. Such sociocultural settings might also be powerful enough to durably shape a person's manner of apprehending uncertainty. Of course, this would need to be explored. The idea this suggests is that even rupture is not a context-free event.

In the five case studies appear a variety of perceived ruptures. Analyses enable the identified rupture to be relocated within life-trajectories. From that perspective, it appears that, on one side, a person has constructed and evolved her personal culture, her orientations and resources through time. On the other side, she has also a story of past ruptures. Hence, Julia's rupture of coming to university follows the rupture of losing her grandmother. One might say that the first rupture enabled the second, and provided her with resources for it. Thomas' coming to university is just part of a much wider process of transition. And Lewis (chapter 3) considers the current rupture as a way to repair the bad outcome of his last rupture—entering boarding school was tragic, entering university should be an occasion to undo and reshape his identity and position. A rupture is thus a rupture in a series; a person sees a new rupture on the line of sight given by experience or the memories of the previous ones. On that ground, one might wish to modify the logic of that series, or to conserve it. The relationships between ruptures will influence the work of transition in which one might engage. Resources might first of all be used to maintain and reinforce oneself, or to promote change, or create ruptures and call for reinvention. Hence, a rupture in a given life trajectory appears bounded by a story of previous ruptures.

What Symbolic Resources? What Uses for a Given Cultural Element?

Some cultural elements are recurrent through the cases, such as Orwell's work, biographies, and the Bible. What does it tell us? It might reveal shared needs and longings, typical for people of a certain age, in a certain state of society. For example, Orwell's novels are both fashionable and part of school programs. Yet it is striking that, 60 years after their publication, these are still moving young people like Julia and Max. If might be that, although politics and technique have changed over that time, the fears a young person has when approaching the adult world remain. Orwell's novels still give form to a diffuse anxiety, and distrust of the hypocrisy of a normative life, which subsists in the early years of the second millennium.

Biographies of driven people also correspond to another *Zeitgeist* discourse: one has to be a *successful*. Reading such biographies is a way to reread one's own situations, and possibly to reflect on aspects of one's personality that might lead to a successful trajectory. Biographies are constructed like imaginary identity narratives (escalation or metamorphosis genres, see Bakhtin, 1979/1986), framed as real-life stories (it really happened!). They appear as proofed identity tools.

What about the Bible, then? If we admit that the Bible is an excellent dictionary of possible aspects of human psyche, conduct, and relationships—from the most luminous to the most hideous, in its complexity and ambiguity—then we see it offers a very wide range of potential uses.

These three recurrent families of books seem to fulfil specific needs. When examined through the model of uses of symbolic resources, they can be seen as having quite different *aboutness*. For a young person that mistrusts the modern society into which she is entering, an Orwell book might offer symbolic resources that enable one, *primarily*, to elaborate one's relationship to the world. In contrast, biographies appear to be used much more towards oneself, for crafting one's future. Biographies appear as symbolic resources *primarily* useful for elaborating one's identity. Finally, even if uses of the Bible are potentially infinite, it is mostly religious people who use it—that is, people who are included within clearly bounded communities, and who try to follow a consistent system of orientation developed within the community. For them I would suggest, the use of the Bible *primarily* supports or reinforces one's system of orientation; the Bible can, for example, support bridges between high-semiotic mediation (L4) and concrete actions (L1) through metaphorical examples that become categories for thinking (L2, L3).

However, this is not so simple. One does not only react to the explicit message of a cultural element. One does not only empathize with the main character. One also reacts to structural and semantic aspects, sounds and colors, background figures and forms.[10] Because numerous lateral nonconscious linking can be awakened by a cultural experience (chapter 2), what the use of symbolic resources can do to a person is potentially infinite. Consequently, cultural elements are open to many uses; by themselves, they do not prescribe how they are to be used. *The Beach*—a traveller's novel set in Thailand—is used by someone as prospective tool in anticipation of a visit to Thailand; another person uses the same novel as a self-soothing device, rereading it every time reality becomes too threatening; a third one uses it to acquire skills that enabled him to observe and understand the body-language of other travellers during his trip in South America. *Anna Karenina* might be read by a person in anticipation of a trip to Russia, by another to relive her memories of a past trip, and by a third as a way through which to deepen his relationship to his beloved.

These logics of use question attempts to objectively evaluate symbolic objects. There have been long debates about the utility or weakness of various forms of cultural elements on the basis of their stylistic qualities, the intellectual demand they exert, their potential alienating power (Adorno, 1991), or the form of emotional commitment they require (Grodal, 1997). In contrast, the data observed here suggest that a given cultural element (the objective, available artefact) necessarily becomes a *different symbolic resource* for two different persons, who have internalized it in some specific conditions, integrated it to their personal culture, and used it to address a particular, personally relevant issue, at a given timespot of their trajectories.

On the basis of such observations, the only criteria of *richness* of a cultural element might be its power to invite various uses, its resistance to these, its openness to multiple interpretation by people in various sociocultural and historical locations, and the breadth of human questions and issues it might possibly help to reflect. The Bible and Tolstoy might seem more resistant to a diversity of needs, intentions, and uses than, possibly, the *Bridget Jones* diaries. But people's creativity in using what is available seems to have no barriers (cf. also Zittoun, 2001, 2004b): Wanda could use these diaries as resource after the loss of her brother (chapter 3). However, uses of symbolic resources are limited by internal and external constraints, as chapter 6 will show.

Processes of Transition

If uses of symbolic resources participate in the work of transition, then they should support identity repositioning and definition, learning and skill development, and meaning construction (chapter 1). The five aspects of cultural experiences described in chapter 2 should participate in such changes.

In terms of *work of identity*, processes of repositioning are very strong in the cases of Julia, Thomas, Pat, and Eli. Their uses of symbolic resources have enabled them to define new groups to which they want to belong, or new spheres of experience where they want to be acknowledged (or differentiated): the *Manic Street Preachers* fans for Julia; not car-stealers, but mountain guides for Pat; groups located outside the island for Thomas. Symbolic resources also mediate each of these people's relationships to others who will confirm that new location, from within or outside that new sphere of experience. Julia is acknowledged as a fan by other fans, or as a leftist by other people; Thomas is no longer considered a social deviant in his new sphere of experience. In turn, these relocations and new legitimacy change how these young people define or perceive themselves—for Julia, there is a clear change from the young Christian-science girl, to the agnostic-leftist; Thomas can now feel comfortable with his choices.

Identity changes promoted through the use of symbolic resources are partly due to the first aspect of cultural experience, their *sociocultural location*. In effect, approaching a given cultural element always implies a move on the societal board. The second aspect of cultural experiences, *manipulation and framing* can also enable identity work; for example, Julia, Max, or Thomas' room decorations reinforce their sense of continuity and consistency; Max's swapping CD's enables him to present his identity to others. Of course, identity work occurs through the *imaginary experience* itself, the third aspect of cultural experience: processes of empathy enable partial identification with the explicit content of the experience (the main characters of biographies read by Thomas), or with the shadow of the other behind it (the singer for Julia's songs, the artist for Max's stencil art). Such processes might alleviate the parts of personal identity which are difficult to bear, which can then be projected on that cultural element—hence Julia's pain of loss might possibly be said to be projected onto the figure of the dead singer. In other cases the imaginary experience supports an identity project, like in Thomas' case. Finally, *post hoc* elaborations, the fourth aspect of cultural experiences, enable these young people to realize these moves and to inscribe them in their personal narrative, itself culturally shaped.

Knowledge change and skill acquisition appear to be developed through the use of symbolic resources thus providing semiotic devices of various levels of mediation. Thomas says he learns to manage stress through his biblical readings, or possibly, through the regularity of his practice. Eli discovered the importance of the contents of fiction in helping him to reflect on his emotions. Julia learns factual and historical information through her explorations of song's lyrics and their related texts. Max's experience of *André the Giant* gives him some understanding of the efficiency of advertising. Thomas then developed metarules ("a novel can be read as a parable") that enable him to see a moral in every story. Through Jewish studies, Eli and Lev develop thinking heuristics that can be applied to other texts.

Hence, some of this learning is procedural, and some is content-based. Procedural knowledge itself can be of various types: thinking heuristics developed in Jewish learning are highly internalized and automatic; Thomas' uses of regulation procedures are more intentional and oriented towards a goal. Content knowledge taken from symbolic resources has various *aboutness*: it can enable self-knowledge, through reflectivity; but it can also suggest knowledge about others, or about the socially shared reality. More generally, contents can bring people to develop new perspectives on internal, interpersonal, or worldly events, and thus enable dialogical constructions of new understandings.

Again, various aspects of cultural experience can support such forms of knowledge. *Framing* activities are often part of the internalization of procedures, through regularity and the ritualization of symbolic uses. *Imaginary experiences* provide contents of knowledge or present metaphors or descriptions of actions. *Post hoc integration* appears important for rendering available information or skills for further uses, as well as for creating distinctions between knowledge that applies only to imaginary experiences, and that which might be relevant for real life.

The use of symbolic resources obviously participates in *emotional elaboration and meaning construction*. This is what we have explored at length: symbolic resources enter semiotic dynamics (the semiotic prism) which, at a microgenetic level, link emotional and experiential content to semiotic devices, which in turn can be linked to one's experience. At an elementary level, Julia's red textiles on her walls directly attach her current disarray to her mother's care. At another level, cultural elements enter similar semiotic dynamics, enabling one to organize or group thoughts and actions within a temporal structure: Eli's experience of coming back becomes shaped and meaningful once articulated through Hesse's novel, *The Glass Bead Game*. Through these two levels of semiotic dynamics, we have suggested, people construct and transform their hierarchies of internalized semiotic units, that serve as systems of orientation, and that offer the necessary distance to develop time perspectives (chapter 2). For example, Pat's scout experience leads him to develop high-morals, that mediate his conduct and support his projects.

Framing processes are important for meaning construction to take place: they create the boundary required for a person to engage in an imaginary experience, mobilizing real emotions. The alchemy of meaning making mostly occurs through the *imaginary* zone opened by the cultural experience, in which a person's inner world is diffracted onto many semiotic-emotional composites that evolve throughout the cultural experience. *Post hoc reflections* facilitate *framing out* procedures, and the process of reassembling after imaginary diffraction (Benson, 2001), that is, one's integration of changed aspects of self. When this fails, cultural experiences can continue to absorb a person, or haunt her, as one can be haunted by a bad dream (Freud, 1900; Tisseron, 2000); this was Xenia's reason for stopping seeing scary movies (chapter 3).

It is thus through such processes enabled by cultural experiences and the use of symbolic resource that emotional experiences might be symbolized and linked to one's memory, so that their unconscious prolongations might be worked out. These are processes of meaning making; and they secrete the two axes—level of mediation and time orientation—that organize the architecture of self. A little more must be said about the construction of a time perspective.

Time Perspective: Past, Present, and Future—and Projects

These case studies are collected in such way that young people have to talk about their past and their future. The question is, how are uses of symbolic resources linked to these past memories and the definition of futures? Do these uses really support these time perspectives? In chapter 4, a transversal analysis of the data suggested that people use symbolic resources to represent facets of past experience, to copresent current events, and to pre-present possible futures. I suggested that all of these time orientations might support change, but that these might be developmental only when past and future perspectives are combined. We have seen uses primarily oriented toward the past (watching framed images), uses accompanying processes of change (Max's explorations of *André the Giant*), and others which are turned to the future (Thomas' uses of biographies). How are these likely to be developmental?

In chapter 4, it was suggested that the use of symbolic resources might require a necessary two-step processes, on the same model as children's acquisition of signs and language. The assumption is that, when faced with uncertainty, humans have the psychological need to, first of all, ensure self-continuity; if it is so, uses of resources oriented towards the past and present are always prior to those towards the future. Hence, for every matter a person in rupture would have to address, or for every use of a particular resource, she would go through the same two step process—first representing and copresenting, and then only, in some cases, prerepresenting. Case studies support such ideas. Julia moves from soothing uses of songs, to their exploratory potential; Pat probably was happy to act as a scout in the here and now, although he now draws on these experiences to define future plans. The hypothesis would thus be that there is a chronology of a person's uses of resources. To move from past to future uses, one must find a form of security and safety—which can be physical and social (a virtual or a real community, a set of rules), or imaginary (a poetic, transitional space). The creation of that space permits the exploration of possibilities, in the case of adults as it is with children.

But do all young people develop a future orientation? And is this always developmental? This depends on the consistency of a person's system of orientation, I suggest.

All young people interviewed express some future orientation, vague, or clearly defined projects. Having a future-oriented project is a requirement dictated by young people's position within the contemporary social world. As future orientations are grounded in one's past, they can be more in continuity or in rupture to the latter (Zittoun, 2001, 2005a). Eli and Pat's symbolic resources are clearly linked to past and continuous experiences, and in both cases they bring to definition future projects in continuity with these past experiences. Thomas uses resources that have a link to his past; however, he defines a project implying a distance toward his past.

Do such projects guarantee better development? Will clearly defined future-representations be attained? The literature on this suggests that there is a long way from projects to their realization. In the literature on youth, goal setting and achievement has been shown to be a complex matter. In effect, some goals are too general and lack the realism to be implemented. The definition of goals does not necessarily coincide with commitments in actions that might possibly lead to their achievement (Charlot & Glasman, 1998; Gollwitzer, Bayer, Scherer, & Seifert, 1999; Nurmi & Salmelo-Aro, 2002). There is a long way for Thomas to go to become an MP; nevertheless, examining his reported conduct, it might be reasonably guessed that he is studying the right discipline in the right university, and that he might indeed be presented with possibilities that might eventually bring him to the political scene. Pat might well be trained as a mountain guide; yet this might be just an excursus for him before coming back to study. What seems important is a relative consistency within a person's system of orientation, and between the latter and a given sphere of experience. Goals must be linked to higher-level commitments, and some other mediations are required to link these to local conduct, which themselves need to be provided by the sphere of experience, so as to be oriented toward that project. Conduct itself can modify these higher mediations. Symbolic resources, that might transform these various levels of mediation, can support their harmonization, and render a person's system of orientation more consistent. In this way, the use of symbolic resources might practically guide one towards some sufficiently realistic and open future representations.

Additionally, goal-oriented actions might not be necessary for all forms of development. In some spheres of experience, an activity might incite development without explicit goals: young people might be engaged in occupational conduct that is enjoyable, or brings money, without it being the means to achieve explicit higher-level goals (Zittoun, 2004a).

Hence, in our frame of analysis, future orientation does not equate to goal-directed projects. Development is seen as enabled if future orientations mediate conduct in a sufficiently consistent way, not if projects or goals are attained.

Bricolage in the Architecture of Self

Using symbolic resources appears more like a messy bricolage than a calculated strategy. One of the five studied persons started to listen to a singer's songs by chance, one has been sent to scouts by his parents, and stickers on the walls struck another. Each of them was going through ruptures, and, traversed by unformulated questions, might have been gasping for bits of meaning. In their field of given constraints, they had to deal with available cultural elements.

Bricolage involves a form of *symbolic thinking* that clinical psychologists, rather than developmental ones, have been examining. To work, bricolage needs to bring together cultural elements or bits of meaning that seem to fit in, or to be relevant for a person's state of unelaborated experiences. In chapter 2, it was proposed that such symbolic thinking would require vertical and horizontal linking. These forms of linking are based on logics of proximity or resemblance, as in the conscious and unconscious mind (symmetrical linking). Hence, a person might respond to a cultural experience because of an emotional resonance (Julia's song for her grief); a semantic similarity (novell about Russia in Russia); a structural analogy (Eli's use of Hesse) (Holyoak & Thagard, 1995) or metaphorical relationship (Ricoeur, 1976). However, resonance to a cultural element also imply processes of displacement, splitting, or condensation of one's thoughts and emotions through one's cultural experience or its memory (Freud, 1900, 1901), and of trespassing codes-boundaries (it is possible to link colors and melody).

Symbolic bricolages are not built on nothing—they transform systems of orientation within the architecture of self. Eli's uses of Hesse are transplanted within a system of orientation developed through his socialization in Jewish culture. Julia's new personal culture is based on the ruins of her Christian system of orientation; Max's ambiguities come from his rejection of some of the Catholicism that structured him, without finding any equivalence.[11] Bricolages require the integration of new symbolic resources within the architecture of the self and its system of orientation.

Symbolic resources can be more or less relevant, or more or less consistent within these structures. Cultural elements are more or less personally significant, depending on how they are emotionally invested—for the quality of the experience they enable, or for being associated to significant others—and how much they awake secondary thoughts, horizontal, unconscious experiences. The more significant they are, the more likely they are to be partly internalized. Consistency might appear very pragmatic: it depends on what is relevant, for that person, in a situation perceived as requiring a new positioning, a learning or the elaboration of emotions. Hence Eli's use of the Bible and *The Graduate* movie are consistent with his religious faith: it provides the semiotic mediators he needs when facing secular life.

Integration of a new bricolage within the architecture of the self is likely to require processes similar to assimilation and accommodation (Piaget, 1964/1967), *provided that emotional needs and personal relevance are satisfied* (what is at times called empathy and identification). Assimilation to the system requires, at the minimum, a semiotic anchorage between new elements and the existing system: Thomas can thus use films as resources, because he expects to see moral lessons in these, as in biblical parables. Accommodation of the architecture of the self is its transformation due to new uses of symbolic resources, like in the case of Julia, whose entire world has been transformed to integrate the message of some songs.

Transformations of a system of orientation can probably take different paths. In the cases we have analyzed, some transformations seem to start from the lower levels of mediations, and slowly move to the highest; other start to affect high-level values and can, in some cases, finally change the bottom ones. Thomas' rupture touches his high-level orientation values; he is using symbolic resources to define goals and commitments, and *then* to promote some forms of action. In contrast, Julia started by mediating her actions and feelings, *before* progressively questioning higher-level values.

Finally, development has been defined as being the sort of changes through processes or transitions, which enable the person to be confronted with new orientations, without alienation.

Our empirical studies suggest that developmental changes seem to occur when there is a mutual irrigation and adjustment between practical conduct, feelings, and one's general definition of the situation. In contrast, if higher-level values do not enable action—because these are unrealistic or not adapted to the current situation, change is *for a while* not generative. Less developmental changes might thus appear when there is a great disjunction between what is given by the shared material and social reality, or what one feels and experiences, and one's existing means for understanding these experiences. Similarly, developmental changes are based on actions consistent with future oriented ideas, whereas thoughts only focused towards the past prevent change. Both levels of generality of semiotic mediation and time orientation rely on the same distancing processes.

However, developmentally speaking, the disjunctions between level of experiences, or between future and past, might be temporary. Violent ruptures in the life of a person who has little experience of similar ruptures might require a long time for her to stabilize new everyday local conduct; then only she might be able to explore possible or future worlds. Some people might have different priorities at certain points of their lives, where they accept that they will not develop a consistent understanding of some issues, while they are engaged in addressing others (Coleman, 1993). Cultural experiences open spaces where the multiplicity of these degrees of elaboration can coexist and be symbolized, thus reflecting the work in process of the architecture of the self. The use of symbolic resources offers varieties of distancing semiotic devices that can participate in the transformation of that system. But of course, all these beautiful effects are highly dependent on societal, situational, and psychological constraints, as we will now see.

NOTES

1. Picture: www.rawvision.com/back/picassiette/picass.html *Picassiette* is the nickname of Raymond Isidore, living and working in northern France. In French, a "pique-assiette" is a "scrounger, sponger or gatecrasher, someone whose interest in stealing a plate would generally be the food on it. 'Picassiette' may well be a pun on 'Picasso,' while 'piqué' can mean 'crazy' or 'nuts'. (...) It's an interesting thought that perhaps the way this nickname was invented was unconsciously mimicking what Isidore was doing. It took pieces of language, broke them up and created something new, just as he did with crockery." www.thejoyofshards.co.uk/pique2.shtml
2. Sociologists of religion observe that modern bricoleurs might have the illusion that they can use symbolic resources as they wish. This might lead to difficulties: some cultural combinations are meaningless or not functional (Bernand, Capone, Lenoir, & Champion, 2001).
3. I thank here the students that collected and analyzed these interviews, and Gerard Duveen who supervised them.
4. Religious Jews try to follow as much as possible the 613 Mitzvoth, the 613 "laws," which include obligations (among which study, prayer, etc.) and interdictions (among which the ones related to food and hygiene), regulated and adapted to various situations by the Halakhah, the law; Yeshiva life is collectively organized around them and facilitates individual's respects for them.
5. Religious Jews study Torah—which includes Talmud (Jewish law and its multiple layers of interpretation and controversies through the centuries, mostly Michnah and Gemarrah), Tanakh (the Pentateuch), the postbiblical

literature, and other issues such as philosophy or liturgy, under the supervision and the authority of rabbis. Students study in pairs of "Haverim," friends, who give each other a response or contradict each other's interpretation of a given text. A great part of the study is linked to the identification and the resolution of contradiction within the text, and the deduction of the application of rules or parts of the text to new hypothetical situations.

6. This side of Judaism has been especially emphasized by humanist Jewish authors such as Buber or Levinas.

7. Some time after this interview I saw the film *Dogville*, by Lars von Trier (2003): a village life with its transparent house, its isolation, its mad rules and people' claustrophobic insanity. Thomas' narration of his hometown gave me a similar impression.

8. It is because of this strong recurrence of the political themes in the architecture of self that I exclude the hypothesis that Thomas' affirmation about his wish to become MP is a joke or a provocation.

9. This event seem have been quite dramatic; the tone of the talk is very different except the last "quite cool." There is a long description of the impregnation of the meat flavoring, which might be an embodied displacement of his discomfort. Also, Max describes how, being "sick of that job," he impulsively decided to go to France.

10. The language of a Beckett gives another shape to one's thoughts and another space to one's emotions, than that of Zola (see Green, 1973/1999, 1992). The music beat of this movie does calm us, more than that other one. The aggressive colors of the film *Kill Bill* awake other zones of our embodied experience than the attenuated colors of *Amélie*.

11. Although these examples might suggest it, I am not stating that these systems of orientation ought to be religious. Other national, familial, cultural, or personal bricolage might have the same functions —see for example Lily and Mary (chapter 4). My emphasis reflects the fact that religious systems of orientation are, from my perspective, much simpler to identify within and through an interviewee's discourse. They can be named and discussed—although what they mean for each person must be carefully examined.

CHAPTER 6

CONCLUSIONS

Youth Transitions, Symbolic Processes and the Lifespan

> *I had arranged a bunk in the upper room and would sit for a long time on the stairs looking out over the Volga. I forgot everything around me. Hermann Hesse's Siddharta came into my thought those times. When Siddharta came to the ferryman, he spent time listening to the river. Dreams came with the flowing of water that I could see in the distance. I saw my past—a full, interesting life.*
>
> —A. H. Schütz, *Davai, Davai! Memoir of a German Prisoner of World War II in the Soviet Union* (1997, p. 58)

> *When did you last read something interesting in the papers?*
>
> —L. Vaculík, *A cup of coffee with my interrogator* (1986/1987, p. 1)

All through this book, we have seen people using symbolic resources, with some intentions, for some results. In this concluding chapter, I will build on these observations and the models developed to account for them. Going beyond mere descriptions, I will address three interrelated questions: What is the role of the use of symbolic resources in development? What kinds of development leads to the use of symbolic resources? And how does the use of symbolic resources itself develop? Raising such questions, this chapter extends reflections on symbolic resources and opens new routes of enquiry.

DEVELOPMENT THROUGH SYMBOLIC RESOURCES

The sceptical reader might now ask, these changes being shown, why would one think that interacting with cultural objects brings forth anything more than the trivial alterations of everyday life? Why should these changes be deep, serious, enduring, and, from a psychological perspective, developmental?

There is an external argument in favor of the idea that using symbolic resources promotes authentic and durable change within the architecture of the self, and with it, in a person's capabilities to feel, think, and act. The external argument is that, if symbolic resources were not powerful tools for change, dictatorships and totalitarian states, as well as modern so-called democracies, would not be so keen to control cultural elements available in people's environment. If a painting, a poem, or the Bible have been considered as counterrevolutionary under communism, it is because they enabled people to feel or see the world in a new or different manner. During World War II, American film studios carefully chose the narrative about Nazis' actions in Europe that they would give, so as to orient public opinion regarding a possible U.S. intervention. On the other hand, it is the case that cultural elements have shaped the sensibility of whole generations—sometimes bringing people to develop critical or disillusioned views of the society in which they lived.

Besides such external arguments, there are, of course, arguments internal to the theoretical framework developed here. Using the notions and models developed in these pages, I will thus try to show how symbolic resources can lead to the emergence of durable change. I will proceed in two steps, answering two questions: first, can changes promoted by symbolic resources allow real newness, that is, for a person to feel things she never felt before, to see the world or herself in a radically different way? Second, admitting that such changes might be substantial, are they necessarily developmental?

Do These Changes Really Bring Newness?

This book started by accepting an initial dynamic assumption—consciousness is a flow, what is presented to the organism is always new, and the transactions between the organism and the world have always to be renegotiated. It was also stated that cultural experiences suppose the mobilization of one's embodied memories. Imagination, I argued, is always reconfiguration. If this is so, how can the use of a symbolic resource bring about anything other than a representation of something already felt or known? How can it produce substantial change and development?

To answer this question, let us come back to the five aspects of a cultural experience as defined in chapter 2, and recall what sort of change they enable. The first two—*location, manipulation*—create the threshold that enables the immersion in an imaginary zone, and the ability to step out of that zone, so as to reenter the socially shared reality. (We have also seen that manipulation and location can reinforce some psychic abilities, and promote repositioning, chapter 5).

During the *imaginary* experience, one's focus of attention is constantly displaced and replaced into new positions, which are created through the meeting of one's embodied memories and the unfolding of the semiotic configuration of the cultural element. These meetings correspond to microsemiotic dynamics: they involve a semiotic mediation of any level of generality of one's previous experience. More exactly, because many semiotic streams have their own logic during the cultural experience, various aspects of the person and her memory simultaneously meet such semiotic units; self can thus be said to be diffracted into (or mapped out on) the imaginative experience. These meetings, the diffraction and displacement, are usually facilitated by some resonance between aspects of the cultural elements—a character, a tonality, or the structure of an event— and aspects of one's experience.[1] These resonances and meetings do not only occur in the focus of one's consciousness: any semiotic aspect of the cultural element can awake in the person lateral and vertical associations to mnemonic traces or embodied experiences. Hence, because of the diffraction of various aspects of the self in these meeting knots, and because of the progression of the cultural experience through time, previous emotional composites, or previous links between aspects of one's experience, can be undone, and new links can be created.

Processes of semiotic mediations within cultural experience can thus unlink existing emotional composites, reassemble their components, relink them through new semiotic mediations, guide them and create new emotional composites. Some of these can acquire semiotic mediation of higher or lower levels; some of these transformations can bring unconscious memory contents to preconsciousness, or preconsciousness to consciousness. New conscious thoughts are thus possible. Eventually, mnemonic traces or unelaborated contents can thus, through new mediations, become objects of consciousness and of articulated thought: new categories of experiences might suddenly be available. In chapter 4, Lily's example illustrates such a transformation of unconscious into conscious ideas through her use of the movie *After Life*.

Post hoc elaborations, consisting of stepping back to one's own real-life position (which might occur during the cultural experience) then enable the contemplation of the change or displacement produced, and might help its reflective integration. In chapter 5, Eli becomes thus aware of his use of symbolic resources afterwards: he realizes how *The Glass Bead Game* changed his understanding of his coming-back experience.

Later on, the *use of symbolic resources* in a given situation requires for a person to remobilize the memory of all these four previous aspects and their significant, transformative effect for the person. Using a symbolic resource might thus imply remobilizing mnemonic traces of a diversity of achieved positions, their changes, or transformations of emotional composites. Hence, any of these changes might be played again, addressing another current experience of the person using a symbolic resource. Julia, in chapter 5, makes deliberate use of her preferred music as a resource. Here again, bringing unconscious to conscious, elaborating emotions, bridging incompatible perspectives, can occur.

Such an analysis suggests that radically new emotions, positions or conscious thoughts might be achieved. If it is so, new experiences are enabled. Because of the irreversibility of time, these moves cannot be undone—as the apple in paradise can never be uneaten.

Is the Change Promoted by the Use of Symbolic Resources Developmental?

Development must be one particular sort of oriented change. In chapter 1, development in transitions was said to require three sorts of interdependent processes (identity change, skill acquisition, and meaning construction). Two criteria for development were identified: change should bring about new situations of rupture and thus open up new possibilities of change; change should not bring radical alienation towards oneself or the others. In the case of youth, development asked for more specific qualitative changes: the creation of links between one's past, and a reasonable future orientation; the construction of a system of orientation, with a relative correspondence and irrigation between its various aspects.

As seen in chapter 4 and 5, the use of symbolic resources can participate in one or more aspects of change. Within case studies, local changes appear to be part of transformative dynamics. A use of symbolic resource that is retrospective and mostly soothing might be just temporary, and might be the prerequisite for a later, future oriented, exploratory use. Hence, change can be observed in local time-spots, but development must be evaluated in the wider picture. Examples such as Lily, Eli, or Julia highlight migrations of the use of a symbolic resource within the architecture of the self, and thus, the transformation of that very structure.

Of course, it is not suggested that the use of symbolic resources *causes* these changes, or that it *alone* explains observed changes. Most people find many types of resources in periods of intense change; and what enables them to change in a developmental manner is a complex conglomerate or resultant of processes. The role played by symbolic resources might be part of these conglomerates; and their role can be that of countenance, guidance, (or scaffolding), or transformation of thoughts and emotions. In that sense, development occurs through symbolic resources.

DEVELOPING USES OF SYMBOLIC RESOURCES

The study of the use of symbolic resources is raised by a particular state of affairs in occidental societies with abundant circulation of cultural artefacts, and experiencing an apparent breakdown of overarching understandings of the world. It is theoretically based on the statement that, when there is no comprehensive and shared worldview—and one can doubt if there is ever such a thing (Nathan, 1990, 1992; Obeyesehere, 1963, 1977; Valsiner, 1998)—people have to engage in the bricolage of producing their own worldviews with what they have at hand, mixing traces of wider systems of meaning with local ones.

Problems people are confronted with, as well as the cultural elements at disposal to address them, are specific to a country, to a state of socioeconomical constraints, and to a societal atmosphere. Some fears or nostalgias common to one generation are usually related to changes in the societal structure—so for the romanticism of the German *Sturm-und-Drang* generation, or occidental tourists' aspiration to find a lost paradise in Ladakh (Gillespie, 2003). Some of these atmospheric characteristics are likely to shape a generation's sensibility. Social and cultural constraints also promote and restrict access to, and use of, cultural elements through the power of media markets, cultural politics, the distribution of economical goods etc.[2] People are thus likely to use resources promoted by that state of society, to answer issues partially shaped by the current time. Here, for example, most English young interviewees would mention the novels of George Orwell as eye openers; the presence of the church infuses most of the discourses with religious values (chapter 5).

In what follows, I examine the development and the use of symbolic resources in people's specific spheres of experiences, where actions and interactions take place in a given material and symbolic setting. These settings coexist next to each other, and are always located within that general context, whose various ideological and material streams traverse and constitute these local settings, interactions, and individual conduct. The thinking space (Perret-Clermont, 2001, 2004) of a person has thus to be seen as constituted and bounded by these many social and symbolic forces.

I will start by identifying the minimal situation of acquisition of symbolic resources—that is, an initial semiotic prism. Redeploying the thinking space in which such prisms occur will enable us to relocate the individual in his spheres of experiences, themselves positioned in a society. Constraints on the use of symbolic resources will thus be identified as resulting from *relative positions*: moving from one sphere of experience to another might constrain or enable the use of symbolic resources; being in a sphere of experience positioned as marginal within the societal space, will also press upon such use. Finally, I will come back to the intrapsychical modalities that might hinder some uses of resources.

Learning to use Symbolic Resources

Learning to use symbolic resources is quite likely to be an extension of the acquisition of early symbolic function in infants, and of language in children. Psychologists from various orientations seem consensually to admit that early symbolic acquisitions require regular patterns of shared and culturally defined actions with adults, that will progressively be internalized by the child, thus provoking qualitative change in her possible thinking and actions in the world (Ammaniti & Stern, 1991; Moro & Rodriguez, 1998; Nelson, 1996; Piaget, 1951, 1945/1994; Valsiner, 1997). In chapter 2, to summarize these ideas, I proposed to consider a primary prism at the origin of the use of symbols, including the infant, a state of the world, a reflecting parent and a symbol with which the parent will reflect the child's recognition of the state of the world (Fonagy, Gergely, Jurist, & Target, 2002; Green, 2002; Nelson, 2002). Not only are basic symbolic abilities fundamental for later use of symbolic resources, but also, I suggested, the use of symbolic resources is likely to emerge within similar interactive patterns. These are likely to occur through some modalities of interpersonal interactions around a cultural experience, where negotiations of meaning and identity take place (Baltes & Staudinger, 1996; Grossen & Perret-Clermont, 1994; Perret-Clermont, Perret, & Bell, 1991), as well as the acknowledgment of mutual emotional experiences (Tisseron, 2000).

In short, the transformation of cultural experiences into usable symbolic resources is likely to occur when two persons interact on a regular basis about a symbolic object, and come to a shared acknowledgment of what the object designates (the shared and objective referent) and a mutual acknowledgment of the fact that it has a personal meaning for each of them (within ones' internal, embodied representational and emotional world). Eventually, these mediations and the presence of another will be internalized, and the child will take a progressive distancing from cultural experiences (Lawrence & Valsiner, 2003). When parents read a goodnight story to their child, or sing her a lullaby when she is anxious, they create just such a semiotic prism that encompasses them, the child, the story or the lullaby, and the emotional state of the child (reflected by the parents, perceived by the child, all adjusting in a loop). The child who then asks for her preferred lullaby or goodnight story is then already an user of a symbolic resource: she uses that element as a way to regulate their emotion, open an imaginary space, in the comforting and mediating presence of her parents. Of course, the parents might, or might not, acknowledge the function of that use. The child might then be confronted by a multitude of such semiotic experiences, in which the parents might be replaced by other adults, or peers; hence the *other* pole of the semiotic prism is changing, until it might become a generalized other pole; the mediating position of these others or the generalized others will eventually be internalized by the child. The developmental hypothesis proposed here is thus that the internalization of such interpersonal semiotic dynamics, or semiotic prisms, will enable further uses of cultural elements as symbolic resources.

Admitting such a constitutive core, what can explain interpersonal differences in the use of symbolic resources? If the use of resources is likely to be developed through constant dynamics between who the person is, what her emotional needs are, what opportunity she is presented with or is looking for, what transitions she has to face and how she is changed through them, who she interacts with and what meanings emerge out of these interactions (see also Brandtsädter & Lerner, 1999), is there any dimension that might help to account for interpersonal differences? In the literature, candidates for explaining such differences are the presence of cultural elements in early spheres of experiences, socioeconomic factors, genres of discourse about cultural experiences, and personal trajectories though spheres of experiences.

First, one might think that the regularities and nature of interactions around cultural experiences during childhood in the family or its equivalent might play an important role (Nelson, 1996; Valsiner, 2000). Children that grow up in houses full of books have different access to books as possible symbolic resources than children that grow up in houses where books are excluded. Milieus where some cultural forms are encouraged are likely to enable a person to experience more shared experiences of these forms, that is, more occasions to learn to reflect upon an experience with significant others, and the person might be more likely to look for such experiences later on. In a study on heavy readers (Nell, 1988), it appears that children of avid, ludic mature readers, are so, too; so are the daughters of literary families (Wolf & Heath, 1992), or the sons of reading-fathers (Lloyd, 1999); a literary home environment appear to be a predictor of early literacy (Saracho, 1997).

Second, some might say that having books at home, or having the TV on all day, reflects some sociocultural and professional attributes of parents. Yet such socioeconomical attributes are certainly not causal factors. It is likely that, as suggested in a study on transitions to parenthood (Zittoun, 2001, 2004b, 2005a), there is no serious ground for thinking that socioeconomical distinctions explain generative uses of resources. In our sample, lower class people have intense interactions with cultural elements, and some who come from higher classes avoid these. Mary, Pat, and Julia, who all come from lower-class families, have recourse to various forms of cultural elements that are highly generative. Of course, one could argue that all the observed cases of the use of symbolic resources in this study are produced by a relatively privileged sample (parental jobs ranked from low-qualification technicians to international diplomats), and that none of the interviewees belonged to inner city youth. Rather than replying to that objection, let me recall where the discussion is located: it is not so much how many books or CDs a household has, or what they are, than *what is done* with the cultural elements at disposal, which is important; and this depends on more general games of constraint than economic ones.

A third explanation for interpersonal differences in the use of symbolic resources might be given by people's most promoted mode of communicating about cultural experiences. In effect, research indicates that sociocultural groups develop different forms of talking about and referring to these experiences (Cairnay & Ashton, 2002; Ochs & Capps, 2001). Pedler and Ethis (1999) indicate that people from various socioeconomic classes have different frequentations of museum and cultural institutions: the frequency of visits and time spent in the institutions differ. Spending more or less time in a museum might reveal how much time parents spend explaining things to their children. Once again, explaining is fine; but how things are explained appears to be more important. Thus, children who go to the museum with mothers that give them *narrative* accounts (stories) of paintings, rather than *paradigmatic* ones (causal and argumentative explanation), develop a better memory and can recall these narratives more easily (Tessler & Nelson, 1994; quoted in Nelson, 1996). Narrative comments develop children's memories and understanding of time. The authors note that such styles of talking and thinking are *not* those encouraged by schools, which promote paradigmatic forms of thinking (Levi-Strauss' engineers, chapter 5).

Hence, one might think that more educated parents might also give more school-compatible paradigmatic explanations to their children. What forms of talking and thinking would the use of symbolic resources require? As we have proposed, cultural experiences are likely to become internalized as potential symbolic resources if their meaning for a person, their emotional impact, their links to others, have been acknowledged and reflected. Paradigmatic discourse does not enable such recognition. The formulation of its communicative content does not offer space to symbolize personal, emotional involvement. Narrative is submitted to secondarity (the principles of secondary processes, see chapter 2) and time structure, and can be formal; yet it can also carry personal meanings and emotional and embodied experiences. Language is one of the ways through which humans can communicate about symbolic thinking as it occurs in cultural experiences. Hence, the more narrative forms of interaction are more likely to encourage the development of the ability to use symbolic resources than paradigmatic modes of discourse.

Modes of discourse are also not likely to strictly reflect parental occupations and socioeconomic positions. For example, one might imagine that the two parents have different roles towards their child: in our sample, it is often mothers who mediate a person's relationship to her preferred cultural experiences. One might thus wonder whether, in some traditional families, mothers encourage a more narrative style of interaction with cultural elements than fathers do.

Fourth, in order to account for interpersonal differences in the use of symbolic resources we have to move away from the person's first cultural encounters in the family. Early patterns of interactions at home can reasonably be expected to be challenged by children's experiences outside home, in school, in leisure time, with other adults and children, or later in their life (Perret-Clermont, 1980; Perret-Clermont & Nicolet, 1986/2001, Pontecorvo, 2004). Educational institutions generally aim at overcoming cultural and social inequalities. However, schools encourage formal thinking skills (paradigmatic or narrative). They do not necessarily support the development of the forms of reasoning required for using symbolic resources, which are associative, metaphorical, and emotionally laden. Studies even suggest that schools discourage children from reporting their experiences of television in the classroom (Hodge & Tripp, 1986). In the same vein, social scientists encourage media literacy teachings, that is, methods for formal analysis of the construction of images, *without* considering their referentiality (what it means for the person herself) (Livingstone & Lunt, 1994; MacBeth, 1996). Hence the official curriculum might not support, if not discourage, uses of symbolic resources as personal meaning-making tools. Nevertheless, schools might offer marginal spaces that encourage reflection upon one's cultural experiences, narrative reasoning and referentiality, for example, in classes where teachers offer quality spaces for discussing history, painting, or literature, and so forth. (Girardet & Fasulo, 1997; Henri, 2003; Ivinson, 2002; Sigel & McGillicuddy-De Lisi, 2003; Valsiner, 2000). Various forms of communities outside of school-settings propose alternative forms of socialization and learning; around activities such as drama or biblical readings, they might encourage children to reflect upon their cultural experiences—for example, in Sunday schools, leisure centers, music or theatre courses (Heath, 1994, 2000; Perret-Clermont, Pontecorvo, Resnick, Zittoun, & Burge, 2004; Zittoun, 1996).

Finally, life offers surprising opportunities to discover cultural experiences and learn to use them as resources. As I was writing these pages, I met a French-speaking actor in a Berlin café; born in Africa from an Italian woman and a French soldier, he had arrived with his mother in a small German village as a child. There he decided to overcome the linguistic obstacle: using a Tolstoy novel, a children's book, a dictionary, and with the help of a local shoemaker, he learned German. Hence, in families, at school in the margins of the official curriculum, or in formal and informal spaces out of school, people might develop modes of reflecting cultural experiences before turning them into resources. Finally, through these situations, children might develop an implicit understanding of what cultural experiences do to them, how they might use them for some aims, in what sort of situation, and how to create these experiences.

Hence, differences in how young adults use different sorts of symbolic resources cannot be simply related to their family's socioeconomic background. Being told stories or Bible narrative by a parent or a grandparent, spending Sunday in museum, talking about novels with a classmate or a shoemaker can support developing uses of symbolic resources; these are not class privileges in our modern societies. In other words, in normal thinking spaces—good enough, satisfying interpersonal, social, and contextual situations—people learn that the world is inhabited by stories and images as much as humans, and that one can gain something from interacting with them. In normal conditions, everyone develops a more or less conscious ability to use symbolic resources. As young adults, people become symbolically responsible. What is then done with this basic ability is another matter, which will depend on individual tastes and interests, chances and opportunities, and on an unfolding personal story.[4] Overall, social and cultural constraints exerted on spheres of experiences along the life trajectory, the modalities of interaction they might lead to, and their internalization into specific modalities of linking, will highly influence what might be done with symbolic resources.

Within the Societal: Peripheral Spheres of Experiences

Spheres of experience are socially located within lines of tensions that structure a society in a given historical-cultural state. Uses of symbolic resources are not immune to the power relationships imposed upon a person's given sphere of experience. Social tensions constrain material access to and use of types of experiences and resources; they also legitimize or sanction individual conduct (Bourdieu, 1979). Hence, society can render illegitimate some forms of conduct for a given person, positioned within a sphere of experience. A mother of many children can thus be stigmatized by the media for being a professional sport person, training 8 hours a day and constantly competing around the world.

This being stated, I would suggest that symbolic resources might acquire a significant importance for people who are, relative to a type of conduct, in a peripheral position. Being in a peripheral position would be to be placed in a slightly marginalized situation, which does not enable the full range of possible conduct or externalizations that might have been given to another person in the same situation (which is a form of *positional* stigma à la Goffman, 1963).

In the group of young English people interviewed, the few cases of systematic exploration of a set of cultural elements, such as in the case of Julia, or the persons who appeared to be heavy readers, are generally women. In the sample, some men are, of course, heavy readers of poetry, books on motorbikes, or heavy movie watchers; but they also might tend to turn that leisure into a socially visible activity: writing movie or music reviews, writing and publishing poetry. Also, it tends to be men that engage in politics or religious commitments. Not surprisingly enough, men seem thus to choose rather public cultural elements with strong hierarchical structures, while women seem to opt for composites, flexible, openly emotional cultural elements, and personal cultures (of course this is not based on a significant statistical analysis; see summary of these cases Appendix 1).

A gender-difference explanation might of course be given here. It might be that some of the interviewees came from homes where classical male-female division of roles were held, or that the University still encourages such divisions (boys go to debating societies, girls to belly-dancing classes). It might also express something about forms of thinking encouraged in women (Gilligan, 1982/1983, 1988). In the past, some forms of proactive leisure occupations might have been encouraged in boys, rather than in girls (see also Duveen & Lloyd, 1990; Psaltis & Duveen, 2004); under stress, this might lead girls to adopt internal regulating strategies (reader, listening to music) when boys might do sports or politics.

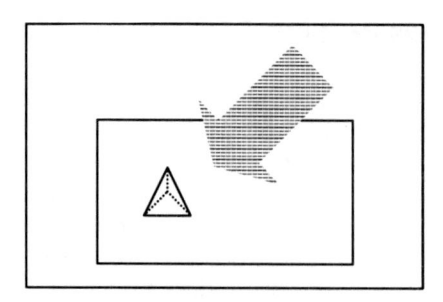

Figure 6.1. Societal constraints on uses of symbolic resources in a given sphere of experience.

However, pursuing my effort to identify structural features and explanations, rather than content specific ones, I would rather suggest considering these differences as positional. It is less the women's condition that is relevant here, than the fact of being in a slightly marginalized position, from which ready-made definitions are lacking or refused, where legitimacy is unclear, and where social resources as well as social arenas are not necessarily available. I would call these *peripheral* positions, from which to display one's symbolic responsibility is restrained, if not denied.

Such a positional argument would be supported if various peripheral positions bring about characteristic types of behavior. For example, one might investigate whether siblings with large age differences, or members of minority groups find themselves in comparable situations and have similar uses of symbolic resources. This is beyond my scope here. However, let me identify some of the features of the use of symbolic resources in various peripheral positions available to my scrutiny.

First, in peripheral situations, a full-blended identity might be forbidden by *a said other* relevant for a given semiotic prism. For Julia or Eli, opting for self-made personal cultures, and accepting guidance from their exploration of books or songs, might translate their active commitment into finding what is good for them beyond prescribed gendered or intergroup positions that would otherwise limit their possible conduct. The use of symbolic resources would thus support and *define self-identity* and meaning. Second, peripheral positions might bring people to relative *isolation* and to spend more time by themselves. Thus might be the case in some sibling positions. For example, Cathy or Elaine, two heavy symbolic resources users, are youngest sisters, at least partly rejected by their older brother's games. Also, parents of wide families might spend less time interacting around cultural experiences with the youngest child (Nelson,

1996). Other peripheral positions that lead to heavy use of symbolic resources would be that of the children of diplomats or professionals called to travel a lot. Hence, Randy became a precocious movie expert while his family was moving through Asia; Ilona became absorbed in fantasy, while following her father's new appointments through the world. As children, they were likely to lack the possibility to develop durable friendships and social networks. Thus, third, people in peripheral situation might be deprived of access to social arenas (because of their symbolic relative position, or because of constant moves) or forbidden some forms of externalization, and thus are in need of arenas for communication and action. These might then be done on an imaginary plane. Cultural experiences enable dialogue with imaginary others, and might bring about the internalization of these others as imaginary companions (Taylor, 1999). Cultural experiences engage indirect, imaginary, but nevertheless emotionally real, actions (Vygotsky, 1926).

Hence, the use of symbolic resources by young women in societal environments that offer very polarized role models would indicate that they neither find experiences that reflect their identities, worries and understanding in main male-oriented values, nor the spaces to express and enact their positions (Lawrence, Benedikt, & Valsiner, 1992). In a comparable peripheral position, Carl Rogers, raised in the countryside and relatively isolated, refusing the professional career that was offered to him, became an intense user of symbolic resources, before reorienting his trajectory (Zittoun, 2003). As a young black man raised in a white community, Malcolm X early realized that his peripheral position would deny him the right to learn what he wanted and express his views; he engaged in an active self-education project, which developed in his year in prison, before externalizing a new project for Black people—a project that was inspired by his wide reading (Gillespie, 2005). In a more dramatic vein, many stories of survival in extreme detention conditions—Primo Levi (1985/1991) in a concentration camp, or Václav Havel (1983/1988) in jail—found resources in books or that they knew by heart.

The use of symbolic resources in peripheral positions might thus be seen as combining these functions—self-sustainment and definition, commitment out of isolation, imaginary acting and interacting—which might help the rereading of one's own story, the conferring of meaning on absurd aspects of one's life, and the definition of new projects. Malcolm X or Vacláv Havel were changed by years of reading in prison. Using cultural resources did not cause these changes: but using them might have supported a general process of change.

Within the Societal: Moving Between Spheres of Experience

Spheres of experience are located within a societal reality. Yet this is not the only determining factor in the forces exerted on the use of symbolic resources. A person always arrives in a new situation with her story of previous situated interactions and transitions. She also has a personal culture and access to cultural elements which might be turned into symbolic resources; her internalized semiotic prisms carry traces of their past uses and of the shadow of real or imagined others (chapter 2 & 5).

If we admit that one cannot use a symbolic resource without triggering full semiotic dynamics, or semiotic prisms, the question of the use of a cultural element as a symbolic resource in a new sphere of experience, becomes the problem of transplanting such semiotic prisms. Do internalized semiotic prisms authorize such application within new spheres of experiences?

First, spheres of experience bring in the presence of given cultural elements, and can enable interactions with significant others, through which these cultural element can become symbolic resources—the initial semiotic prism. Second, these spheres can produce dynamics that legitimize or condemn the use of these symbolic resources in further spheres of experiences.

Let us examine examples of *presentation* and *legitimization* of using a given semiotic resource. Julia discovered an online community that presented her with the lyrics of the *Manic Street Preachers* and their related texts; Thomas' grandmother kept sending (presenting) him his Bible readings. Legitimization applies when using a given cultural element as resource, in that sphere of experience, or in a further one. The presence of his fiancée legitimizes Eli's use of *Anna Karenina* to think his love relationship; the imaginary presence of Mrs. Thatcher legitimizes Thomas' use of biographies to make plans for his future. Legitimization by the *other* of the prism, real, present, absent, or imaginary, whether linked to the situation of presentation of that resource or mediating the recomposition of the semiotic prism, can inflect on the destiny of uses of that resource.[4]

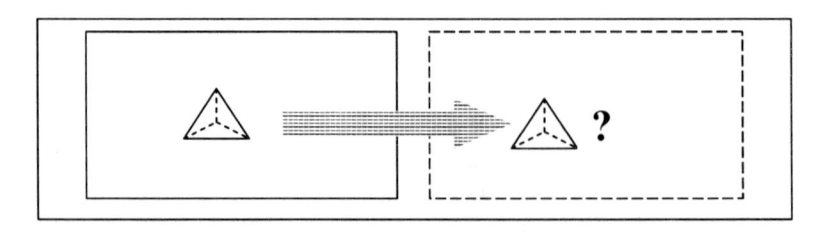

Figure 6.2. Transfer of a semiotic prism in a new sphere of experience.

Consequently, the difficulty of using symbolic resources in new spheres of experiences can be seen as resulting from a lack of validation by *other*. Lev (chapter 2), who lived through a painful transition, had acquired his knowledge of Talmud in the protected sphere of experience of the orthodox community, under the presenting of his rabbi. Moving out of that sphere, it became impossible to use Talmud as a resource to address new everyday life situations, as if Talmud was still linked to its conditions of acquisition, in the shadow of the rabbi condemning Lev's presence in the secular world. Pat seems to have needed to move out of the sphere of school, which had not legitimized his membership of the scouts, to be able to use his scout experience as a resource. In Mary's working life, painting seemed absolutely without legitimacy; it required the apparition of her childhood teacher to represent her with art as resource and legitimize her artistic expertise.

Hence the question of using symbolic resources is not exactly that of transfers of skill or knowledge. For these, a person needs to identify the structure of a situation or some of its contents as requiring some previously acquired skills or knowledge. A pupil must recognize that a problem of bathtubs is a task that requires his understanding of proportions; a medical doctor needs to identify in his patient's symptoms variations on some others he once treated. Such sorts of transfer would be rather hindered if the pupil or the doctor gave too much importance to their emotional reaction to the situation or to their relationship to their teacher or patient. In contrast, such emotional and relational reactions are necessary in the use of a symbolic resource. Using a symbolic resource thus not only requires the identification of structural and content analogies (like in maths) but also emotional and relational relevance, or even more diffuse sensual, emotional, or unconscious correspondences between situations. It is the taste of a Madeleine that calls the memory of Guermance out of Marcel Proust's cup of tea; it is the fact that all readers have had a father and a mother that moves them in Sophocles's *Oedipus Rex* (Freud, 1900). Linking between a person's new experiences and the semiotic constellations constituting a cultural object are fluid and numerous—and fragile.

Intrapsychic Constraints

Sociocultural and interpersonal constraints are exerted on the cultural elements available to a person and on what she can do with them, and these combine with and influence psychic constraints. Here, I address three intrapsychic conditions required for the use of symbolic resources to be developmental.

First, the use of symbolic resources supposes myriad operations of linking, delinking and relinking (Green, 2000). To be transformative, these operations must have some semiotic aliveness, that is, be representational and emotional, in touch with, on the one side, a person's conscious and unconscious thoughts, and on the other side, her experiences of the real world. This aliveness corresponds to the semiotic dynamics that have been represented in the semiotic prism (chapter 2). It might thus be argued that transitions need to have such an aliveness for identity processes, learning, and emotional elaboration to occur. On the other hand, shocking events, psychical breakdowns, or excessive violence can be described as modifying modalities of semiotic linking. Links might lose their intentionality, their emotional quality, or their contact with the real world. In the worst case, some brutal experience will resist any form of semiotic mediations.

Second, the use of symbolic resources require clear boundaries between a person's zones of experience—what is her inner life, what belongs to the shared reality, and what belongs to the imaginary zone where the cultural element and her inner life meet. Such boundaries are necessary for the avoidance of the acting out of fictional ideas, or to distinguish between one's feelings for others, and feelings created by the cultural experience.

Third, to be transformative, open to reflectivity, and to the exploration of the future, these processes need to be oriented in time: they need to be connected to memory which can be mobilized, and to find a field of future oriented thoughts. If someone's memories are not accessible (repressed or cleaved for traumatic reasons) or if a person's sense of self is so fragile that it can not be brought to think about what is to come, then the use of symbolic resources cannot be transformative.

Symbolic resource use requires access to these three dimensions and zones of experience and to specific modalities of linking. Drawing on clinical literature, we can envisage and name various alterations of the processes of symbolization that have been documented (Bion, 1977; Winnicott, 1971/2001). The nomenclature proposed her is taken from the work of Anne Alvarez (1992) and Hanna Segal (1991).

Having a cultural experience without acknowledging its internal resonance might be called a *cold* use. Taking the cultural experience (or some of its parts) for real, without locating it in an imaginary zone, involves *symbolic equations*. Soothing uses can also be seen as turned primarily toward the inner zone and ignoring the socially shared value of the experience. *Playful* semiotic mediations involve all these spaces, but do not need to be oriented in time. The addition of time brings *explorative* uses. Hence uses of symbolic resources depend on the quality of the boundaries between real, internal and imaginary zones of experience. In youth, developmental uses of symbolic resources require such *explorative* uses, fully acknowledging boundaries, and a time-dimension, as well as involving complex semiotic dynamics.

Although these categories have been developed in clinical psychology, it might be suggested that such modalities of linking coexist in each of us.[5] We can thus identify within the data the occurrence of various modalities. Coming back to the secular world, the religious Ron practices his daily hours of biblical studies. He does not question what it means; as he explains, it is the fact that he is doing it, that is important. In effect, it constitutes him in whom he wants to be; it also helps him to avoid encounters with secular people. Hence symbolic resources are used to reinforce the boundaries between inner and outer worlds; these operations are *cold* and disinvested, and thus exclude the exploration of the inner world. Similarly, René, presenting himself as a film and art critic, talks about his preferred movies in terms of their construction, their contributions to the arts and so forth; he refuses to envisage that these might be somehow linked to his personal experience. The construction of meaning which is thus done is cut from the link to himself, and the object appears as strangely disinvested, as indicated by the low and blasé tone of his discourse. In these two cases, the symbolic elements appeared as *cold*: they are decoded and used in a technical sense, but stay unrelated to any internal experience or affect. In contrast, Sarah enjoys all her rich repertoire of resources—literature, music, and arts—as ways to retain past personal feelings. The outer world is excluded from her prism; lost in her inner world, Sarah's modalities of uses are close to *symbolic equations*.

It is important to highlight that initial semiotic prisms are constantly reworked through life; consequently, during all life, societal, social, and political, interpersonal conditions can create pressure upon actualization of the prism and thus disturb these modes of linking. From a cultural-social development point of view, this implies the examination of the historical, social, and symbolic conditions in which a person is inserted, and her own historicity. Typically, a situation of economic crises like in the 80s brought many young people to see future orientations as delegitimized; the *no future* generation could therefore become wildly *playful* in its uses of resources (which it did), but not *explorative*. Propaganda and advertising in general tend to be exerted on the real-imaginary-inner boundaries: it presents imaginaries representations of inner wishes as real. Max's explorations of stencils and posters, that enable him to master these techniques, were seen as aiming at the reinforcement of such boundaries (chapter 5).

Also, we have seen that considering personal historicity implies acknowledging the location of transitions within full developmental trajectories. In that respect, using a given cultural element as a resource under a given modality is temporary, and can also be the condition for subsequent uses of the same resources under a different modality. Julia, unhappy, started to use music for purely inner functions under *semiotic equations*. These modalities evolved until they became *explorative*. The manipulation of containing or isolating symbolic resources can progressively transform the dominant modes of linking (Tisseron, 1999) and thus enable playing (Winnicott, 1968a, 1968b, 1971/2001).

Finally, various modalities of semiotic linking coexist or succeed themselves as normal parts of human functioning. Given the intended and unintended effects of the use of resources, these might operate simultaneously on these various modes. Also, if a person uses a symbolic resource in a privileged mode for a given group of thoughts, that resource might acquire a general psychic function (the purple fabric on Julia's walls became her psychic *container* (Zittoun, 2001, 2004b). As long as *symbolic equation* and *cold* symbols are not the dominant modes of thinking of a person, her conduct remains nonpathological. In youth transitions explorative and playful modes of linking are necessary for development. In consequence, social, cultural, or personal constraints that impose other semiotic modalities hinder development.

EXPERTISE IN USING SYMBOLIC RESOURCES

People use symbolic resources—and to some extent, we all do. But can people know what they do? Is using a symbolic resource voluntary, deliberate conduct? And if it is, do some people develop a certain skill in using symbolic resources? In this section, I examine various degrees of awareness when using symbolic resources. I thus propose to identify a set of symbolic competencies—symbolic skills, or know-how—that constitute an expertise in using symbolic resources (Zittoun, 2001, 2004b).

Awareness must be distinguished from intention. As proposed earlier, a cultural experience has *per definition* an intentional nature (it is about something, it is representational, chapter 2). I have distinguished between intentions that are linked to the explicit content of the cultural element, and intentions that exceed it: in the latter case, for a given person, the cultural element points toward something external to the element.

The question of awareness concerns the experience that a person might have when interacting with a cultural element or remembering that cultural experience, not necessarily the fact of having consciously chosen to have that cultural experience itself. Hence, one might have a cultural experience at random: sitting in a coffeehouse and suddenly paying attention to the background music; stopping in the street in front of the poster for an art exhibition, or to listen to a street band; reading a short story in a Sunday magazine, and so forth. Finally, one can willingly have a cultural experience and intend to feel some of its effects, but also one can be changed by unintentional consequences of that experience. Hence, Julia listened to her preferred pop band for the soothing function of the music; the unintended effect of this use is Julia's progressive awareness of political issues and her subsequent identity changes.

In what follows, various modalities of use are proposed. An individual person can alternate various modalities of use; such a typology of processes is not a typology of persons. These distinctions are, for now, based on observed patterns of use, as analyzed in these pages. This typology is provisory. Its underlining idea is more important: a person can use symbolic resources in various ways; alone or with the help of others, she might develop modes of use that enable her to gain different, personally relevant insights.

Zero Use

Let us first admit a *degree zero* of use of cultural elements. People can have cultural experiences and appreciate these experiences for the direct and immediate impression they cause, or meanings they carry. A movie is seen because it is good fun, a painting is nice because it is well done or has beautiful colors, and so forth. In such a degree zero, a person would not have to be aware that the cultural experience might point at aspects of her experience that matter to her or are relevant within her sphere of experience. This does not mean that the experience is not significant; but the shaping of the experience is somehow occurring within its flow, without distancing. The experience *is* change. In other words, there is no pointing at something that exceeds the cultural experience, that is no use as resource. The semiotic prism would miss the *meaning for person* pole. A particular case of zero use is the *literate expert use*: here, the cultural elements might be addressed formally or historical-critically, but again, without any links to personal resonance (a *cold* mediation). Zero uses are likely to take place during most people's cultural experiences; other modalities of uses might then follow.

For some people, *zero uses* are the dominant mode of apprehending cultural experiences. This might have different origins. People might simply lack elementary reflectivity, or might not have developed reflectivity upon their cultural experiences. This might be due to a lack of occasions to share and discuss such experiences. It might also be linked to internalized rules or positions delegitimizing the fact that a cultural experience has moved or affected oneself (some social spheres would not be sympathetic to the fact that one cried when seeing *Titanic*). Literate over-expertise must also have been developed through the training of some skills and the negation of personal emotionality. Zero use can thus, indirectly, also be part of work of positioning, identity making, or group belonging.

Quasi Use

Mostly, people have a vague sense that cultural experiences do affect them, make them feel things and change them. *Quasi use* designates this vague acknowledgment. At the minimum, it would be the fact of seeing a good movie and feeling good afterwards, or listening to some music and realizing one's state of mind. This would involve a L1 mediation of experience. It is likely that most voluntary engagements in cultural experience are guided by the memory of such an effect and the expectation of its reproduction. The border between quasi uses and intuitive uses is thin.

Intuitive Use

Intuitive uses indicate an acknowledgment, even if not clearly conscious, of one or many effects of having a cultural experience or remembering it. Bringing objects back from holiday, with the intention of conferring on them a memorial value; putting homely objects on the walls; carrying with oneself one's favorite books, can be seen as actualizations of such acknowledgments: these are intuitive uses of symbolic resources. People seem in effect to guide conduct on the basis of a basic understanding that symbolic resources might maintain memories, support self-continuity, indicate identities, and so forth. Because these help form conduct, these might be said to achieve a L2 mediation of conduct.

Deliberate Use

The use of resources can be said to be deliberate when a person is actively looking for a cultural element that might be used as a resource to achieve a certain end. This requires for her to be, more or less consciously, aware of the functioning of resources and their possible effects.

Examples would be people calling upon a vignette from a text or the Bible or a movie, to choose possible conduct. Another deliberate use would be the systematic exploration of chosen cultural elements to prepare oneself for a future trip to a foreign country. Deliberate uses can have been slowly developed out of a progressive reflective understanding of intuitive practices. They can also be systematically trained and automatized as expert skills, as it is the case in groups of Bible readers. Deliberate uses might require L2 and L3 mediations.

Reflective Use

Deliberate uses might become objects of one's reflectivity: a person might clearly know that she does such uses, and reflect upon her uses and the changes these enable, so as to integrate that awareness. Hence, Eli had been able to bridge his religious system of orientation and his use of secular resources, and to reflect upon his own symbolic activities, so as to formulate the hypothesis that some symbolic resources might be used in life-situations. Mediations here are located at least at L2 and L3, possibly L4.

A person aware of the impact of using symbolic resources, deliberately looking for them, might also start to transform existing elements or ways to use them (such as in mixing music), or creating his own resources (writing poems). This leads us to another problem that might be seen as the logical extension of what precedes—that of the creation of cultural elements—which I will not examine here.

Expert Uses of Symbolic Resource, or Symbolic Competencies

Deliberate and *reflective* uses can be called *expert uses* of symbolic resources. These enable planning and exploring possibilities, in link to what the person is currently facing. Such uses achieve the full symbolic functions of cultural elements: personally relevant *aboutness*, inscription within a time perspective, and changes of level of mediations (minimally from L1–L2, to L3–L4). Reflective uses are likely to be the more transformative, as they can accompany the process of reorganizing systems of orientation and linking symbolic resources to concrete situations, so as to develop new perspectives on one's conduct.

Symbolic expertise, or symbolic competencies including deliberate and reflective uses of symbolic resources, not only requires acknowledging the shared sense or aesthetic value of a cultural element. Summarizing our previous discussions, we might say that it also requires:

1. Acknowledging the fact that a cultural experience or its memory has a full meaning for oneself;
2. The recognition of the emotional-sensual impact of that cultural experience (that is, an acknowledgment of its referentiality);

3. A good enough ability to separate experiences occurring within the zones of the real from those occurring in the zone of the imaginary, and to accept the playfulness and exploration required by the latter;
4. A possibility of stepping back or changing perspective after the cultural experience, to reflect upon the transformations enabled by it. The distanciated perspective can be given by the mediation of another person (such as in an interview!), by one's knowledge of the construction of the cultural elements itself, or by an internalized other perspective within the architecture of self;
5. A reflective position on the correspondences and resistance between one's transitions, difficulties, feelings (past and future), and the semiotic organization offered by the cultural element;
6. Such a reflective position requires accepting to leave the safe shore of rational, logical, and causal reasoning, and narrative (linear) thinking to engage in deliberate *symbolic thinking* (cf. chapter 5) that would enable one to trace back the processes through which a cultural experience has become personally significant and involved in the transformation of self—on the same model as the interpretation of dreams aims at tracing back the dream work (Freud, 1900).

People might use symbolic thinking indistinctly, in a nonaware way—similarly to the fact that one might think back to one's dream, associating around it, without a systematic attempt to get at its sense. However, symbolic thinking enables the full use of cultural elements as symbolic resources, which participate in change and development.

OPENINGS

The scope of this book has been to describe uses of symbolic resources and to build theoretical tools to understand them in their variety. Of course, such an enquiry raises many questions; some have been addressed, other are ignored; here, I indicate a few more, that enable me to describe the limits of the present work.

What Symbolic Resources, What Other Resources?

In this book, the choice has been made to consider symbolic resources implying the use of cultural elements, defined as satisfying *three* criteria. These cultural elements are (1) discrete groups of organized semiotic units; (2) other people have intentionally constituted them to carry meaning they found in their lived experiences; (3) they suppose entry into an imaginary zone of experience, where emotions are real but their contents and consequences are not. To be considered as symbolic resources, these cultural elements have to be used about something that exceeds them; that is, they become objects of secondary uses. I have thus considered two types of cultural elements: artifacts like books, songs, novels, paintings, that have a material support and a clear boundary; parts of symbolic system such as religious or cultural elements, which are diffracted through a variety of supports. This has been my choice, and has also implied a selection of theoretical tools to account for imaginary experiences.

Of course, one could have made different choices. The *imaginary* condition might be eliminated, and then argumentative styles, talk shows or newspapers, the body of knowledge linked to a profession, might be treated as a cultural element and a candidate for symbolic resources. The *intentional constitution* of the cultural element might be suppressed, and one could examine people who use the sky, the moon, or the trees as resources to guide their lives.

Readers are invited to try to redefine criteria and to explore what can be done with other sorts of cultural resources in transitions. My task has been to identify the role of symbolic resources that imply imagination—fiction and transcendence, for it is at the same time repeatedly declared one of the most characteristic richness of humans, and systematically excluded from the field of scientific investigation. However, it might also be important to compare what one can do with symbolic resources that trigger imagination, and those that address the real first; and this, I hope, will allow the specification of the symbolic resources I have chosen to consider. Finally, to those who worry that such an investigation would destroy the poetics of cultural experiences, I would say that I do not think that it would threaten their quality; having the experience and analyzing it are two different moments and attitudes. The latter might help us to understand and protect the importance of spaces for cultural experiences.

The Development of Using Symbolic Resources Through the Lifespan

In this book, I have examined the use of symbolic resources in youth transitions. At this time of their lives, people have usually already had quite a long socialization story—they have usually been exposed to the transmissions of their families and schools, they have started to develop their own choices and might have modified their personal trajectories.

They have also developed various forms of thinking, including those prescribed by schools and professions, and possibly some understanding of relationships, of others and of themselves. Finally, they are coming to exert their symbolic responsibility.

It is rather likely that symbolic resources are used in childhood, in adulthood and in old age. It is also rather likely that these uses might differ widely. Different cultural elements might become relevant, their uses might have different primary functions, and expertise in uses might vary.[6] It might of great interest to propose a developmental account of uses of symbolic resources.

For example, as biographical novels suggest, childhood memories of cultural elements might have a strong impact—as one has had less experiences. The use of symbolic resources might be closely linked to childhood fears and imagination, that is to unconscious, and to immediate sensual and embodied impressions—see for example the importance of the smell of paper and the touch of book covers in Amos Oz's autobiographic account (2003). In contrast, uses of symbolic resources in older people might come after innumerable cultural experiences. Their memories might be more distanced from their original cultural elements; used very much as symbolic resources, these might have been deeply internalized and mingled in the stuff of one's life. Older people might thus develop some very condensed images as a synthesis of many symbolic resources, or *ultrasymbolic resources* (Trier, Zittoun, & Perret-Clermont, 2004; Zittoun, 2006a). Such suggestions of course open a whole field of investigations.

Promoting the use of Symbolic Resources?

Social scientists worry about intoxicating cultural elements and the passivity of readers, TV watchers, or other consumers. They have thus encouraged media consumers to become critical, which implied analyzing the syntactic and semantic properties of the cultural elements, rather than thinking about its referential values (its *aboutness*). Referential uses are considered to reveal people's credulity and inability to realize how they have been manipulated (Liebes & Katz, 1990/1994; Livingstone & Lunt, 1994). More optimistically, Lembo (2000) observes that TV watchers develop various forms of mindfulness—choosing specific programs, or deciding to watch TV just for the purpose of resting, or using the remote control to regulate what they are exposed to, on the basis of various criteria—critical expertise à la Liebes and Katz, or referential or emotional resemblance (Pasquier, 1999).

It still appears to me that these worries about the mindlessness of people that have cultural experiences are highly biased by an intellectual scepticism about *simple people's* credulity. Of course, dangerous uses of media *do* exist. People can be captivated by images and words, take for real contents that are of an imaginary nature, or become prisoner of images that awaken traces of unelaborated fears or desires (Tisseron, 2002, 2003). *Misuses* of symbolic resources can of course be identified: uses that bring alienation, that close possibilities, but also, that induce violence and negation of the other. Our investigation suggests that misuses of symbolic resources are due less to cultural elements themselves, than to psychical and sociocultural constraints exerted upon uses.

Can expert uses of symbolic resources be encouraged? Families, schools, and other socialization arenas can support children's and adult's use of symbolic resources, by creating situations that enable a full deployment of semiotic prisms, that provide cultural elements, legitimize their use, and offer protected spaces that invite people to explore, try out and play by using these resources. Practically, Tisseron (1999, 2000) proposes to encourage children's expertise in using symbolic resources in a double way: (1) children must acquire some media literacy, so as to be able to understand how images have been made; this enables the reinforcement of the real-imaginary-inner life boundaries; (2) children have to be guided to reflect upon the feelings triggered by a cultural experience, and to reflect on how it affects the child's relationship to herself, others and the world. In other words, adults in charge of children are encouraged to create good enough prism-like semiotic dynamics. They are asked to mediate both the relationship of the child to the cultural element itself, in link to the real world, and the child's relationship to herself, in link with the cultural elements. And they are asked to indicate the boundaries between the imaginary aspects of these experiences, those that concern the shared social reality, and those that are irreducibly part of their interiority.

However, if such situations can be promoted in children it is much less likely that they can be imposed on adults. It is indeed very difficult to imagine how specific forms of internalization or externalization might be encouraged to support symbolic expertise in adults, without violating their symbolic responsibility. What can be done is bear in mind what we know about the role of cultural experiences in transitions. Then, it is also possible to indicate how social spaces might be organized so as to offer possibilities for people *not to misuse* symbolic resources.

Hence, it seems reasonable to assume a few facts. First, people use symbolic resources *anyway*. Second, they use them in periods of transition, because they have increased emotional and meaning needs, and this is what cultural elements provide them with. Third, such uses can be developmental only when legitimized by significant others in a given sphere of experience. Fourth, uses of symbolic resources require conditions in which a person can maintain boundaries between her various zones of experience—imaginary experience (in all their absurdity and non-normativity), inalienable inner life, and the socially shared reality (that needs to be ruled and regulated). Additionally, the person might need to develop means to relink these three zones of experiences, so as to become reflective on her uses.

Correspondingly, for individual uses of symbolic resources to take place, some minimal social conditions must be fulfilled. For example, local social authorities or wider societal institutions should acknowledge these three zones of human experience, and recognize the differentiated responsibilities they have towards them. In the best of worlds, authorities should organize and regulate social and political life; they should not intervene in inner lives; and they should encourage the making and the circulation of cultural elements, so as to allow people to find spaces for imaginary anarchies and fantasies. And in the best of worlds, authorities would renounce the powerful manipulation tool of mixing imaginary fantasies with the organization of social and political life. Misuses of symbolic resources might thus be reduced.

CONCLUDING WORDS

This book has explored a very simple and everyday experience—that of thinking about a movie when being in a particular situation, of humming a little song without knowing why, or of being impressed and moved by a painting. The initial intuition was that such everyday experiences are important, and might participate in learning and change. The book has established the fact that people in effect use cultural elements in their everyday life. Through case studies and comparisons, it has described such use of symbolic resources, distinguished the modalities of their use, and examined some of their consequences.

In order to account for these descriptions, theoretical models have been proposed. These models are inscribed within the frame of a developmental cultural psychology. They raise some questions, and open possible routes for generalization.

To develop a psychology of development that accounts for dynamics of change, I have identified a unit of analysis: the sequence *rupture-transitions*, that might bring new regularities. A psychology of transitions is a psychology that identifies accelerated or catalyzed dynamics of transformation within the ever-changing flow of inner life, the world and their mutual transactions. Transitions can be of various amplitudes and sources; yet looking at the structures of such sequences and the processes involved might help us see the similarities and differences in a great variety of phenomena of change.

In the more specific field of a developmental psychology of young people and adults, the notion of *symbolic responsibility* has been proposed to give more attention to the specific relationship grown ups have with cultural objects, artefacts and media messages. They are exposed to this constant shower of symbolic messages like children; yet they are in position to be responsible for what they accept to consider seriously, they can look for cultural elements that are relevant for them, and they can decide what to do with them—whether they will give some a central role in their personal culture or structure of understanding, and how much they will allow them to reshape their discourses and actions. The person's active role in internalization and externalization dynamics is thus highlighted, as well as the social and cultural forces exerted upon them (Valsiner, 1997).

Other theoretical elaborations are specifically addressing symbolic thinking in such a developmental psychology. The central proposition of this book is the model of *use of symbolic resources*. This model is pointed at the relationship between people's imaginary experiences enabled by cultural elements, and their conduct which is oriented toward the *real*—shared social reality and interiority. This model proposes three dimensions for analyzing such links: first, it highlights the multiple *aboutness* of the use of symbolic resources; second, it addresses their orientation within psychic time; third, it distinguishes the degree of generality of the semiotic mediations that they promote, that is, their power to mediate distancing dynamics. In complement, a five-step analysis of *cultural experiences* has been proposed to give visibility to the processes through which these might trigger change, and thus be brought into use as resources.

In order to ground the model of uses of symbolic resources, two additional theoretical constructs have been proposed. First, a basic *semiotic prism* accounts for the relationships between a person, a cultural element, its meaning for the person and others in the social world, and their possible transposition onto an intrapsychic plane. This semiotic prism emphasizes necessary conditions for internalization and externalization dynamics to take place, in an ontogenetic perspective, and perhaps in a microgenetic one. The double nature of this model, both psychosocial and intrapsychical, invites reflection on the puzzling nature of the transactions between shared reality, imaginary, and interiority.

Second, the notion of sphere of experience within societal contexts highlights dynamics of social legitimacy when using symbolic resources. It also indicates how peripheral positions in spheres of experience might induce transformative uses of symbolic resources.

These theoretical constructs aim at suggesting codependent dynamics. Hence, beyond description, they open the route for explanatory analysis of the use of symbolic resources.

This book has mobilized and woven various streams of psychological and psychoanalytical theorization, so as to define an understanding of semiotic dynamics in psychological change. Books, movies, and songs are the magnifying glass through which the alchemy of embodied meaning making has been observed. This book might invite further theoretical discussions, and empirical explorations of comparable phenomenon; thus, it would be engaged in the development of psychological knowledge. Also, the use of symbolic resources appear to offer powerful means for everyday knowledge and development, and this book might help thinking about the good-enough conditions for people to engage in such uses. It is, after all, in being used about something else that this book might become a resource itself.

NOTES

1. In that context, the notion of *empathy* would designate the process of being displaced by the progression of the cultural element.
2. Atmospheric characteristics also shape the work of researchers; there must thus be a blind spot to each study. Yet addressing such a blind spot would require another research enterprise (an *archaeology of knowledge* à la Foucault, or an exhumation of *themata*) (Marková, 2000; Moscovici, 2000)).
3. I exclude here personalistic explanations for interpersonal differences, in contrast to Nell (1988) for whom there are two types of heavy readers: those who use books as distraction or escape, and those who use reading as a means to heighten their awareness. Typically, personality explanations are here circular and redundant (Valsiner, 2000)
4. Dynamics of legitimation of the use of symbolic resources thus orient change and development; as such, they can be said to set zones of preferred development, as indicated by Valsiner (1997, 1998) (Gillespie, personal communication, January/2005).
5. The problem of knowing when the use of symbolic resources is impossible is another. The use of symbolic resources is threatened by the same constraints as other elementary forms of symbolization. Pathological modalities of early interactions might endanger some people's capacity to symbolize. Forms of psychic-emotional suffering are linked to a diminution of symbolization (depression, addiction) (Green, 1973/1999; Rapaport, 1942). Some events of traumatic nature threaten the balance of psyche and can damage linking processes and thus symbolization in some areas associated to that traumatic zone (Abraham & Torok, 1978/1994; Bion, 1977; Tisseron, 1996). Also, forms of constant threat or real or symbolic violence exerted by the immediate interpersonal social context, or by wider social and political conditions damage symbolization abilities. Practically, it would of course be interesting to examine in a clinical perspective, what

sort of suffering radically forbids access to the use of symbolic resources, or how these can be alleviated through the use of symbolic resources, as it has been done with tales, myths, and traditional stories (Bettelheim, 1976/1985; Kaës, 1996; Zajde, 1993/1995).
6. This of course is also dependent on the general development of thinking and interpreting, see for example, Feldman, Bruner, Kalmar, and Renderer (1994).

APPENDIX A

Name Age	Religion	Sibs	About 0 Bored 1 Self 2 Other 3 Group 4 World	Time orient. 1 Past 2 Present 3 Future	Level of Mediation 1 Affects 2 Case 3 Cat.-Self 4 High-Level	Reflect. 1 None 2 Notes 3 Seeks 4 Creates	Domin Ress	SymRes	From ?	Extern- alization	Transition/ Rupture?
Lina		Br					Others Arts, etc. Friends	-	Father art		
Lily 23	-	1b	1, 2, 3, 4	1, 2, 3	1, 2, 3, 4	3, 4	Books, Cinema & Friends	Cinema	Mother reads a lot, 2nd hand.	Writes cine critics, paints, talks	Choices after College
Gustav 23	Chris- tian?	?(o)	1, 3	2, 3	3	2, 3	Nonfiction Debating Play	-	Grand- father	Talks with grandfa- ther Debating.	Bullied at col- lege; back gap (China)
Wanda 19	Catholic	2b 1 dead	1, 2, 3	1, 2	1, 2, 3, 4	2, 3, 4	Literture Family & group support	Poetry, books	Mother- family	?	Death & Hand- icap brother Coming to University
Felix 20		1b	1, 2	1, 2	1	2, 3	Music, Encyclope- dia F1, TV thrillers, running	Music	Father F1	Plays guitar	-
Greg 19	church of England	1B	4	2, 3	1, 2, 3, 4	2, 3	Music, poetry, nov- els, sings.	Novels & Bible	School Religion family	Plays	Choosing secu- larity-
Robert 19	-	1b	1, 3	1, 2	1, 2, 4	2, 3	Poetry, music play and listen	Poetry & music	Mother (book, guitar)	Plays	Leaving mother?

Xenia 19	Buddhist	2B	1	1, 2	1, 2, 3	1	Music, novel-dairies Children book	Id.	Mother reads	?	Going to boarding school
William 21	-	1S	1, 3	1, 3	1	0, 3	Literary critic; music, films, visual arts & music	? films?	music with dad/ art with friend	Writes critics	Changing faculty Or 13-14
Adam 21	Christian.	1S	1, 2, 4	2	1, 2, 3, 4	3	Bible & Christian act. *James Bond*	Bible	Community.	Teaches	Gap year (South America & local community work)
Max 20	Catholic.	1S	1, 2, 3, 4	1, 2	1, 2, 3, 4	2, 3, 4	Graphics Novels Other people, music	Stickers, books – (does graphs)	Brother Ideal Artist?	Does graphics	Gap year Factory, building & pub
Anne 20	-	-	1, 2, 3,	1, 2	1	2	Music, various foods, novels	?	Food/ music Mother		Culture parents? Coming to University?
Wolf 20	-	1s	2, 3, 4	3	2	3	Russian literature, Biodict. Biographical Music	Novel	Mother & Father-read		Gap year Russia?
Julia 19	Chistian	1b	1, 2, 3, 4	1, 2, 3	1, 2, 3, 4	2, 3, 4	Cover rooms in purple, pictures, *Manic Street Preacher*	*Manic Street Preacher*, *Manic Street* literature			Coming to University/ Death Grandmother

Name Age	Religion	Sibs	About 0 Bored 1 Self 2 Other 3 Group 4 World	Time orient. 1 Past 2 Present 3 Future	Level of Mediation 1 Affects 2 Case 3 Cat.-Self 4 High-Level	Reflect. 1 None 2 Notes 3 Seeks 4 Creates	Domin Ress	SymRes	From ?	Extern- alization	Trans./ Rupture?
Paris 20	Chris- tian.	-	3	2	1, 2	1	Job exp Father, design architect Sports	Architect.			?
Lewis 20	-	2S	1, 2, 3, 4	1, 3	1, 3	2	Western, Bond, Chan sports	Beach, guides			Back from gap year without memories
Thomas 20	Chrisian.	1s	1, 2, 3, 4	1, 2, 3	1, 2, 3, 4	3	Bible Political Biography	Bible Political. biography	Family grand- mother bible		? (gap year no problem)
Randy 20	-	1S, 1B	1, 2, 3	1, 2	1, 3, 4	3, 4	Cinema	Cinema	Father?		Been on the move
Lev 21	Ortho- dox Jew	2B, 1s	1, 2, 3, 4	2	1, 3	3, 4					Out Yeshiva
Eli 24	Ortho- dox Jew	1S	1, 2, 3	2, 3	1, 2, 3, 4	3, 4					Out yeshiva
Ron 21	Ortho- dox Jew	1S, 1s	1, 2	2	1, 2, 3, 4	1					Out yeshiva
Ilona 25	Jew-Mix	1s	1, 2, 3	1, 2	1, 2, 3	2	Cinema Fantasy	Fantasy	Mother- sister boy- friend		On the move
Moshe 25	Ortho- dox J – alt	2b 1s	1, 2, 3, 4	2	4	4					On the move

Name	Religion							Sources		Stage
Esther 22	Orthodox Jew	1S	1, 2, 3	2, 3	1, 2, 3, 4	3, 4	Life exp. Others Scouts Books, films non rel	Scouts ethics	parents	Out of yechiva
Pat 20	-	2S	1, 2, 3, 4	2, 3	1, 4	1				Out of school, & defining job
Charles 20	-	-	0, 1	1, 2	1	2	Novels Film	Novels Film	?	Out of school
Orson 21	atheist	1B, 1S	1	2	1, 3	3	Exp, others Novels	Novels?		Out of school
Mary 25	-	2B, 1b, 1s	1, 2	1, 2	1	1	professional, personal exp. others Tales Novels Museum	Novels (arts)	Mother, brothers tales, and paint	In job
Elaine 20	Mixed, none	2B	0, 1, 2	1, 2	1, 2, 3	2	Music, Books, Arts	Novels	Mother Every res.fam.	Coming to University
Olivia 23	Ex-Neo Apostolic	1S	0, 2	2	1	1	Friends, counsellors Music, radio novels	??? Radio?	-	professional choice

APPENDIX B

Framework for Interview

This research is about culture and the role it plays in our lives. I am going to ask you some general and some specific questions about different aspects of your experiences. I will also sometimes ask you to concentrate on more specific memories of given events, if this is ok for you. You are free to refuse to enter any question. The data has to be recorded; it will be transcribed anonymously, and if any part is used for a report, I guarantee that it will be impossible to recognize any person or place involved.

Starting point—how did you come to University, what did you expect? What is/is it different?

1. IF the person took a gap year: what was the gap year program?
2. When did you prepare yourself for coming here? (package, etc.).
3. What did you take with you? Did you take any novels, books, pictures, CD, with you, and so forth? Which one? How did you choose them?
4. What do you have in your room (books, music, pictures, posters, etc.)?
5. How similar is your new room from your previous room?

6. When do you listen music/what sort? Since you came here, did you read books (nontext-books)—things you brought with you? Can you describe a recent example when such a thing happened?
7. What is the last movie you saw, in two words? How did you choose? Did you go alone?
8. Did you ever read a novel a few times, or choose to see a movie a few times? What? Can you remember what it was about/can you remember at what moment of your life it came? Would you still do so? Do you know what changed?
9. Is there a particular event of reading a novel, or of watching a movie, theatre, church ... that was particularly important for you? How did you come across?
10. Is it the case that, in everyday situation, you would suddenly think about this (or any) novel, book, song, movie you like?
11. Do you have the memory of having read/being told stories with your parents/grandparents?
12. Were you close from your grand parents? Did you meet them often?
13. Did you have a religious education?
14. Do you have any idea about what will happen after University?

REFERENCES

Abbey, E., & Davis, P. (2003). Constructing one's identity through autodialogue: A cultural psychological approach. In I. Josephs (Ed.), *Dialogicality in development: Of advances in child development within culturally structured environments* (Vol. 5, pp. 69-86). New York: Elsevier.

Abbey, E., & Valsiner, J. (2003a, August). *Going to No-where: The role of diagnosis in educational practice*. Paper presented at the New Encounters for Educational Psychology symposium, Padova, Italy.

Abbey, E., & Valsiner, J. (2003b, August). *Emergence of meaning through ambivalence*. Paper presented at the European Conference on Developmental Psychology, Milano, Italy

Abbey, E. (in press). Triadic frames for ambivalent experience. *Estudios de Psicologia*.

Abraham, N., & Torok, M. (1994). *The shell and the kernel*. Chicago: University of Chicago Press.

Adams, G. R., Montemayor, R., & Gullotta, T. P. (Eds.). (1996). *Psychosocial development during adolescence*. Thousand Oaks, CA: Sage.

Adorno, T. (1991). *The culture industry* (selected papers). London: Routledge.

Alléon, A. M., Morvan, O., & Lebovici, S. (1990). *Devenir "adulte?"* [Becoming "adult?"]. Paris: Presses Universitaires de France.

Alvarez, A. (1992). *Live company: Psychoanalytical psychotherapy with autistic, borderlines and abandoned children*. London: Routledge.

Amato, P. R., & Booth, A. (1997). *A generation at risk: Growing up in an era of family upheaval*. Cambridge, MA: Harvard University Press.

Ammaniti, M., & Stern, D. N. (Eds). (1991). *Psychoanalysis and development: Representations and narratives*. New York: New York University Press.

Anastasopoulos, D. (1988). Acting out during adolescence in terms of regression in symbol formation. *International Review of Psychoanalysis, 15*, 177-194.

Anatrella, T. (1988). *Interminables adolescences. Les 12-30 ans, puberté, adolescence, postadolescence. Une société adolescentrique* [Endless adolescences: 12–30, puberty, adolescence, postaldolescence]. Paris: Cerf/Cujas.

Anatrella, T. (1999). *Adolescences au fil des jours* [Adolescences day after day]. Paris: Cerf/Cujas.

Anderson, D. R., Huston, A. C., Schmitt, K. L., Lineburger, D. L., & Wright, J. C. (2001). Early childhood television viewing and adolescent behaviour: The recontact study. *Monographs of the Society for Research on Child Development, 264,* 1-66.

Anderson, J. A. (1998). Qualitative approaches to the study of the media: Theory and methods of hermeneutical empiricism. In J. K. Asamen & G. L. Berry (Eds), *Research paradigms, television and social behaviour* (pp. 205-236). Thousand Oaks, CA: Sage.

Arnett, J. J. (1998). Learning to stand alone. The contemporaneous American transition to adulthood in cultural and historical context. *Human Development, 41,* 295-325.

Aumont, B., & Mesnier, P. M. (1992). *L'acte d'apprendre* [The act of learning]. Paris: Presses Universitaires de France.

Bagnoli, A. (2003). Imagining the lost other: The experience of loss and the process of identity construction in young people. *Journal of Youth Studies, 6*(2), 203-217.

Bajoit, G., & Franssen, A. (1995). *Les jeunes dans la compétition culturelle* [Young people in the cultural competition]. Paris: Presses Universitaires de France.

Bakhtin, M. M. (1981). Discourse in the novel. In M. Holquist (Ed.), *The dialogical imagination: Four essays by M. M. Bakthin* (C. Emerson & M. Holquist, Trans.) (pp. 259-420). Austin, Texas: University of Texas Press. (Original work published 1934-1935)

Bakhtin, M. M. (1981). Forms of time and chronotype in the novel. In M. Holquist (Ed.), *The Dialogical Imagination: Four essays by M. M Bakthin.* (C. Emerson & M. Holquist, Trans.) (pp. 84-258). Austin, Texas: University of Texas Press. (Original work published 1937-1938)

Bakhtin, M. M. (1986). *Speech genres and other late essays* (V. McGee, Trans.). Austin, Texas: University of Texas. (Original work published 1979)

Baltes, P. B. (1997). On the incomplete architecture of human ontogeny. Selection, optimization and compensation as foundation of developmental psychology. *Amercian Psychologist, 52*(4), 366-380.

Baltes, P. B. (2000). Autobiographical reflections: From developmental methodology and lifespan psychology to gerontology. In J. E. Birren & J. J. F. Schroots (Eds), *A history of geropsychology in autobiography* (pp. 7-26). Washington, DC: American Psychological Association.

Baltes, P. B., Lindenberger, U., & Staudinger, U. M. (1998). Life-span theory in developmental psychology. In R. M. Lerner (Eds.), *Handbook of child psychology: Vol. 1. Theoretical models of human development* (5th ed., pp. 1179-1143) New York: Wiley.

Baltes, P., B., & Staudinger, U. M. (1996*). Interactive minds. Life span perspectives on the social foundation of cognition.* New York: Cambridge University Press.

Bandura, A. (Ed.). (1971). Analysis of modelling processes. In *Psychological modelling: Conflicting theories* (pp. 1-62). Chicago: Aldine-Atherton.

Bangerter, A., Grob, A., & Krings, F. (2001). Personal goals at age 25 in three generations of the twentieth century: young adulthood in historical context. *Swiss Journal of Psychology*, *60*(2), 59-54.

Bar-On, D. (1995). *Fear and hope: Three generations of the holocaust*. Cambridge, MA: Harvard University Press.

Barrett, P. M., & Holmes, J. (2001). Attachment relationships as predictors of cognitive interpretation and response bias in late adolescence. *Journal of Child and Family studies*, *10*(1), 477-496.

Bartlett, F. C. (1995). *Remembering: A study in experimental and social psychology*. New York: Cambridge University Press. (Original work published 1932)

Bedell, G. (2002, February). Why don't we just grow up? *The Observer*, p. 4.

Benson, C. (1993). *The absorbed self: Pragmatism, psychology and aesthetic experience*. London: Harvester Wheatsheaf.

Benson, C. (2001). *The cultural psychology of self*. London: Routledge.

Bergson, H. (1911). *Creative evolution* (A. Mitchell, Trans.) New York: Henry Holt.

Bernand, C., Capone, S., Lenoir, F., & Champion, F. (2001). Regards croisés sur le bricolage et le syncrétisme. A propos de Mary (André) [Crossed perspectives on bricolage and syncretism: About Mary (André)]. *Archives de Sciences Sociales des Religions*, *114*, 39-60. Available: http://www.ehess.fr/centres/ ceifr/assr/ N114/BERNAND.htm

Bettelheim, B. (1985) *The uses of enchantment: The meaning and importance of fairy tales*. Harmondsworth, England: Penguin. (Original work published 1976)

Bideaud, J., Houdé, O., & Pedinelli, J. L. (1993). *L'homme en développement* [Human in development]. Paris: Presses Universitaires de France.

Bion, W. R. (1977). *Seven servants: Four works by W. R. Bion*. New York: John Aronson.

Blanchet, A. (1991). *Dire et faire dire, l'entretien* [Saying and making say, the interview]. Paris: Armand Colin.

Blandin, B. (2002). *La construction du social par les objets* [The construction of the social by the objects]. Paris: Presses Universitaires de France.

Blos, P. (1966). *On adolescence*. New York: Free Press. (Original work published 1962)

Blumer, H., & Hauser, P. M. (1933) *Movies, delinquency and crime*. New York: Macmillan.

Boesch, E. E. (1991). *Symbolic action theory and cultural psychology*. Berlin, Germany: Springer.

Boesch, E. E. (1995). *L'action symbolique: Fondements de psychologie culturelle*. Paris: L'Harmattan.

Boesch, E. E. (2001). Symbolic action theory in cultural psychology. *Culture & Psychology*, *7*, 479-483.

Bourdieu, P. (1984). *Distinction: A social critique of the judgment of taste*. London: Routledge. (Original work published 1979)

Brandstädter, J., & Lerner, M. L. (Eds.). (1999). *Action and self-development: Theory and research through the life span*. Thousand Oaks, CA: Sage.

Brentano, F. (1995). *Psychology from an empirical standpoint*. London: Routledge. (Original work published 1874)

Brentano, F. (1995). *Descriptive psychology*. London: Routledge. (Original work published 1887)

Bruner, J. S. (1990). *Acts of meaning*. Cambridge, MA: Harvard University Press.

Bruner, J. S. (1996). *The culture of education*. Cambridge, MA: Harvard University Press.

Bruno, P. (2000). *Existe-t-il une culture adolescente?* [Is there an adolescent culture?] Paris: In Press Editions.

Buchmann, M. C. (2001). Youth culture, sociology of. In N. J. Smelser & P. B. Baltes (Eds.), *International encyclopedia of the social and behavioral sciences* (pp. 16661-16664). Oxford, England: Elsevier.

Bynner, J., Chisholm, L., & Furlong, A. (Eds). (1997). *Youth, citizenship and social change in a European context*. Aldershot, England: Ashgate.

Bynner, J., Ferri, E., & Shepherd, P. (Eds). (1997). *Twenty-something in the 1990s: Getting on, getting by, getting nowhere*. Aldershot, England: Ashgate.

Byrne, R. M. (1990). Mental models. In M. W. Eysenck, A. Ellis, E. Hunt, & P. Johnson-Laird (Eds), *The Blackwell Dictionary of cognitive psychology* (pp. 224-225). Cambridge, MA: Blackwell.

Cairnay, T., & Ashton, J. (2002). Three families, multiple discourses: Parental roles, constructions of literacy and diversity of pedagogic practices. *Linguistics and Education, 13*(3), 303-345.

Campiche, R. J. (Ed.). (1997). *Cultures jeunes et religions en Europe* [Youth culture and religions in Europe]. Paris: Cerf.

Canestrari, R. (1989). Recent researches in the transition from adolescence to adulthood. In Bosinelli & F. Giuberti (Eds), *The age of adolescence and youth and the psychosocial profile of the university student* (pp. 14-35). Bologna, Italy: Cooperativa Libraria Universitaria Editore.

Carugati, F. (2004). Learning and thinking in adolescence and youth. How to inhabit new provinces of menaing. In A.-N. Perret-Clermont, C. Pontecorvo, L. Resnick, T. Zittoun, & B. Burge (Eds), *Joining society: Social interaction and learning in adolescence and youth* (pp. 119-140). New York: Cambridge University Press.

Carugati, F., & Selleri, P. (1996). *Psicologia sociale dell'educazione* [Social psychology of education]. Bologna, Italy: Il Mulino.

Cavalli, A. (1989). The sociological viewpoint in the adolescence-adulthood transition. In M. Bosinelli & F. Giuberti (Eds.), *The age of adolescence and youth and the psychosocial profile of the university student* (pp. 37-42). Bologna, Italy: Cooperativa Libraria Universitaria Editore.

Cavalli, A., & Galland, O. (Eds.). (1993). *L'allongement de la jeunesse* [The lengthening of youth] Paris: Actes Sud.

Certeau, Michel de. (1984). *The practice of everyday life* (S. Randall, Trans.). Berkeley, CA: University of California Press. (Original work published 1980)

Charlot, B., & Glasman, D. (Ed.). (1998). *Les jeunes, l'insertion, l'emploi* [Youth, insertion, work]. Paris: Presses Universitaires de France.

Charlot, B., Bautier, E., & Rochex, J. Y. (1992). *École et savoir dans les banlieues et ailleurs* [School and knowledge in the suburbs and elsewhere]. Paris: Armand Colin.

Chevalier, T. (1999). *Girl with a pearl earring*. London: Harper Collins.

Clémence, A., Rochat, F., Cortolezzis, C., Dumont, P., Egloff, M., & Kaiser, C. (2001). *Scolarité et adolescence. Les motifs de l'insécurité* [Schooling and adolescence: The cause of insecurity]. Bern, Switzerland: Haupt.

Cole, M. (1995). Cultural-historical psychology: A meso-genetic approach. In L. M. W. Martin, K. Nelson, & E. Tobach (Ed.), *Sociocultural psychology: Theory and practices of doing and knowing* (pp. 168-204). New York: Cambridge University Press.

Cole, M. (1996). *Cultural psychology. A once and future discipline*. Cambridge, MA: The Belknap Press of Harvard University Press.

Coleman, J. (1993). Adolescence in a changing world. In S. Jackson & H. Rodriguez-Tomé (Eds.), *Adolescence and its social worlds* (pp. 251-268). Hillsdale, NJ: Erlbaum.

Coleman, J. C., & Hendry, L. (1999). *The nature of adolescence* (Rev. ed.). London: Routledge. (Original work published 1980)

Cornish, F. (2004a). Making "context" concrete: A dialogical approach to the society-health relation. *Journal of Health Psychology, 9*(2), 281-294.

Cornish, F. (2004b) *Constructing an actionable environment: Collective action for HIV prevention among Calcutta sex workers*. Unpublished doctoral dissertation, London School of Economics.

Cottle, T. J. (2001). *Mind fields: Adolescent consciousness in a culture of distraction*. New York: Peter Lang.

Coulon, A. (1997). *Le métier d'étudiant* [The profession of student]. Paris: Presses Universitaires de France.

Cranach, M. V. (1992). The multi-level organization of knowledge and action—an integration of complexity. In M. V. Cranach, W. Doise, & G. Mugny (Eds.), *Social representations and the social basis of knowledge* (pp. 10-21). Bern, Switzerland: Hogrefe & Huber.

Crapanzano, V. (2004). *Imaginative horizons: An essay in literary philosophical anthropology*. Chicago: University of Chicago Press.

Crockett, L. A., & Silbereisen, R. K. (Eds.). (2000). *Negotiating adolescence in times of social change*. New York: Cambridge University Press.

Csikszentmihaly, M., & Larson, R. (1984). *Being adolescent: Conflict and growth in the teenage years*. New York: Basic Books.

Csikszentmihaly, M., & Schneider, B. (2000). *Becoming adult: How teenagers prepare for the world of work*. New York: Basic Books.

Csikszentmihaly, M. (1998). *Living well. The psychology of everyday life*. London: Phoenix. (Original work published 1997)

Csikszentmihaly, M., & Rochber-Halton, E. (1981). *The meaning of things: Domestic symbols and the self.* Cambridge, England: Cambridge University Press.

Cupchik, G. C. (2002). The evolution of psychical distance as an aesthetic concept. *Culture & psychology, 8*(2), 155-187.

De Bruin, J. (2001, February). *Qualitative analysis of media content: The representation of sexuality in teen magazines and ethnicity in soap operas*. Paper presented at the Faculty of Social and Political Sciences, University of Cambridge, England.

De Rivera, J. (Ed.) (1976). *Field theory as human-science: Contributions of Lewin's Berlin group*. New York: Gardner Press.

De Rosny, E. (1985). *Healers in the night* (R. R. Barr, Trans.). New York: Orbis. (Original work published 1981)

De Rosny, E. (1992). Les nouveaux guérisseurs africains: Réaménagments de l'espace thérapeutique [The new African healers: Reframing the therapeutic setting]. In M. Grossen & A. -N. Perret-Clermont (Eds.), *L'Espace thérapeutique. Cadres et contextes* (pp. 249-267). Paris: Delachaux et Niestlé.

Deconchy J. P. (1973). Systèmes de croyances et comportements orthodoxes [Systems of beliefs and orthodox behaviours]. *La Recherche, 4*(30), 35-42.

Deconchy, J. P. (2003). Croyances et idéologies. Systèmes de représentations, traitement de l'information sociale, mécanismes cognitifs [Beliefs and ideology: Systems of representations, treatment of social information, cognitive mechanisms]. In S. Moscovici (Ed.). *Psychologie sociale* (pp. 335-362). Paris: Presses Universitaires de France..

Dewey, J. (1910). *How we think*. Lexington, MA: D.C. Heath.

Dewey, J. (1917). Duality and dualism. *The Journal of Philosophy, Psychology and Scientific methods, 14*(18) 491-493.

Dewey, J. (1934). *Art as experience*. London: George Allen & Chumin.

Diriwächter, R. (2003, June). *What really matters: Keeping the whole*. Paper presented at the 10th biennale conference for the International Society for theoretical psychology, Istanbul, Turkey.

Diriwächter, R. (2004). Völkerpsychologie: The synthesis that never was. *Culture & Psychology, 10*(1), 85-109.

Doise, W. (1986). *Levels of explanation in social psychology*. New York: Cambridge University Press.

Dominicé, P. (Ed.) (1985). *Pratiques du récit de vie et théories de la formation* [Practices of life narrative and theories of training]. Genève, Switzerland: Faculté de Psychologie et des Sciences de L'éducation.

Dubois, N., & Trognon, A. (1989). L'apport de la notion de norme d'internalité à l'approche des pratiques de formation [The contribution of the notion or internality norm to approaches of training practices]. In J. L. Beauvois, R. V. Joule, & J. M. Monteil (Eds.), *Perspectives cognitives et conduites sociales* (pp. 213-224). Cousset, Switzerland: Delval.

Dudzik, P. (1998). La mondialisation de la société [The mondialisation of society]. *La Revue Pour les 150 ans de l'État Fédéral et les 200 ans de l'Helvétique*, 4-6.

Duffell, N. (2000). *The making of them. The British attitude to children and the boarding school system*. London: Lone Arrow Press.

Durkin, K. (1995). *Developmental social psychology: From infancy to old age*. Malden, MA: Blackwell.

Duveen, G. (1997). Psychological development as a social process. In L. Smith, J. Dockrell, & P. Tomlinson (Eds), *Piaget, Vygotsky and beyond: Future issues for developmental psychology and education* (pp. 67-90). London: Routledge.

Duveen, G. (1998). The psychosocial production of ideas: Social representations and psychologic. *Culture & psychology, 4*(4), 455-472.
Duveen, G. (2000). Introduction: The power of ideas. In S. Moscovici (Ed.), *Social representations: Explorations in social psychology* (pp. 1-17). Cambridge, England: Polity.
Duveen, G. (2001). Representations, identities, resistance. In K. Deaux & G. Philogene (Eds.), *Social representations: Introductions and explorations* (pp. 257-20). Oxford, England: Blackwell.
Duveen, G., & Gilligan, C. (2004, March). *A conversation on interviewing*. Cambridge, England: University of Cambridge.
Duveen, G., & Lloyd, B. (Eds.). (1990). *Social representations and the development of knowledge*. Cambridge, England: Cambridge University Press.
Elkind, D. (1970). The origins of religion in the child. *Review of Religious Research, 12*, 35-42.
Elkind, D. (1999). Religious development in adolescence. *Journal of Adolescence, 22*, 291-296.
Erikson, E. H. (Ed.). (1975). "Identity Crisis" in autobiographical perspective. In *Life history and the historical moment* (pp. 17-46). New York: W. W. Norton.
Evans, K., & Furlong, A. (1997). Metaphors of young transitions: Niches, pathways, trajectories or navigations. In J. Bynner, L. Chisholm, & A. Furlong (Eds), *Youth, citizenship and social changes in a European context* (pp. 17-41). Aldershot, England: Ashgate.
Fabbri, D., Mari, R., & Valentini, A. (1992). *La Paura di Capire, Modelli di socializzazione e nuova patologia nei primi anni dell'adolescenza* [The fear of understanding: Models of socialisation and new pathologies of the first years of adolescence]. Milano, Italy: FrancoAngeli.
Fairey, S. (1990). *Manifesto*. Available: www.obeygiant.com
Fallada, H. (2002). *Seul dans Berlin* (A. Virell & A. Vandervoorde, Trans.). Jeder stirbt für sich allein [Each man dies his own death]. Paris: Denoël/Folio. (Original work published 1947)
Falmagne, R. J. (2001). The dialectic of critique, theory and method in developing feminist research on inference. In J. R. Morss, N. Stephenson, & H. Van Rappard (Eds.), *Theoretical issues in psychology* (pp. 145-157). Dodrecht, The Netherlands: Kluwer Academic Press.
Falmagne, R. J. (2003). *A contextual approach to the study of "mind": Cognition, discourse and society*. Paper presented of the University of Athens Cognitive Science program, Clark University, MA.
Feldman, C., Bruner, J., Kalmar, D., & Renderer, B. (1994). Plot, plight and dramatism: Interpretation at three ages. In W. F. Overton & D. S. Palermo (Eds.), *The nature and ontogenesis of meaning* (pp. 255-279). Hillsdale, NJ: Erlbaum.
Fine, G. A., Mortimer, J. T., & Roberts, D. F. (1990) Leisure, work., and the mass media. In S. S. Feldman & G. R Elliott (Eds.), *At the threshold: The developing adolescent* (pp. 225-252). London: Harvard University Press.
Flammer, A., & Alsaker, F. (2000). Adolescent electronic media use: Instead of doing what? *International Journal of Group Tensions, 29*(1-2), 163-190.

Flammer, A., & Alsaker, F. (2001). *Entwicklungspsychologie der Adoleszenz. Die Erschliessung innerer und äusserer Welten im Jugendalter* [Developmental psychology of the adolescent: The resolution of inner and outer world in youth]. Bern, Switzerland: Verlag Hans Huber.

Flaubert, G. (1999). *Madame Bovary: Life in a country town* (G. Hopkins, Trans.). Oxford, England: Oxford University Press. (Original work published 1857)

Flyvbjerg, B. (2001). *Making social science matters: Why social inquiry fails and how it can succeed again.* Cambridge, England: Cambridge University Press.

Fonagy, P., Gergely, G., Jurist, E. L., & Target, M. (2002). *Affect regulation, Mentalisation, and the development of the self.* New York: Other Press.

Fornäs, J., & Bolin, G. (1995). *Youth culture in late modernity.* Thousand Oak, CA: Sage.

Fouquet, A. (2004). Joining society in Europe: Convergence or sustainability of national specificities. In A. -N. Perret-Clermont, C. Pontecorvo, L. Resnick, T. Zittoun, & B. Burge (Eds.), *Joining society: Social interaction and learning in adolescence and youth* (pp. 267-285). New York: Cambridge University Press.

Freud, S. (1900). The interpretation of dreams. *S. E., 4-5*, 1-630.

Freud, S. (1901). On dreams. *S. E., 5*, 631-678.

Freud, S. (1908). Creative writers and day-dreaming. *S. E., 9*, 141-153.

Freud, S. (1914). Remembering, repeating and working through. *S. E., 12*, 145-156.

Freud, S. (1920). Beyond the pleasure principle. *S. E., 18*, 7-64.

Freund, A. M. (2003). Die rolle von zielen für die entwicklung [The role of goals for development]. *Psychologische Rundschau, 54*(4), 233-242.

Friedrich, W., & Hossakovski, A. (1962). *Zur Psychologie des Jugendalters [For a psychology of youth].* Berlin, Germany: Volk und Wissen, Volkeigener Verlag.

Fuhrer, U. (2004). *Cultivating minds: Identity as meaning-making practices.* New York: Routledge.

Galland, O. (1995). Une entrée de plus en plus tardive dans la vie adulte [An always-later entrance in adult life]. *Economie et Statistique, 3-4*(283-284), 33-52.

Galland, O. (1997). *Sociologie de la jeunesse* [Sociology of youth]. Paris: Armand Colin.

Geertz, C. (1972). Religion as a cultural system. In C. Geertz (Ed.), *The interpretation of culture* (pp. 87-126). New York: Basic Books.

Giddens, A. (1994). Living in a post-traditional society. In U. Beck, A. Giddens, & S. Lash, (Eds.), *Reflexive modernization: Politics, tradition and aesthetics in the modern social order* (pp. 56-110). Cambridge, England: Polity Press.

Gigerenzer, G. (2002). *Reckoning with risk: Learning to live with uncertainty.* London: Penguin Books.

Gillespie, A. (2003). Surplus & supplementarity: Moving between the dimensions of otherness. *Culture & Psychology, 9*(3), 209-220.

Gillespie, A. (2004). *Returning surplus: Constructing the architecture of intersubjectivity.* Unpublished doctoral dissertation, University of Cambridge, England.

Gillespie, A. (2005). Malcolm X and his autobiography: Identity development and self-narration. *Culture & Psychology, 11*(1), 77-88.

Gilligan, C. (1983). *In a different voice: Psychological theory and women's development.* London: Harvard University Press. (Original work published 1982)

References 231

Gilligan, C. (1988). Adolescent development reconsidered. In C. Gilligan, J. V. Ward, & J. Mclean Taylor (Eds.), *Mapping the moral domain*. Cambridge, MA: Harvard University Press.

Ginsburg, H. P. (1997). *Entering the child's mind: The clinical interview in psychological research and practice*. Cambridge, England: Cambridge University Press.

Girardet, H., & Fasulo, A. (1997). I bambini riscrivono la storia: La costruzione retorica del punto vista [Children rewrite history: Rhetorical construction of the point of view]. *Rassegna di Psicologia, 14*(1), 139-176.

Goffman, E. (1963). *Stigma: Notes on the management of spoiled identity*. Englewood Cliffs, NJ: Prentice-Hall.

Goffman, E. (1975). *Frame analysis: An essay on the organisation of experience*. Cambridge, MA: Harvard University Press.

Gollwitzer, P. M., Bayer, U., Scherer, M., & Seifert, A. E. (1999). A motivational-volitional perspective on identity development. In J. Brandtädter & R. M. Lerner (Eds), *Action and self-development: Theory and research through the life-span* (pp. 283-314). Thousand Oaks, CA: Sage.

Goodnow, J. J. (1999). Families and development. In M. Bennett (Ed.), *Developmental psychology: Achivements and prosects* (pp. 72-88). London: Psychology Press.

Green, A. (1969). La lecture psychanalytique des tragiques [A psychoanalytical reading of tragic]. *Un oeil vivant: Le complexe d'Oedipe dans la tragédie* (pp. 10-47) Paris: Éditions de Minuit.

Green, A. (1992). *La déliaison. Psychanalyse, anthropologie et littérature* [Unlinking: Psychoanalysis, anthropology and literature]. Paris: Hachette Littératures/Les belles lettres, Pluriel.

Green, A. (1999). *The fabric of affect in the psychoanalytical discourse* (A. Sheridan, Trans.). London: Routledge. (Original work published 1973)

Green, A. (2000). *André Green at the Squiggle Foundation* (J. Abrams, Ed.). London: Karnac Books.

Green, A. (2002). *Abrégé de psychanalyse* [Introduction to psychoanalysis]. Paris: Presses Universitaires de France.

Griffin, C. (1993). *Representations of youth: The study of youth and adolescence in Britain and America*. Cambridge, England: Polity Press.

Grob, A. (2001). Transition from youth to adulthood across cultures. In N. J. Smelser & P. B. Baltes (Eds.), *International encyclopaedia of the social and behavioural sciences* (pp. 16678-16682). Oxford, England: Elsevier.

Grob, A., Krings, F., & Bangerter, A. (2001). Life markers in biographical narratives of people from three cohorts: A life span perspective in its historical context. *Human Development, 44*(4), 171-190.

Grodal, T. (1997). *Moving pictures: A new theory of film, genres, feelings and cognition*. Oxford, England: Clarendon Press.

Grossen, M. (1988). *Construction de l'intersubjectivité en situation de test* [The construction of intersubjectivity in test situation]. Cousset, Switzerland: DelVal.

Grossen, M. (2001, August-September). *Constructing meaning and context in teacher-student interactions*. KeyNote address, EARLI 9th conference, Fribourg, Germay.

Grossen, M., & Perret-Clermont, A. -N. (Ed). (1992). *L'espace thérapeutique. Cadres et contextes* [The therapeutic space: Frames and contexts]. Paris: Delachaux et Niestlé.

Grossen, M., & Perret-Clermont, A. -N. (1994). Psychosocial perspective on cognitive development: Construction of adult-child intersubjectivity in logic tasks. In W. de Graaf & R. Maier (Eds.), *Sociogenesis re-examined* (pp. 243-260). New York: Springer.

Grossen, M., Liengme Bessire, M. J., & Perret-Clermont, A. -N. (1997). Construction de l'interaction et dynamiques socio-cognitives [Construction of interaction and sociocognitive dynamics]. In M. Grossen & B. Py (Eds.), *Pratiques Sociales et Médiations Symboliques* (pp. 221-247). Bern, Switzerland: Peter Lang.

Grotevant, H. D. (2001). Developing new insights form a process approach to adolescent development. *Human development, 44*, 55-58.

Guichard, J. (1993). *L'école et les représentations d'avenir des adolescents* [School and adolescents' future representations]. Paris: Presses Universitaires de France.

Gutton, P., & Jeammet, P. (Eds.). (1998). Pertinence de l'œuvre d'André Green pour une théorisation de l'adolescence [Relevance of the work of André Green for a theory of adolescence]. *Adolescence, 17*(1).

Habermas, T. (1999a). *Geliebte Objekte: Symbole und Instrumente der identitätsbildung* [Loved objects: Symbols and tools for identity construction]. Frankfurt, Germany: Suhrkamp. (Original work published 1999)

Habermas, T. (1999b). Persönliche Objekte und bindungen im prozess der Ablösung vom elternhaus [Personal objects and attachments in the process of separation from the parental house]. In U. Fuhrer & I. E. Josephs (Eds.), *Persönliche Objekte, Identität und Entwicklung* (pp. 109-133). Göttingen, Germany: Vandenhoeck & Ruprecht.

Hacking, I. (1999). *The social construction of what?* London: Harvard University Press.

Harris, P. L. (2000). *The work of the imagination*. Oxford, England: Blackwell.

Harris, P. L. (2002). What do children learn from testimony? In P. Carruthers, M. Siegal, & S. Stich (Eds.), *Cognitive bases of science* (pp. 316-334). Cambridge, England: Cambridge University Press.

Harter, S. (1990). Self and identity development. In S. Feldman & G. Elliott (Eds.), *At the threshold: The developing adolescent*. Cambridge, MA: Harvard University Press.

Hartup, W. W. (1999). Peer experience and its developmental significance. In M. Bennett (Ed.), *Developmental psychology: Achievements and prospects* (pp. 106-125). Philadelphia: Psychology Press.

Haskell, V. M., & McHale (2004, July). *Symbolic processes in a toddler's efforts to move forward in face of uncertainty*. Paper presented at the 18th biennial meeting of the International Society for the study of behavioural development, Ghent, Belgium.

Haskell, V. M., Valsiner, J., & McHale, J. P. (2003). *Toddlers' processing of affect in symbolic self-soothing: The early development of symbolic play skills*. Poster session presented at the 33rd annual meeting of the Jean Piaget Society, Chicago.

Hasse, C. (2001). Institutional creativity: The relational zone of proximal development. *Culture & Psychology, 7*(2), 199-221.

References 233

Havel, V. (1988). *Letters to Olga: June 1979-September 1982*. Boston: Faber & Faber. (Original work published 1983)

Heath, A., & Yi Cheung, S. (1998). Education and occupation in Britain. In Y. Shavit & W. Muller. (Eds.), *From school to work: A comparative study of educational qualifications and occupational destinations* (pp. 71-101). Oxford, England: Clarendon Press.

Heath, S. B. (1994). Stories as ways of acting together. In A. H. Dyson & C. Genishi (Eds.), *The need for story: Cultural diversity in classroom and community* (pp. 206-220). Urbana, IL: National Council of Teachers of English.

Heath, S. B. (1996). Ruling places: Adaptation in development by inner-city youth. In R. Jessor, A, Colby, & R. A. Shweder (Eds.), *Ethnography and human development: Context and meaning in social inquiry* (pp. 225-251). Chicago: University of Chicago.

Heath, S. B. (2000). Seeing our way into learning. *Cambridge Journal of Education, 30*(1), 121-132.

Heaven, P. C. L. (1994). *Contemporary adolescence: A social psychological approach* South Melbourne, Australia: MacMillian.

Hendry, L. B., Shucksmith, J., Love, J. G., & Glendinning, A. (1993). *Young people's leisure and lifestyles*. New York: Routledge.

Henri, C. (2003). *De Marivaux et du Loft. Petites leçons de littérature au lycée* [About Marivaux and Big Brother: Little stories about literature at college]. Paris: P.O.L.

Hermans, H. J. M., & Kempen, H. J. G. (1993). *The dialogical self: Meaning as movement*. San Diego, CA: Academic Press.

Hermans, H. J M. (1996). Voicing the self: From information processing to dialogical interchange. *Psychological Bulletin, 119*, 31-50.

Hill, A. (2002, February). Meet Maria and Mathew—they live miles apart, but they're happy being together. *The Observer*, p. 10.

Hodge, R., & Tripp, D. (1986). *Children and television: A semiotic approach*. Cambridge, England: Polity Press.

Holyoak, K. J., & Thagard, P. (1995). *Mental leaps: Analogy in creative thought*. London: MIT Press.

Hundeide, K. (2001). Reactivation of cultural mediational practices. *Psychology and Developing Societies, 13*(1), 1-24.

Hundeide, K. (2004). A new identity, a new life-style. In A. -N. Perret-Clermont, C. Pontecorvo, L. Resnick, T. Zittoun, & B. Burge (Eds), *Joining society: Social interaction and learning in adolescence and youth* (pp. 86-108). New York: Cambridge University Press.

Hutchins, E. (1995). *Cognition in the wild*. London: MIT Press.

Iacovou, M., & Berthoud, R. (2001). *Young people's lives: A map of Europe*. Colchester, England: University of Essex, Institute for Social and Economic Research.

Iannaccone, A., Ghodbane, I., & Rosciano, R. (in press). La "ricerca del significato" nel contesto universitario: Il mestiere di studente. [The search for meaning in university context: The profession of student]. *Psicologia Scolastica*.

Inhelder, B., & Piaget, J. (1958). *Growth of logical thinking*. London: Routledge & Kegan Paul. (Original work published 1955)

Ivinson, G. (2002, August) *The construction of knowledge: School art as uncanny objects*. Paper presented at the International Conference on social representation, Stirling, Scotland.

James, W. (1884). What is an emotion? *Mind, 9*(34), 188-205.

James, W. (1984). *Psychology: Briefer course*. London: Harvard University Press. (Original work published 1892)

Janet, P. (1926). *De l'angoisse à l'extase. Tome I* [From anxiety to ecstasy. Vol. 1]. Paris: Librairie Félix Alcan.

Janet, P. (1928). *De l'angoisse à l'extase. Tome II*. [From anxiety to ecstasy. Vol. 2]. Paris: Librairie Félix Alcan.

Janet, P. (1929). *L' évolution psychologique [The psychological evolution of personality]*. Paris: Chahine.

Janet, P. (1935). *Les débuts de l'intelligence* [The beginnings of intelligence]. Paris: Flammarion. (Original work published 1934)

Jodelet, D. (2002). Les représentations sociales dans le champ de la culture [Social representations in the field of culture]. *Informations sur les Sciences Sociales, 41*(1), 111-133.

Joffe, M. L. (1998). *Adolescence*. New York: Wileys.

Johnson, J. G., Cohen, P., Smailes, E. M., Kasen, S., & Brook, J. S. (2002). Television viewing and aggressive behaviour during adolescence and adulthood. *Science, 295*, 2468-2471.

Josephs, I. E (1997). Talking with the dead: Self-construction as dialogue. *Journal of Narrative and Life History, 71*(1-4), 359-367.

Josephs, I. E. (1998). Constructing one's self in the city of the silent: Dialogue, symbols, and the role of "as if" in self-development. *Human Development, 41*, 180-195.

Kaës, R. (1994). *La parole et le lien* [The word and the link]. Paris: Dunod.

Kaës, R. (Ed.). (1996). *Contes et divans. Médiation du conte dans la vie psychique* (3ème édition), [Tales and couch: The mediation of the tale in psychic life (3rd ed.)]. Paris: Dunod.

Kaës, R. (Ed.). (1998). *Différences culturelles et souffrances identitaires* [Cultural differences and identity sufferance]. Paris: Dunod.

Kahneman, D. (2003). A perspective on judgment and choice: Mapping bounded rationality. *American Psychologist, 58*(9), 697-720.

Kamberelis, G., & Dimitriadis, G. (1998). Talkin' Tupac: Speech genres and the mediation of cultural knowledge. In C. M. Carthy, G. Hudak, S. Allegretto, & P. Saukko (Eds.), *Sound identities: Popular music and the cultural politics of education* (pp. 119-150). New York: Peter Lang.

Keating, D. P. (1990). Adolescent thinking. In S. Feldman & G. R Elliott (Eds.), *At the threshold. The developing adolescent* (pp. 54-89). London: Harvard University Press.

Keating, D. P., & Sasse, D. K. (1996). Cognitive socialisation in adolescence: Critical period for a critical habit of mind. In G. R. Adams, R., Montemayor, & T. P. Gullotta (Eds.), *Psychosocial development during adolescence* (pp. 232-258). Thousand Oaks, CA: Sage.

Koepping, K. P. (Ed.). (1997). The Ludic as creative disorder: Framing, de-framing and boundary crossing. In *The games of Gods and Man: Essays in play and performance* (Vol. 2, pp. 1-39). Hamburg, Germany: Lit Verlag.

Kögler, H. H. (2000). Empathy, dialogical self, and reflexive interpretation: The symbolic source of simulation. In H. H. Kögler & K. R. Stueber. (Eds.), *Empathy and agency: The problem of understanding in the human sciences* (pp. 194-221). Oxford, England: Westview Press.

Kohlberg, L. (1981). *The philosophy of education: Moral stages and the idea of justice.* San Francisco: Harper & Row.

Koreeda, H. (1998). *Wandafuru raifu* [Film]. Japan [After Life].

Kraus, W. (1996a). *Adolescent identity projects as Narratives. The Quest for a Dynamic Perspective* (No. 60). University of Munich.

Kraus, W. (1996b). *Das Erzählte Selbst. Die narrative Konstruktion von identität in der Spätmoderne.* [Narrated self: Narrative construction of identity in late modernity]. Pfaffenweiler, Germany: Centaurus.

Kraus, W. (2000). Making identities talk. On qualitative methods in a longitudinal study. *Forum: Qualitative Social Research* (On-line journal), *1*(2). Available: http://qualitative-research.net/fqs/fqs-e/2-00inhalt-e.htm

Labouvie-Vief, G. (1992). A neo-Piagetian perspective on adult cognitive development. In R. J. Sternberg & C. A. Berg (Eds.), *Intellectual development* (pp. 197-228). Cambridge, England: Cambridge University Press.

Laird, J. D. (in press). *Feelings: The perception of self.* New York: Oxford University Press.

Lakoff, G., & Johnson, M. (1980). *Metaphors we live by.* London: University of Chicago Press.

Lakoff, G. (1987). *Women, fire, and dangerous things: What categories reveal about the mind.* London: Chicago University Press.

Lambie, J. O., & Marcel, A. J. (2002). Consciousness an the varieties of emotional experiences: A theoretical framework. *Psychological review, 109*(2), 219-259.

Lnge, C. (1922). The emotions. In E. Dunlap (Ed.), *The emotions* (pp. 33-92). Baltimore: Williams & Wilkins.

Laser, S., Josephs, & Fuhrer, U. (1999). Die Bedeutung von Dingen für die Identität Jugendlicher [The meaning of things for youth identity]. In U. Fuhrer & I. E. Josephs (Eds.), *Persönliche Objekte, Identität und Entwicklung* (pp. 134-147). Göttingen, Germany: Vandenhoeck & Ruprecht.

László, J. (1999). *Cognition and representation in literature: The psychology of literary narratives.* Budapest, Hungary: Akadémiai Kiadó.

Laufer, M., & Laufer, E. (1984). *Adolescence and developmental breakdown: A psychoanalytic view.* New Haven, CT: Yale University Press

Lawrence, J., Benedikt, R., & Valsiner, J. (1992). Homeless in the mind: A case-history of personal life in and out of a close orthodox community. *Journal of Social Distress and the Homeless, 1*(2), 157-176.

Lawrence, J., & Valsiner, J. (1993). Conceptual roots of internalisation: From transmission to transformation. *Human development, 36,* 150-167.

Lawrence, J., & Valsiner, J. (2003). Making personal sense: An account of basic internalisation and externalisation processes. *Theory & Psychology, 13*(6), 723-752.

Lembo, R. (2000). *Thinking through television*. Cambridge, England: Cambridge University Press.
Lerner, R. M., & Galambos, N. L. (1998). Adolescent development: Challenges and opportunities for research, programs and policies. *Annual review of psychology, 49*, 413-436.
Lerner, R. M., Freund, A. M., De Stefanis, I., & Habermas, I. (2001). Understanding developmental regulations in adolescence: The selection, optimisation and compensation model. *Human development, 44*, 29-50.
Les orphelins des trente glorieuses. [Orphans of the glorious thirties]. (1996, October) *Esprit*.
Leudar, I., & Costall, A. (Eds.). (2004). Special issue: Theory of mind. *Theory & Psychology, 14*, 5.
Levi, P. (1991). *Other people's trades* (R. R. Rosenthal, Trans.). London: Abacus Sphere Books. (Original work published 1985)
Levi-Strauss, C. (1966). *The savage mind* (J. Weightman & D. Weightman, Trans.). Chicago: University of Chicago Press. (Original work published 1962)
Lewin, K. (1939). Field theory and experiment in social psychology: Concepts and methods. *The American Journal of Sociology, 44*(6), 868-896.
Lewin, K. (1951). *Field theory in social sciences: Selected theoretical papers* (S. Cartwright, Ed.). New York: Harper & Brothers.
Liebes, T., & Katz, E. (1990/1994) *The export of meaning: Cross-cultural readings of Dallas* (2nd ed.). Cambridge, England: Polity Press. (Original work published 1990)
Lightfoot, C. (1997a). The clarity of perspective: Adolescent risk taking, fantasy, and the internalization of cultural identity. In B. D. Cox & C. Lightfoot (Eds.), *Sociogenetic perspectives on internalization* (pp. 135-156). Mahwah, NJ: Erlbaum.
Lightfoot, C. (1997b). *The culture of adolescent risk-taking*. London: Guilford Press.
Lindlof, T. R., & Meyer, T. P. (1998). Taking the interpretative turn: Qualitative research of television and other electronic media. In J. K. Asamen & G. L. Berry (Eds.), *Research paradigms, television and social behaviour* (pp. 237-267). Thousand Oaks, CA: Sage.
Livingstone, S., & Lunt, P. (1994) *Talk on television: Audience participation and public debate*. London: Routledge
Livingstone, S. (1997). The work of Elihu Katz: Conceptualizing media effects in context. In J. Corner, P. Schlesinger, & R. Silverstone (Eds.), *International media research* (pp. 18-47). New York: Routledge.
Livingstone, S. (1998). *Making sense of television: The psychology of audience interpretation*. New York: Routledge.
Lloyd, T. (1999). *Reading for the future: Boys' and fathers' views on reading*. London: Save the Children.
Luria, A. R. (1969). *The mind of a mnemonist: A little book about a vast memory*. London: Cape.
Luria, A. R. (2003). *The making of mind: A personal account of soviet psychology* (M. Cole, Trans.). Cambridge, MA: Harvard University Press. (Original work published 1908) Available: http://www.marxists.org/subject/psychology/index.htm
Lutte, G. (1988). Libérer l'adolescence [Freeing adolescence]. Paris: P. Mardaga.

MacBeth, T. M. (Ed.). (1996). *Tuning in to young viewers: Social sciences perspectives on television*. Thousand Oak, CA: Sage.
Malewska-Peyre, H. Z., Tap, P. V. (Eds.). (1999). *La socialisation de l'enfance à l'adolescence* [Socialisation from childhood to adolescence]. Paris: Universitaires de France.
Marková, I. (2000). Amédée or how to get rid of it: Social representations from a dialogical perspective. *Culture & Psychology, 6*(4), 419-460
Markus, H. R., & Kitayama, S. (1991). Culture and the self: Implications for cognitions, emotions, and motivation. *Psychological Review, 98*, 224-253.
Marshall, H., & Wooelett, A. (2000). Changing youth: An exploration of visual and textual identifications. In C. Squire (Ed.), *Culture in psychology* (pp. 118-131). New York: Routledge.
Matte Blanco, I. (1975). *The unconscious as infinite sets: An essay in bi-logic*. London: Duckworth.
Mc Adams, D., & Bowman, P. J. (2001). Narrative life's turning points: Redemption and contamination. In D. Mc Adams, R. Josselson, & A. Lieblich (Eds.), *Turns in the road: Narrative studies of life in transitions* (pp. 3-34). Washington, DC: American Psychological Association.
Mc Gowan, H. (2001). *Schooling*. London: Faber & Faber.
Meeus, W. (1993). Occupational identity development, school performance, and social support in adolescence: Findings of a Dutch study. *Adolescence, 28*(112), 809-818.
Meeus, W., Iedema, J., Helsen, M., & Vollebergh, W. (1999). Patterns of adolescence identity: Review of literature and longitudinal analysis. *Developmental Review, 19*, 419-461.
Mischler, E. (1996) Missing persons: Recovering developmental stories/histories. In R. Jessor, A. Colby, & R. A. Shweder (Eds.), *Ethnography and human development: Context and meaning in social inquiry*. Chicago: Chicago University Press.
Mørch, S. (2003). Youth and education, *Young, 11*, 1, 49-73.
Moro, C., & Rodriguez, C. (1998). Towards a pragmatical conception of the object: The construction of the uses of the objects by the baby in the prelinguistic period. In M. D. P. Lyra & J. Valsiner (Eds.), *Construction of psychological processes in intepersonal communication* (Vol. 4, pp. 53-72). Norwood, England: Ablex.
Moro, M. R. (1998). *Psychothérapie transculturelle des enfants de migrants* [Transcultural psychotherapy of migrants' children]. Paris: Dunod.
Morrow, V., & Richards, M. (1996). *Transitions to adulthood*. York, England: John Rowntree Foundation.
Moscovici, S. (1973). *La psychanalyse, son image, son public* [Psychoanalysis, its image, its public]. Paris: Presses Universitaires de France.
Moscovici, S. (2000). *Social representations: Explorations in social psychology* (G. Duveen, Ed.). Cambridge, England: Polity.
Moscovici, S. (2003). Introduction. Le domaine de la psychologie sociale [The domain of social psychology]. In S. Moscovici (Ed.), *Psychologie sociale* (pp. 5-22). Paris: Presses Universitaires de France. (Original work published 1984)
Muuss, R. E. (1996). *Theories of adolescence*. New York: McGonvile. (Original work published 1996)

Nathan, T. (1990). Dionysos dé-contenancé. Irruptions psychopathologiques et métamorphoses de l'identité chez les jeunes de la seconde génération (l'exemple de la toxicomanie) [Startled Dionysos: Psychopathological irruptions and metamorphoses of identity in young people of the second generation (the example of drug-addiction]. In A. M. Alléon, O. Morvan, & S. Lebovici (Eds.), *Devenir "adulte?"* (pp. 193-212). Paris: Presses Universitaires de France.

Nathan, T. (1992). Tuer l'autre ou la vie qui est en l'autre [Killing the other or the life which is in the other]. *Nouvelle revue d'ethnopsychiatrie, 19*, 37-54.

Nathan, T. (1993). *...fier de n'avoir ni pays, ni amis, quelle sottise c'était* [...Proud to have no land, no friends, how foolish it was...]. Grenoble, France: La Pensée Sauvage.

Nathan, T. (Ed). (1998). *Psychothérapies* [Psychotherapies]. Paris: Odile Jacob.

Nathan, T. (2001). *Nous ne sommes pas seuls au monde* [We are not alone in the world]. Paris: Les Empêcheurs de Penser en Rond.

Neimeyer, R. A., & Hevitt, L. H. (2001). Coping and coherence: A narrative perspective on resilience. In C. R. Snyder (Ed.), *Coping with stress: Effective people and process* (pp. 47-67). Oxford, England: Oxford University Press.

Nell, V. (1988). *Lost in a book: The psychology of reading for pleasure*. London: Yale University Press.

Nelson, K. (1981). Social cognition in a script framework. In J. H. Flavell & L. Ross (Eds.), *Social cognitive development* (pp. 97-118) Cambridge, England: Cambrige University Press.

Nelson, K. (1996). *Language in cognitive development: Emergence of the mediated mind*. Cambridge, England: Cambridge University Press.

Nelson, K. (2002, September). *Entering a symbolic world*. Paper presented at the workshop "Exploring psychological development as a social and cultural process," Cambridge, England.

Notterman, J. M. (2004). Persistent conceptual issues in psychology: A selective update. *Theory & Psychology, 14*(2), 239-260.

Nurmi, J. E., & Salmela-Aro, K. (2002). Goal-construction, reconstruction and depressive symptoms in a life-span context: The transition from school to work. *Journal of Personality, 70*(3), 386-420.

Obeyesekere, G. (1963). Pregnancy cravings (Dola-Duka) in relation to social structure and personality in a sinhalese village. *American Anthropologist, 65*, 323-392.

Obeyesekere, G. (1977). Psychocultural exegesis of a case of spirit possession in Sri Lanka. In V. Crapanzo & V. Garrison (Ed.), *Case studies in sprit possession* (pp. 235-294). London: Wiley.

Ochs, E., & Capps, L. (2001). *Living narrative: Creating lives in everyday storytelling*. London: Harvard University Press.

Ouaknin, M. A. (1994). *Bibliothérapie* [Bibliotherapy]. Paris: Seuil.

Ouaknin, M. A. (1995). *The burnt book: Reading the Talmud* (L. Brown, Trans.). Princeton, NJ: University Press. (Original work published 1986)

Oxford English dictionary. (2004). Oxford, England: Oxford University Press. Available: http://dictionary.oed.com/entrance.dtl

Oz, A. (2003/2004). *A tale of love and darkness*. London: Chatto & Wintus.

Paìn, S. (1985). *La fonction de l'ignorance* [The function of ignorance]. Bern, Switzerland: Peter Lang.
Palmonari, A. (1984). *Notes sur l'adolescence* [Notes on adolescence]. Cousset, Switzerland: DelVal.
Palmonari, A. (Ed.). (1993). *Psicologia dell'adolescenza* [Psychology of adolescence]. Bologna, Italy: Il Mulino.
Park, K. S. (2003). *Thinking about friends: Learning resources.* Unpublished master's thesis, University of Cambridge, England.
Pasquier, V. (1999). *La culture des sentiments. L'expérience télévisuelle des adolescents* [The culture of feelings: Adolescents' televisual experience]. Paris: Editions de la Maison des Sciences de l'Homme.
Pasupathi, M., Staudinger, U. M., & Baltes, P. B. (2001). Seeds of wisdom: Adolescents' knowledge and judgement about difficult life problems. *Developmental psychology, 37*(3), 351-361
Pedler, E., & Ethis, E. (1999). La légitimité culturelle en questions [Cultural legitimacy on questions]. In B. Lahire (Ed.), *Le travail sociologique de Pierre Bourdieu: Dettes et critiques* (pp. 179-203). Paris: La Découverte.
Peirce, C. S. (1868a). Questions concerning certain faculties claimed for man. *Journal of Speculative Philosophy, 1,* 103-114.
Peirce, C. S. (1868b). Some consequences of four incapacities claimed for man. *Journal of Speculative Philosophy, 2,* 140-157. Available: http://members.door.net/arisbe/arisbe.htm
Peirce, C. S. (1878). How to make our ideas clear. In R. B. Goodman (Ed.), *Pragmatism: A contemporary reader* (pp. 37-49). London: Routledge.
Perret, J. F., & Perret-Clermont, A. -N. (2001). *Apprendre un métier technique dans un contexte de mutations technologiques* [Learning a technical trade in a period of technological development]. Fribourg, Switzerland: Éditions Universitaires de Fribourg.
Perret-Clermont, A. -N. (1980). *Social interaction and cognitive development in children.* New York: Academic Press.
Perret-Clermont, A. -N. (1997). Revisiting young Jean Piaget in Neuchâtel among his partners in learning. In L. Smith, J. Dockrell, & P. Tomlinson (Eds.), *Piaget, Vygotsky and beyond* (pp. 91-121). New York: Routledge.
Perret-Clermont, A. -N. (2001). Psychologie sociale de la construction de l'espace de pensée [Social psychology of the construction of the thinking space]. In J. J. Ducret (Ed.), *Actes du colloque. Constructivisme: Usages et perspectives en éducation* (Vol. I, pp. 65-82). Genève, Switzerland: Département de l'Instruction Publique: Service de la Recherche en Éducation.
Perret-Clermont, A. -N. (2004). Thinking spaces of the young. In A. -N. Perret-Clermont, C. Pontecorvo, L. Resnick, T. Zittoun, & B. Burge (Eds), *Joining Society: Social interaction and learning in adolescence and youth* (pp. 3-10). New York: Cambridge University Press.
Perret-Clermont, A. -N., & Carugati, F. (2001). Social factors in learning and instruction. In N. J. Smelser & P. B. Baltes (Eds.), *International encyclopedia of social and behavioral sciences* (pp. 8586-8588). Oxford, England: Elsevier.
Perret-Clermont, A. -N., Carugati, F., & Oates, J. (2004). A sociocognitive perspective on learning and cognitive development. In Oates, J. & Grayson, A.

(Eds.), Cognitive and language development in children (pp. 305-332). Oxford, England: Blackwell.

Perret-Clermont, A. -N., & Nicolet, M. (Eds.). (2001) *Interagir et connaître. Enjeux et régulations sociales dans le développement cognitif [Interacting and knowing]* (2nd edition). Paris: L'Harmattan. (Original work published 1986)

Perret-Clermont, A. -N., & Zittoun, T. (2002) Esquisse d'une psychologie de la transition [Sketch for a psychology of transition]. *Education permanente. Revue Suisse pour la Formation Continue, 1*, 12-15.

Perret-Clermont, A. -N., Perret, J. F., & Bell, N. (1991). The social construction of meaning and cognitive activity in elementary school children. In L. B. Resnick, J. M. Levine, & S. D. Teasley (Eds.), *Perspectives on socially shared cognition* (pp. 41-62). Washington DC: American Psychological Association.

Perret-Clermont, A. -N., Pontecorvo, C., Resnick, L., Zittoun, T., & Burge, B. (Eds.). (2004). *Joining society: Social interaction and learning in adolescence and youth*. New York: Cambridge University Press.

Perriault, J. (1989). *La logique de l'usage: Essai sur les machines à communiquer* [The logic of use: Essay on the communicating machines]. Paris: Flammarion.

Phillips, P. (1999a). Genre, star and auteur—critical approaches to Hollywood cinema. In J. Nelmes (Ed.), *An introduction to film studies* (2nd ed., pp. 162-207). New York: Routledge.

Phillips, P. (1999b). The film spectator. In J. Nelmes (Ed.), *An introduction to film studies* (2nd ed., pp. 129-160). New York: Routledge.

Piaget, J. (1951). *Play, dreams and imitation in childhood*. London: Heinemann.

Piaget, J. (1967). *Six psychological studies* (A. Tenzer & D. Elkind, Trans.). New York: Random House. (Original work published 1964)

Piaget, J. (1976). *The child's conception of the world*. Totawa, NJ: Littlefield. (Original work published 1926)

Piaget, J. (1981). *Intelligence and affectivity: Their relationship during child development*. Palo Alto, CA: Annual Review. (Original work published 1954)

Piaget, J. (1994). *La formation du symbole chez l'enfant. Imitation, jeu et rêve, image et représentation*. Lausanne, Switzerland: Delachaux & Niestlé. (Original work published 1945)

Pontecorvo, C., & Pirchio, S. (2000) A developmental view on children's arguing. The voice of the other. *Human Development, 43*(6), 361-363.

Pontecorvo, C. (2004). Thinking with others: The social dimension of learning in families and schools. In A. -N. Perret-Clermont, C. Pontecorvo, L. Resnick, T. Zittoun, & B. Burge (Eds), *Joining society: Social interaction and learning in adolescence and youth* (pp. 227-240). New York: Cambridge University Press.

Potek, C. (1967). *The chosen*. New York: Ballantine.

Poulet, G. (1980). Criticism and the experience of interiority. In J. P. Tompkins (Ed.), *Reader-response criticism: From formalism to post structuralism* (pp. 41-50). London: John Hopkins University Press. (Original work published 1972)

Prieur, C. (2002). Unions, enfants, ruptures: l'Insee explore la précocité familiale des détenus [Unions, children, ruptures: The Insee explores on the precociousness of prisoners]. *Le Monde, 15*(2), 12.

References 241

Psaltis, C., & Duveen, G. (in press). Social relations and cognitive development: The influence of conversation type and representations of gender. *European Journal of Social Psychology*.

Rabardel, P. (1999). Le langage comme interprétation, éléments pour une théorie instrumentale élargie [Language as interpretation, elements for an enlarged instrumental theory]. In Y. Clot (Ed.), *Avec Vygotsky* (pp. 241-265). Paris: La Dispute.

Rapaport, D. (1942). *Emotions and memory*. Baltimore: Williams & Wilkins.

Rayner, E. (1995). *Unconscious logic: An introduction to Matt-Blanco's bi-logic and its uses*. London: Routledge.

Resnick, L. (2004). Prospects for youth in post-industrial societies. In A. -N. Perret-Clermont, C. Pontecorvo, L. Resnick, T. Zittoun, & Burge, B. (Eds), *Joining Society: Social interaction and learning in adolescence and youth* (pp. 11-25). New York: Cambridge University Press.

Ricoeur, P. (1974). *The conflict of interpretations*. Chicago: Northwestern University Press. (Original work published 1969)

Ricoeur, P. (1976). *Metaphor and symbol: Interpretation theory*. Fort Worth, Texas: Texan Christian University Press.

Ricoeur, P. (1988). *Time and narrative, Vol. 3* (K. Blamey & D. Pellauer, Trans.). Chicago: University of Chicago Press. (Original work published 1985)

Ricoeur, P. (1991). On interpretation (K. Blamey & J. B. Thompso, Trans.). Evanston, IL: Northwestern University Press. (Original work published 1965)

Rommetveit, R. (1979). On the architecture of intersubjectivity. In R. Rommetveit & R. M. Blakar (Eds.), *Studies of language thought and verbal communication* (pp. 93-108). London: Academic Press.

Rönkä, A., Oravala, S., & Pulkkinen, L. (2002). "I met this wife of mine and things got onto a better track": Turning points in risk development. *Journal of Adolescence, 24,* 47-63.

Rosenthal, G. (1993a). Reconstruction of life stories: Principles of selection in generating stories for narrative biographical interviews. In R. Josselson & A. Lieblich (Eds.), *The narrative study of lives* (Vol. 1, pp. 59-91) New York: Sage.

Rosenthal, G. (1993b). *Erlebte und erzählte Lebensgeschichte. Gestalt und Struktur biographischer Selbstbeschreibungen* [Experienced and narrated life story: Form and structure in self-description]. Frankfurt, Germany: Campus Verlag.

Rossier, L. (1997). *L'adolescence et la psychologie de l'accommodation. Thèse de doctorat* [The adolescent and the psychology of adolescence]. Lausanne, Switzerland: Université de Lausanne.

Roulleau-Berger, L. (1991). *La ville intervalle. Jeunes entre centre et banlieue* [The town-interstice: Youth between centre and suburbs]. Paris: Meridiens Klincksieck.

Rowe, A. (1999). Film form and narrative. In J. Nelmes (Ed.), *An introduction to film studies* (2nd ed., pp. 92-128). New York: Routledge.

Russell, J. A. (2003). Core affect and the psychological construction of emotion. *Psychological review, 110*(1), 145-172.

Rutter, M., & Rutter, M. (1993). *Developing minds: Challenge and continuity across the life-span*. London: Penguin books.

Ryan, P. (2001). The school to work transition: Problems and indicators. In A. -N. Perret-Clermont, C. Pontecorvo, L. Resnick, T. Zittoun, & B. Burge (Eds.), *Joining society: Social interaction and learning in adolescence and youth* (pp. 286-299). New York: Cambridge University Press.

Salomon, G. (1979). *Interaction of media, cognition and learning*. San Francisco: Jossey-Bass.

Salomon, G. (1993). No distribution without individuals' cognition: A dynamic interactional view. In G. Salomon (Ed.), *Distributed cognitions: Psychological and educational considerations* (pp. 111-138). Cambridge, England: Cambridge University Press.

Saracho, O. N. (1997). Perspectives in family literacy. *Early Child Development and Care, 3*(11), 17-128.

Sayers, J. (1998). *Boy crazy: Remembering adolescence, therapies and dream*. New York: Routledge.

Schone, M. (2003, November 9). The matrix defense. *Boston Sunday Globe*, pp. D1-5.

Schubauer-Leoni, M. L., & Grossen, M. (1993). Negotiating the meaning of questions in didactic and experimental contracts. *European Journal of Psychology of Education, 8*(4), 451-471.

Schütz, A. (1945). On multiple realities. *Philosophy and Phenomenological Research, 5*(4), 533-576.

Schütz, A. (1951). *On phenomenology and social relations: Selected writings* (H. R. Wagner, Ed.). Chicago: University of Chicago Press.

Schütz, A. D. H. (1997). *Davai, Davai! Memoir of a German prisoner of World War II in the Soviet Union*. London: McFarland.

Searle, J. R. (1983). *Intentionality: An essay in the philosophy of mind*. Cambridge, England: Cambridge University Press.

Sebeok, T. A. (1994). *An introduction to semiotics*. London: Finter.

Segal, H. (1991). *Dream, fantasy and art*. London: Routledge.

Seiffge-Krenke, I. (1997). Imaginary companions in adolescence: Sign of deficient or positive development? *Journal of Adolescence, 20,* 137-154.

Sigel, I., & McGillicuddy-De Lisi, A. V. (2003). Rod Cocking's legacy: The development of psychological distancing. *Applied Developmental Psychology, 24*(6), 697–711.

Silbereisen, R. K. (2001a). Adolescents: Leisure-time activities. In N. J. Smelser & P. B. Baltes (Eds.), *International Encyclopaedia of the social and behavioural sciences* (pp. 122-125). Oxford, England: Elsevier.

Silbereisen, R. K. (2001b, July). *New research in antecedents and consequences of puberty and its timing on psychosocial development*. Paper presented at the VIIth European congress of psychology, the Barbican centre, London.

Simão, L. M. (2003). Beside rupture—disquiet; beyond the other—alterity. *Culture & Psychology, 9*(4), 449-459.

Staudinger, U. M., & Baltes, P. B. (1994). Psychology of wisdom. In R. J. Sternberg (Ed.), *Encyclopaedia of human intelligence* (pp. 1143-1152). New York: MacMilan.

Steinberg, L. (1993). *Adolescence* (3rd ed.). New York: McGraw Hill.

Steinberg, L., & Morris, A. S. (2001). Adolescent development. *Annual review of psychology, 52,* 83-110.
Steinsaltz, A. (1996). *The thriteen petalled rose.* New York: Basic books.
Steinsaltz, A. (Ed). (2001). *Le Talmud. Berakhot I.* Paris: Pocket.
Stern, D. (1996, September). *Self-narrative self.* Paper presented at the Iscrat conference, Piaget-Vygotsky Congress, Geneva, Switzerland.
Sugar Skateboard Magazine. (2000, August). André the Giant, a monstrous wrestler. *Sugar Skateboard Magazine,* 21. Retrieved August, 2000, from http://obeygiant.com/articles/sugar-english.html
Sutton-Smith, B. (1997). *The ambiguity of play.* Cambridge, MA: Harvard University Press.
Taracena, E. (1994). La construction psychique de l'enfant sous l'influence de modèles identitaires différents [The psychic construction of the child under the influence of various identity models]. In C. Labat & G. Vermes (Eds.), *Cultures ouvertes, sociétés interculturelles* (Vol 2, pp. 165-175). Paris: L'Harmattan.
Taylor, M. (1999). *Imaginary companions and the children who create them.* New York: Oxford University Press.
Tessler, M. A., Nelson, K. (1994). Making memories: The influence of joint encoding or later recall by young children. *Consciousness and Cognition, 3,* 307-326.
Thatcher, M. (1993). *The downing years.* London: Harper & Collins.
Thom, R. (1975). *Structural stability and morphogenesis.* New York: Benjamin.
Thompson, N. S. (2000). Shifting the natural selection metaphor to the group level. *Behavior and Philosophy, 28,* 83-101.
Tilton-Weaver, L. C., Vitunski E. T., & Galambos, N. L. (2001). Five images of maturity in adolescence: What does "grown up" mean? *Journal of Adolescence, 24,* 143-158.
Tisseron, S. (1996). *Secrets de famille mode d'emploi* [Family secrets—instructions]. Paris: Edition Ramsay.
Tisseron, S. (1998). *Y a-t-il un pilote dans l'image?* [Is there a pilot in the picture?]. Paris: Aubier.
Tisseron, S. (1999). *Comment l'esprit vient aux objets* [How spirit comes to objects]. Paris: Aubier.
Tisseron, S. (2000). *Enfants sous influence. Les écrans rendent-ils les jeunes violents?* [Children under influence: Do screen make youth violent?] Paris: Armand Colin.
Tisseron, S. (2002). *Les bienfaits des images* [The benefits of images]. Paris: Odile Jacob.
Tisseron, S. (2003). *Comment Hitchcock m'a sauvé la vie?* [How Hitchcock saved my life]. Paris: Armand Colin.
Tomasello, M. (1999). *The cultural origins of human cognition.* Cambridge, MA: Harvard University Press.
Toomela, A. (1996). How culture transforms mind: A process of internalisation. *Culture & Psychology, 2*(3), 285-306.
Toomela, A. (2000). Activity theory is a dead end for cultural-historical psychology. *Culture & Psychology, 6*(3), 353-364.
Trier, U. P., Zittoun, T., & Perret-Clermont, A. -N. (2004, May). *Entre générations: Histoires de vie et ressources symboliques* [Between generations: Life story and

symbolic resources]. One-day graduate workshop meeting at the Institut de Psychologie, Université de Neuchâtel, Switzerland.

Tudge, J. (2000). Theory, method, and analysis in research on the relations between peer collaboration and cognitive development. *The Journal of Experimental Education, 69*, 98-112.

Turner, J. S., & Helms, D. B. (1989). *Contemporary adulthood* (4th ed.). Chicago: Holt, Riverhart & Winston. (Original work published 1979)

Uexküll, J. Von. (1956). *Mondes animaux et mondes humains, suivi de théorie de la signification* [Animal worlds, human worlds, followed by theory of meaning]. (P. Müller, Trans.). Paris: Gonthier. (Original work published 1934)

Uexküll, J. Von. (1982) The theory of meaning (B. Stone & H. Weiner, Trans.). *Semiotica, 42*(1), 25-82. (Original work published 1940)

Vaculík, L. (1987). *A cup of coffee with my interrogators. The Prague chronicles of Ludvík Vaculík*. London: Readers International. (Original work published 1986)

Valsiner, J. (1987). *Culture and the development of children's action: A cultural-historical theory of developmental psychology*. New York: Wiley.

Valsiner, J. (1989). *Human development and culture: The social nature of personality and its study*. Lexington, MA: Lexington Books.

Valsiner, J. (1997). *Culture and the development of children's action: A theory of human development* (2nd ed.). New York: Wiley.

Valsiner, J. (1998). *The guided mind: A sociogenetic approach to personality*. Cambridge, MA: Harvard University Press.

Valsiner, J. (2000). *Culture and human development*. Thousand Oaks, CA: Sage

Valsiner, J. (2001a). *Cultural developmental psychology of affective processes*. Unpublished manuscript.

Valsiner, J. (2001b). Process structure of semiotic mediation in human development. *Human Development, 2&3*(44), 84-97.

Valsiner, J. (2002). Irreversibility of time and ontopotentiality of signs. *Estudios de Psicologia, 23*(1), 49-59.

Valsiner, J. (2003). Beyond social representations: A theory of enablement. *Papers on Social Representations, 12*, 7.1-7.16. Retrieved from http://www.psr.jku.at

Valsiner, J. (2004a). Editorial. Three years later: Culture in psychology—between social positioning and producing new knowledge. *Culture & Psychology, 10*(1), 5-28.

Valsiner, J. (in press). Soziale und emotionale Entwicklungsaufgaben im Kulturellen Kontext [Social, emotional and personality development]. In J. Asendorpf & H. Rauh (Eds.), *Soziale, emotionale und Persönlichkeits-entwicklung*. Göttingen, Germany: Hogrefe.

Valsiner, J. (2004c, July). *The promoter sign: Developmental transformation within the structure of dialogical self*. Paper presented at the symposium for the developmental aspects of the dialogical self, Ghent, Belgium.

Valsiner, J. (2004d, September). *Transformative and flexible forms: Where qualitative psychology begins*. Keynote conference meeting at the Inaugural Conference of the Japanese Association of Qualitative Psycholgy, Kyoto, Japan.

Valsiner, J., & Cappezza, N. (2002). *Creating arenas for action: Videogames and violence*. Invited lecturer at the 5th International Baltic Psychology Conference, Tartu, Estonia.

Valsiner, J., & Connolly, K. J. (2003). The nature of development: The continuing dialogue of processes and outcomes. In J. Valsiner & K. J. Conolly (Eds), *Handbook of developmental psychology* (pp. ix-xviii). Thousand Oaks, CA: Sage.

Valsiner, J., & Lawrence, J. A. (1997) Human development in culture across the life span. In J. W Berry, P. R. Dasen, & T. S. Saraswathi (Eds.), *Handbook of cross-cultural psychology* (Vol. 2, pp. 69-106). Needham Heights, MA: Allyn & Bacon.

Valsiner, J., & Sato, T. (in press). Historically structured sampling (HSS): How can psychology's methodology become tuned in to the reality of the historical nature of cultural psychology? In J. Straub, C. Kölbl, D. Widenman, & B. Zielke (Eds.), *Pursuit of meaning: Advances in cultural and cross-cultural psychology*. Bielefeld, Germany: Transcript.

Valsiner, J., & Van der Veer, R. (2000). Pierre Janet's world of tensions. In *The social mind: Construction of an idea* (pp. 61-137). Cambridge, England: Cambridge University Press.

Van Geert, P. (2003). Dynamic system approaches and modeling of developmental processes. In J. Valsiner & K. J. Conolly (Eds), *Handbook of developmental psychology* (pp. 640-672). Thousand Oaks, CA: Sage.

Von Trier, L. (Diretor). (2003). *Dogville* [Film]. Denmark.

Viderman, S. (1970). *La construction de l'espace analytique* [The construction of the analytical space] Paris: Gallimard.

Vygotsky, L. S. (1926). Esthetic education. In *Educational Psychology* (chapter 13), Available: http://www.marxist.org

Vygotsky, L. S. (1933). *Play and its role in the mental development of the child*. (N. Schmotlze, Trans.). Available: http://www.marxists.org/archive/vygotsky/works/1933/play.htm

Vygotsky, L. S. (1986). *Thought and language*. Boston: MIT Press. (Original work published 1934)

Vygotsky, L. S. (1971). *The psychology of art*. London: MIT Press. (Original work published 1928)

Vygotsky, L. S. (1978). Tool and symbol in child's development. In M. Cole, V. John-Steiner, S. Scribner, & E. Souberman (Eds.), *L. S. Vygotsky, Mind in Society: The development of higher psychological processes* (pp. 19-30). London: Harvard University Press. (Original work published 1930)

Vygotsky, L. S. (1994). Imagination and creativity of the adolescent In R. Van der Veer & J. Valsiner (Eds.), *The Vygotsky reader* (pp. 266-288). Cambridge, MA: Blackwell. (Original work published 1931)

Vygotsky, L. S., & Luria, A. (1994). Tool and symbol in child development. In R. van der Veer & J. Valsiner (Eds.), *The Vygotsky reader* (pp. 99-174). Oxford, England: Blackwell. (Based on a 1930 English-language manuscript given by Luria to Michael Cole)

Waddell, M. (1998). *Inside lives. Psychoanalysis and the growth of personality*. London: Duckworth.

Werner, H., & Kaplan, B. (1963). *Symbol formation: An Organismic-Developmental Approach to Language and the Expression of Thought*. New York: Wiley.

Wertsch, J. V. (1998). *Mind as action*. New York: Oxford University Press.

Wertsch, J. V. (1999). Cognitive development. In M. Bennett (Ed.), *Developmental psychology: Achievements and prospects* (pp. 309-322). Philadelphia: Psychology Press.

Wertsch, J. V. (2000). Vygotsky's two minds on the notion of meaning. In C. D. Dee & P. Smargorinsky, (Eds.), *Vygotskian perspectives on literacy research: Constructing meaning through collaborative activity* (pp. 19-30). Cambridge, England: Cambridge University Press.

Williams, K., & MacGillicuddy-De-Lisi, A. (1999). Coping strategies in adolescents. *Journal of Applied Developmental Psychology, 20*(4), 537-549.

Winnicott, D. W. (1968a). On "The Use of an Object." In C. Winnicott, R. Shepherd, M. Davis (Eds.), *Psycho-analytical explorations* (pp. 217-227). Cambridge, MA: Harvard University Press.

Winnicott, D. W. (1968b). Playing and culture: A talk given to the imago group, 12 March 1968. In C. Winnicott, R. Shepherd, & M. Davis (Eds.). *Psycho-analytical explorations* (pp. 203-206) Cambridge, MA: Harvard University Press.

Winnicott, D. W. (2001). *Playing and reality*. Philadelphia: Bruner-Routledge. (Original work published 1971)

Winnicott, D. W. (1989). *Psycho-analytic explorations* (C. Winnicott, R. Shepherd, & M. Davis, Eds.). London: H. Karnac.

Wiser, M. (2004, July). *A socio-constructivist perspective on the internalization of microworlds*. Paper presented at the XVIIIth ISSBD conference, Ghent, Belgium.

Wiser, M., & Amin, T. (2001). "Is heat hot?" Inducing conceptual change by integrating everyday and scientific perspectives on thermal phenomena. *Learning and Instruction, 11*(4-5), 331-355.

Wittgenstein, L. (2000). *Philosophical investigations*. Cambridge, MA: Blackwell. (Original work published 1953)

Wolf, S. A., & Heath, S. B. (1992). *The braid of literature: Children's worlds of reading*. Cambridge, MA: Harvard University Press.

Wyn, J., & White, R. (1997). *Rethinking adolescence*. Thousand Oaks, CA: Sage.

Zagórska, W., & Tarnowski, A. (2004, July). *Historical re-enactment in young adulthood: Experiences and psychological functions*. Poster presented at the XVIIIth ISSBD conference, Ghent, Belgium.

Zajde, N. (1995). *Enfants de survivants* [Children of survivors]. Paris: Odile Jacob. (Original work published 1993)

Zittoun, T. (1996). Non sono tutti fascisti. Immagini di sé e degli altri nei ragazzi della scuola ebraica [They aint' all fascists! Images of self and other in children from a Jewish school]. *La Rassegna Mensile di Israel, 62*(3), 155-187.

Zittoun, T. (1999). *Tradition juive et constructions de sens. Une introduction à la transmission traditionnelle de l'herméneutique juive et à son utilisation contemporaine. Centre romand d'études herméneutiques* [Jewish tradition and the construction of meaning. An introduction to the traditional transmission of Jewish hermeneutics and its contemporary use]. Neuchâtel, Switzerland: Université de Neuchâtel.

Zittoun, T. (2001). *Engendrements symboliques. Devenir parent: le choix du prénom*. Thèse de Doctorat en Sciences Humaines [Symbolic generations. Becoming a parent: The choice of the first name]. Neuchâtel, Switzerland: Université de Neuchâtel.

Zittoun, T. (2003). The hidden work of symbolic resources in emotions. *Culture & Psychology, 9*(3), 313-329.

Zittoun, T. (2004a). Preapprenticeship as a transitional space. In A. -N. Perret-Clermont, C. Pontecorvo, L. Resnick, T. Zittoun & B. Burge (Eds), *Joining society: Social interaction and learning in adolescence and youth* (pp. 153-176). Cambridge, United Kingdom: Cambridge University Press.

Zittoun, T. (2004b). Symbolic competencies for developmental transitions: The case of the choice of first names. *Culture & Psychology, 10*(2), 161-171.

Zittoun, T. (2004c). Janet's emotions in the whole of human conduct. *From past to future, 5*(1), 25-29.

Zittoun, T. (2004d). Memorials and semiotic dynamics. *Culture & Psychology, 10*(4), 1-19.

Zittoun, T. (2004e). *Difficult secularities: Talmud and Hesse as symbolic resources.* Unpublished manuscript.

Zittoun, T. (2005a). *Donner la vie, choisir un nom. Engendrements symboliques* [Giving life, choosing a name: Symbolic begetting]. Paris: L'Harmattan.

Zittoun, T. (2006a). *Dynamics of inferiority: Ruptures and transitions in the self development.* In L. M. Simão & J. Valsiner (Eds.), Otherness in question: Labyrinths of the self. Greenwich, CT. Information Age.

Zittoun, T. (2006b). The role of symbolic resources in human lives. In J. Valsiner & L. A. R. Rosa (Eds.), *Handbook of social/cultural psychology.* New York: Cambridge University Press.

Zittoun, T., & Cesari Lusso, V. (1998). Bagage culturel et gestion des défis identitaires [Cultural baggage and dealing with identity challenges]. *Cahiers de Psychologie, 34,* 1-63.

Zittoun, T., Duveen, G., Gillespie, A., Ivinson, G., & Psaltis, C. (2003). The uses of symbolic resources in transitions. *Culture & Psychology, 9*(4), 415-448.

Printed in the United States
203005BV00006B/13/A